RESOURCES FOR WORSHIP

RESOURCES

FOR WORSHIP

CLARICE M. BOWMAN

ASSOCIATION PRESS

NEW YORK

Dedicated
to you,
Frances and Harry Britt,
with
appreciation and love
for what you are,
and with
high confidence for what
you will be
and
help others to be
in your life
ministry

Acknowledgment

Grateful acknowledgment is made to all authors, publishers, and editors whose creativity and friendly helpfulness have made possible the bringing together of these ideas and aids for worship. Our apology is extended herewith to any person for whose material we were unable to secure information or in whose quoted work omissions or errors may have occurred inadvertently.

Gratitude is expressed also to the wider circle of unnamed people: writers of centuries past, and of now; innumerable young folk and adults whose shared thoughts in camps, workshops, and conversations have contributed "sacred flame" in the forging of what is here. May what appears in this book lead others to contribute on beyond.

Special thanks: to Dr. William R. Locke, whose brilliant mind and magnificent spirit constantly counsel and guide; to my mother, for daily radiance and kindly humor; to Association Press, for Mr. James Rietmulder's vision and faith to dare, and for Miss Lucile Lippitt's discerning insight and care in preparation of the manuscript.

CONTENTS

in the daily round . . . Worship related with
recreation . . . Worship as we give and serve . . .
Worship at times of catastrophe or confusion . . .
Worship when community or world situations are
in crisis . . . Worship in business sessions . . .
Worship in situations of study and learning . . .
Worship at times of misunderstanding or conflict
. . . Worship at high, holy times . . . Worship
in enlarging fellowships . . . Worship a means of
strengthening the individual person . . . Worship a
means of stretching horizons . . . Worship a test
for individuals and groups

Corporate worship, when "something greater" happens . . . Worship as the drama of the soul . . .
Outward order reflecting inward movement of spirit
. . . In summary
The leadership of the spirit . . . The function of
aids in spirit-led worship . . . Criteria for choice
and use of aids . . . Ways of training individuals
and groups . . . Ways of planning for group worship services

Part Two.   Resources for Planning

Topical Guide to Aids for Worship

(By chapter numbers in Part Two)

Guide to Various Aspects of Worship Planning

(*By chapter numbers in Part Two*)

Authors Quoted

(I indicates Part One; II, Part Two; arabic numerals refer to the chapters.)

INTRODUCTION

❧

You AND I—and apparently millions of other creatures whose address is Planet Earth—are *venture-spirited*. We want to move out beyond what we now know . . . to try more than we can now do.

Space has beckoned man for, lo, how many centuries? And just now we are learning to send objects—is it up, out, down, or around? Problems solved bring new ones in their train. People by the thousands go into research . . .

But there is a vastly more important adventure worth our devotion of research, time, and life-energies. This is a *personal* adventure, in contrast to adventures in the realm of *things*. We are far behind. Too little progress has been made in this area through the centuries. Perhaps one reason is that dealing with things is far easier. But it is not enough . . .

Now is the hour. This adventure has your name on it and mine, for it is the personal privilege of learning more of our God and of ways to communicate with him and with each other. The method is spiritual. It must be individual. We can try it only in the "living laboratories" of our own thoughts and acts. We can share, compare experiences, and encourage one another. Best of all, we strive not alone. One who created us leads us along, and does far more than we.

Because this adventure leads us to look Godward, to seek in eager humility for fellowship with him, and to pray that our lives and our world be brought into the orbit of his will, *we cannot lose.*

The Call—to Venture Personally

Words such as "worship" and "prayer" we have heard all our lives. They have more or less meaning for us, depending upon what our experiences have been. Maybe some of us have not stopped very long to ask what worship or prayer now means— or *could* mean—to us, and perhaps through us, to others and even, in some chain-reacting influence, to the world's on-going way . . .

Perhaps in certain groups to which we belong, "devotions" or "worship services" are held. Do these times mean all they might to us as individuals or to our groups? If not, why not?

One can, of course, take a casual attitude, viewing worship merely as one of many activities characterizing creatures called human. Groups, even under the roofs of churches and synagogues, may go for years listening as spectators to ministers or leaders, perhaps going through habitual customs such as rising, singing, and the like without thinking much about the meaning of it all. Campers may enjoy aesthetic responses to nature's wonders, without moving out of themselves to take the further step of answering to the Call of the Creator upon their own lives.

Meanwhile, baffled, fearful, direction-hungry people all about us are asking for answers big enough to match their need. Who of us is not frightened, lonely, bewildered? Even when many rush out after other goals, wistfully they wish that they might know if there is a God who cares, and if—and how —they might find fellowship with him, and meaning and joy for their personal daily round.

Tensions smolder in the world at large—where small groups want to find pathways to mutual understanding yet grow farther apart in smoking angers, and where millions in the many nations grovel and yearn that the chains of old war-ways might somehow be broken, that the blood shed on all battlefields and the bleeding hearts of all loved ones may not at last have been in vain and that before some awful instant of releasing the powers of doom, man might somehow rise and know "the things that belong to his peace."

How have our expanding knowledge of the physical uni-verse and our abilities, paltry as they are, to use its forces, come? Only as persons have patiently focused their minds, energies, time to the utmost upon its secrets. They have asked questions of the universe, and developed precision instruments for receiving answers.

No less a call—but one demanding even greater dedica-tion—comes now for frontiersmen of the realm of the Spirit. We must seek, with more than scientific care and with com-mitment more than matching the great researchers of all time, for fuller understanding of communication with the Divine and with one another. What happens in worship and prayer? What helps may we employ, such as methods, aids, settings? But most importantly, how does God call and lead?

The call is to venture *personally*, to "take the leap," to risk all, to let ourselves go on the mercies of God, to widen our thoughts by the concerns of God, to tender our spirits by the love of God.

And the call is to venture in our groups, beyond merely putting on comfortable programs in beautiful settings with enjoyable music and messages. Suppose people's consciences, God-prodded through strenuously sincere prayer together, should grow more sensitive about issues affecting neighbors of a different color, or nations of differing ideologies? Could we pray that we might go out from our worship services with more wisdom and even courage for taking stands? Suppose our status, as individuals and in the smaller or larger groups of which we are a part, became involved . . . or our popularity . . . or our purses. Could we, depending all the more upon the leading and strengthening which come only from above, follow through and never give up keeping on?

Worship and prayer never leave us as we are . . . They call us to take pilgrim journeys in living, loving, serving, helping.

Pioneers through all ages have had to be those who were able to "take it." Pioneering of the least costly kind is in geography, even in space. Pioneering in human relations and in God-relations is infinitely more costly.

But this kind makes the most difference, for it leads straight to the roots of sins and wrongs that spawn the evils which cause destruction and suffering, and it leads to the God who holds all worlds in his hand, and his Son the Christ who can meet all crises.

We all know in sober truth that our world may now be at its last bending-time in all history, unless personalities come forth, God-led, to show a better way. The trumpet sounds over the hill.

The world can be saved by one thing, and that is worship.
For to worship is to quicken the conscience by the holiness
  of God,
To feed the mind with the truth of God,
To purge the imagination by the beauty of God,
To open the heart to the love of God,
To devote the will to the purpose of God.[1]

[1] All numbered notes are found at the end of the book by chapters.

PART ONE

Resources for Inward Preparation

I. FORWARD STEPS IN
PERSONAL PRAYER LIFE

❧

WE CAN NEVER EXPECT to understand or define *all* that happens when we pray and worship. But each new experience shows us more. We are like Columbus landing on a new bit of territory, little dreaming of the vast continent lying beyond.

But more importantly, we *become* more. We learn a bit more, each time we pray or gather with others in worship, about what God is like. We learn a bit more about what it means to be persons and how God works with persons and how persons, under God, may work with one another. We use helps that have come to us from the Bible and from others of earlier times and now. But above all human resources, the Eternal God is our Teacher.

Why, then, do not more of us pray more often? Why do not our daily lives and our decisions in groups small and great give more evidence of our having been with God?

One practical, embarrassing reason is that we fail to set aside regular times for daily devotion. Who of us has not said to himself, "Soon I will set up a plan"? But we may put off doing so for a lifetime. Douglas Steere says that persons lack-

25

ing daily prayer times for spiritual inbreathing are as souls without air. Problems are involved in providing for ourselves such times. Let us face and deal with them as best we can.

Time

"So busy." Next question, "Doing what?" Can we find time for doing what we most *want* to do? The habit may be hard to start. At first, too, our minds may wander, flitting from one to another task to be done. But as we earnestly seek to "focus Godward," somehow God seems to work through unknown laws of our mental life and we grow in powers of concentration. Less time is wasted in woolgathering, or in "getting down" to the Center. Our prayer may grow deeper in shorter time-periods. But likewise we shall *want* to adventure further, so that we shall find still more time.

When is our best time? Each one must answer for himself. Some people like a prayer-period first thing in the morning when minds are fresh. The day is different, they will say, when they have begun it with God. Martin Luther wrote:

By the grace of God I desire to lay down the rule not to speak to man until I have spoken with God; not to do anything with my hand until I have been upon my knees; not to read letters or papers until I have read something of the Holy Scriptures. . . . Too much work without corresponding prayer. . . . Today setting myself to pray, the Lord forthwith seems to set a holy dew upon my soul. . . . Was enabled to spend part of Thursday in the church praying. Have had great help in study since then.[1]

The very personal discipline of your time, your moods, and your emotions to make possible a daily devotional period develops strength of spirit. When habit patterns are established, you feel a pang of lostness without your regular prayer period.

Some people keep a brief morning time (as a kind of "grace" for the day) and then a longer, less hurried period in the twilight time, or in the evening before going to bed. We each must seek to understand our own temperament and need. Our prayer time should *not* be when we are least keen and alert!

We marvel at the vast insights about God, daily life, loving neighbors, and national righteousness that have come to us from our spiritual forefathers of Bible times. Maybe one secret was that they *took time;* they gave their lives and all their dealings a "time exposure to the Infinite."

We may not follow quiet vocations such as keeping sheep on the hillsides. But despite our rushed ways and days, the same laws of the spirit hold: that as we learn to "be still" do we come to know that "he is God. . . ." This is more than intellectual and emotional knowing. Unconscious motives and acts are affected. Unworthy attitudes and ways drop away as dead leaves vanish when spring brings new life. Greater love animates our hearts, so that we find time for kindlier actions, too.

We *know* that such life-transforming possibilities await us. Can we not then take the simple, practical step of charting some periods that can be kept regularly, free, private, and for God alone?

When we read our Bibles or devotional helps, we need time to prepare our thoughts before beginning, and then after praying, as we get ready for transition into the busy affairs of our day.

When there is good news, a glad surprise, a dream fulfilled, a hoped-for response, we need time to thank God.

When grief comes, or fear grips, or vexation poisons, we need time to let the infinite Quietness of God and his healing Love assure and direct us.

When we become caged in small self-concerns or grow steely and unsympathetic or pass by on the other side from where someone is suffering, we need time for God to stretch, limber, and tender our thoughts.

Today, as in all times past, we grow only as we "take time to be holy." In our youth and adult groups, let us not be so busy having meetings that we fail to chart special times to seek growth in worship life—through discussing, quiet waiting in silence, sharing, Bible study, and learning of others' aids.

But any group grows in its worship-life only as its members grow. Some persons ask, "Does 'practicing the Presence'[2] or 'praying without ceasing'[3] mean that I do not need to set aside a *special* time for prayer?" "We can pray at any moment," say others. But *do* they? Without that habitual time for attuning thoughts to God, do we not tend to get wrapped up in lesser concerns—to *forget* to pray? "Only when I have first dedicated the day do I find myself sending those little 'flash prayers' all through the day," contributes one. "I compare prayer-time to light," suggests another; "after the quiet time, persons, problems, and even *things* of my day have a different 'look'—a more 'God-illumined' view, somehow."

From giant devotional spirits of the past come whimsical

phrases, descriptive of what we, too, experience: "swift darts of longing love," "exclamation points of prayer," ejaculalations," "nosegays" to lend their fragrance all through the day.[4] The hallowing of prayer affects attitudes, actions, re-actions.

As one picks up a pencil to write, he prays that the words it forms may be in line with God's loving will and in no way harmful. As one bakes bread, he does it "unto the Lord," thankful for the good smell and the joy of feeding one's dear ones. Driving a car, running a vacuum sweeper, matching bolts on an assembly line or ploughing a farm—one thanks the Giver for life and motion, strength, and the sacramental privilege of constructive work.

Place

Privacy is hard to come by in crowded apartments, homes, or dormitories. Let us ask co-operation from others involved in not interrupting us at our specified times. Where we can be sure of privacy, we can perhaps arrange for ourselves helpful settings or reminders, using symbols particularly meaningful in associations to us.

But we cannot always be alone. Through determination, we can practice mentally entering "the little postern gate" as Walter Rauschenbusch said, so that "we can be where God is."[5] Even in crowds, we may thus be "alone" with God. G. A. Studdert-Kennedy said, "Create a secret chamber in the innermost core of yourselves." When you wish to pray in uninspiring surroundings, you can call to the mind's eye remembered pictures of beautiful scenes; you can imagine

Galilee and a young, fearless prophet who walked there; you can picture a hilltop, the sea.

Muriel Lester enjoys a morning walk, feeling the steady rhythm of stepping along and thanking God for pulsing life and fresh air. But usually for most of us, a quiet spot apart is *necessary* for a deep and growing devotional life.

Aids

Our Bibles are probably our first, and most vital, aid. If we are not so familiar with our Bibles that we can turn to favored passages, we can grow in familiarity through use of them. Each of us no doubt has passages of special personal meaning. Rather than merely "reading through" mechanically, we would plan to use such passages, and search ever for new ones, to inspire our thoughts and set them into motion in prayer. The Psalms are especially rich in devotional guidance. We can *study* our Bibles (reading and thinking through historical portions, law, writings, prophets) in times set aside for learning.

Many like to purchase copies of their church hymnals (here is a good idea for gifts). Reading the words of hymns (or singing them over in one's mind) will help bring new thoughts, and enable us particularly to express our *praise*. We may find in unfamiliar hymns words that lift our thoughts to new meanings. When later certain hymns we have used in private are sung in group worship, we enter into their meaning more fully.

We collect poetry, stories, or prose passages for use in our devotions. We do not need *many* materials; an especially vital quotation may be used over and over again, as an esas some would say, probing the Styxian depths and making us come to grips with these sentient beings we call ourselves, a subtle temptation lurks—a very dangerous one. So dark is this valley that we can easily persuade ourselves that our vocation here is to accustom our eyes to darkness, to think and speak of how dark it is, to sense the pain of our aloneness to the uttermost like an exposed nerve. But this is the polar opposite of Bible teaching, and the meaning of our faith. We dare move to the existential depth of awareness, yes, but rather than indulging in cultic despair (the ultimate of self-pity) we think of God rather than self, we look upward rather than inward! And in that moment, if trustingly we hold our total lives utterly and honestly open and "limber" to his leading, we are drawn—maybe imperceptibly at first, but strongly, even as the moon draws tides.

The test of sincerity, thus, is required of all of us. No "cover up a little and it won't show." Before God, no camouflage. Surrender means willingness to let God see all the way in. A newly Christian African girl prayed, "O God, light a candle in my heart, that I may see to sweep the rubbish from thy dwelling place." "Just as I am without one plea." No play acting, no pretending. We may fool some of the people some of the time, but we cannot fool ourselves or our God. Putting on pious faces as we near the sanctuary does not make us religious. Singing with gusto does not mean that we are praising God. Even "leading" in prayer does not mean that we are praying. About this attitude of existential honesty and sincerity, we can do something.

"But suppose," someone asks, "that I really *want* to pray, but on this particular occasion I cannot seem to get 'in the mood' and I don't seem to feel the right emotions. What should I do, leave the room?" No! God knows if we *want* to find and be found of him. He finds us. We do not have to "feel" in some particular way. (For too long, perhaps, and too much we've indulged looking inward, using emotions as a barometer of spiritual vitality.) Rather, religion is measured by inward *intent*, our eager God-reaching in humble love. "Ye that do truly and earnestly *seek* . . ." The little girl had the right attitude when she said, "I try to make my thoughts go with my prayer." God-centered prayer does not take time for self-interested introspection, to check as to whether certain emotions are felt. One girl said, "I used to pray, but I didn't get a 'bang' out of it, so I decided there was no use." Rather, let us see to it that our very expectations get out of the way, make room for the workings of the Spirit, for in true prayer we are prayed through. Former feelings may be breathed through transformingly. Rather than asking for rosy glow sensations or peace of mind palliatives, let there be a steady, self-losing centering upon God! *From small, "selfy" attitudes, prepare a Highway for our God!*

God's initial act of grace . . . is to show to man his sinfulness in such a way that man, seeing himself thus, in abhorrence strips off his masks, and exposes himself as he is wholly to God, imploring forgiveness.[6]

Who can describe the Ways of the Spirit, the whisperings of the "still, small voice" above our clamorings? But each of us can know "from the inside . . . out" that we have been helped to grow, as a tree by rivers of water, each tree in its unique unfolding ways.

Worship is like a tree, reaching upward for the higher rain. Who ever knew a tree to reach in vain?[7]

Another less worthy motive is to worship and pray for fear of what might happen to us in this life or the next if we did not, or for reward here or in eternity—"what we shall get out of it." When we start with this motive, we might find ourselves as a next step trying to persuade God to come over to "our side," or to give us what we want . . . rather than asking ever humbly what he would have us become.

Or we may turn toward God, but only halfway, wanting to hold on to our independence and our pet pursuits. We may put off the time of true surrender: "Thy kingdom come—but not yet!"[8] "Begin with the other fellow, please." "Try me tomorrow." Or we may be spiritually lazy, clutching the easy back seat, not wanting to be called upon to "do anything." We wish not to engage in such disciplines of spirit as will be necessary for spiritual growth and athleticism.[9] We fear that real prayer may cost the making of some changes in our usual way of life.

Or, in our customary worship services, we may become preoccupied with forms and procedures we "like," efficiency and organization we "enjoy," until the work becomes our own and "God cannot get through."

Or we may have become inoculated, through years of "not expecting much to happen" so that we find it hard to lift our spirits in expectation as we begin to pray.

Or, to summarize, we may not yet be willing to come with our total selves, that the God who seeks such to worship him may fill us with his power and call us to his frightening new paths of service. "Ye shall seek me, and find me, when ye shall search for me with all your heart."[10]

Yes, Lord, I will follow . . . But first let me straighten things out before I come. You know how it is, Lord. I must collect all that is due me and, of course, I must pay all my debts. I cannot leave these matters untended. It will take only a little time, Lord, then I shall follow thee.

Yes, Lord, I will heed thy call . . . But first let me go to my family. To them I must say farewell. Let me linger awhile. After I have done this, Lord, then I shall follow thee.[11]

An attitude of unforgiveness toward others, or of unreadiness to accept God's forgiveness of ourselves may hold back our worship and prayer-life. Our guilt may make us ashamed and afraid to venture toward the Presence. We may tremble just outside the door. But God has not shut us out. We turn ourselves away. Forgiveness is there if we but claim it, and show our sincerity by a forgiving spirit to all. When we center our thoughts upon ourselves and our sinfulness, we are as wheels spinning the more deeply into mud. Or we may lack courage to face ourselves in absolute honesty, retreating into various escapisms or rationalizations, or attempting to persuade ourselves that we are no worse than these, our neighbors. Only utter soul searching and resolute confession will free our spirits for fresh communion, for the God who cares meets our hesitant, awkward, unsure steps. The Shepherd comes looking for his wayward sheep. The prodigal's father looks yearningly for his return. God bears the real burden.

> But none of the ransomed ever knew
> How deep were the waters crossed,

Nor how dark was the night that the Lord went through
Ere he found the sheep that was lost.[12]

*Another self-centered attitude is to seek the Adventure of
worship and prayer for our own sake.* Mindful that God has
gifts beyond what we have yet received, we begin a prayer:

Father, we would not miss this Adventure of commun-
ing with thee. We realize that thou hast made us more
than machines or animals, that thou hast given us spirit
and freedom, and this mysterious yearning for communication with thy Spirit. Give us power and peace, then, as we
pray . . .

but now a bigger prayer rises in our thoughts . . . as if God
himself were helping us to *learn* better how to pray, *for that
first was scarcely a prayer at all!* We were thinking mostly of
ourselves and what we wanted. When we turn to think
mostly of God, we can no longer stop with asking what would
help *us* feel joyful or grow, for God is Love. Love is over all.
Love, melting our selfishness, creates within us something
bigger, more Godlike: concern for others. Like a boat lifted
on a tide coming in, we are brought upward to a larger view
where we see *all* lives bound up together under God. We can
no longer ask for ourselves what we would not wish shared.
We cannot ask forgiveness if we are unwilling to forgive.
Now a larger prayer wells up:

Our Father, who lovest all . . . teach me more truly
how to pray . . . not for my sake, but for thy sake and
others' sake. Lead me in thy Plan for all. Teach me to

love thee and to love all in thee. Help me to learn to give
and live for thee and for all of thine. Amen.

And now, as we venture further into learning more about
worship and prayer, may we continue to hold this attitude as
a compass pointing ever true.

Augustine said long ago in his Confessions, "Blessed is he
who loves Thee, and his friend in Thee, and his enemy for
Thee. For he alone loses no one dear to him, to whom all are
dear in him who can never be lost."

Prayer in Times of Particular Urgency

Danger threatens. Need prods. Grief stabs. We are led to
pray with particular intensity, as a burning glass draws into
itself rays from the sun.

How often Lincoln's words may have been true of us, that
"the soul goes to its knees when there is nowhere else to go."
We know we *ought* always to pray and not wait for times
when we are faint. Do we? But even if we have not prayed
regularly, this should not *keep* us from praying in special
need. Groups, too, experience catastrophic happenings:
death, disappointments, dreams dashed to pieces, even danger
(such as a camp in a forest fire).

Douglas Horton suggests the picture of a swimmer, swept
off a small boat into a lake. Would he pause, first, to analyze
the nature of air? to recall the chemical formula for water?
to phrase definitions of swimming? He would struggle to
find air, and finding, he would *breathe* it—gladly, fully. He
would "experience" the air as the element for which his
lungs were made, and which he could not live without. "So

the Christian worshiper knows that he could not exist without God as revealed in Christ."[13]

Because God, in compassion infinite and incomprehensible, knows our need, and "remembers that we are dust," he gives according to the measure of his love (*not* in proportion to the frantic fever of our beseeching). We should pray prayers of petition boldly and honestly, in need. God knows.

No one can explain "answers" to prayer on life rafts, in burning hotels, or at death's door. For a few dramatic situations publicized, there may be hundreds where divine help was falling like the dew, scarcely recognized; or where the very operation of this love necessitated a still further suffering or difficulty on the part of the one praying. "My thoughts are not as your thoughts," says the Lord.

One asks, "But surely, if we have not been praying all along, we have no right to pray frantically in time of trouble. That would not be good sportsmanship with God, would it?" We should pray. He knows our need, even the need below the surface one, to *pray*.

But, even in emergencies, should we not seek to keep *central*—not our selfish clamoring problem—but a loving trust in God who wills the best for us at all times. Prayer is not to enlist extra resources from Up Yonder for our own ends.

Praying in a spirit of love for God and others and acceptance of self even in one's trouble is more than a dutiful tacking onto our prayers, "if it be thy will." If our prayer-habit is to seek ever to will first the loving Will of God, then in emergency we will mean this, too. In his Presence is answer; in his Will is our peace.

Learning to Pray Through Praying

God is not merely the "Thou" whom we address in prayer. He is the "I" who addresses us . . .

The profoundest discovery that the human heart can make is that one is not alone in an unfriendly universe. As Browning said,

> So, the All-Great, were the All-Loving too—
> So, through the thunder comes a human voice
> Saying, "O heart I made, a heart beats here![14]

As the sheep in the story could never wander so far away but that the shepherd would keep on searching, so we are never beyond the reach of God's call. Diognetus wrote many centuries ago, "God is love—nourisher, father, counselor, teacher, physician, light, mind, honor, glory, strength, and life—who takes away all anxieties. God wants us, each one of us: he wants us to believe in his love."[15]

He has planted within us yearning for communication, a potential responsiveness to the Great Responder. Evelyn Underhill suggests that in some sense perhaps all life has its own levels of response, a thought also found in certain Psalms:

> Worship, in all its graces and kinds, is the response of the creature to the Eternal; nor need we limit this definition to the human sphere. There is a sense in which we think of the whole life of the Universe, conscious and unconscious, as an act of worship, glorifying its Origin, Sustainer, and End.[16]

We human beings did not invent worship and prayer. As personal love, God bends to the orbit of our weakness and need, bidding us to righteousness, and supplying our lack. As the lisping efforts of a child to make itself understood are caught and interpreted by the loving insights of a parent, so our faltering human efforts to pray seem grasped by a Love greater. William Law once said, "The sun meets not the springing bud that stretches toward him with half the certainty as God, the source of all good, communicates himself to the soul that longs to partake of him."[17] A girl wrote,

> I have just found God . . .
> After all these years of search,
> Trying to find some obscure way,
> Seeking wise men, going to church;
> Then suddenly I knew he was a part
> Of me, myself . . . the only Life I had.
> And there, deep down in my heart,
> I have found God.[18]

The Divine Activity Far Beyond Our Own

God establishes special pathways to each of us, for communication with himself—pathways uniquely ours. He has not bestowed life, energy, sensitivity, and need and left us to weather our way in a cold, bewildering universe alone. "Speak to him for he hears, and spirit with spirit can meet."[19]

Several may be gathered in a worship service together. Each may experience God's love and call in a different way, yet for each the experience is authentic, real. One needs a quieting of anxious fears. Another needs prodding challenge. At times our worship may be for us like a spring shower: quickening, vivifying, releasing within us springs of forgiveness as we are forgiven. At times our worship may comfort, reassure. At times it may startle and thunder through us, calling us up out of ourselves to new concerns and self-giving: "For he knows our need." A tap on the shoulder may be for us alone.

Nor need we have all the answers to all our questions, even about belief, before we can begin praying. We start *just where we are.* A college girl related at a conference how for years she had struggled to learn about God, trying to arrange her beliefs in neat structures, and meanwhile feeling unable to pray. One day, a couplet she chanced upon gave her a new thought about God, a new invitation:

Who takes one step toward God through doubtings dim,
God will advance a thousand miles in blazing light to him.[20]

We *experience* what we can never fully explain: that when we reach trustfully Godward in our prayer and worship, we are "answering back" to One who has first called us. Have you ever awakened from a dream, tremblingly sure your name was being called? The beloved Negro spiritual whispers, "Hush, hush, Somebody's calling my name . . ." Another says, "I'll be somewhere, listening . . ."

Our need, then, is not so much to find definitions in scientific exactness, but to launch forth from where we are. As an artist develops a picture, brush stroke after brush stroke, so our living concepts of God and worship and prayer will grow.

As an aid for the growing, we recall high and special moments when somehow we knew for a surety that we were not alone, that our lives were encountered, made different.

As we read our Bibles or hymnals or materials such as are

found here or in other sources, echoes reverberate within us and we exclaim, "Why, I have experienced something like this, too!" Value these holy insights. They point directions, as climbing to a hilltop opens far vistas before our eyes.

Times come when, as we set ourselves to pray, we conclude that we are "just not in the mood." Or we try earnestly, yet find ourselves groping. Our prayers don't seem to rise "into orbit." Testimony from the spiritual giants of the past, as well as from almost everyone with whom we may talk, is that people *do* have times of fog, maybe "dark nights of the soul."[21] But continuing steadfast *through* darkness is one test of our trust; and we grow imperceptibly meanwhile. Our feeble efforts are not all! In Michelangelo's painting, the Hand of God reaches actively and powerfully toward the faltering hand of Adam . . .

> Let me no more my comfort draw
> From my frail hold of thee;
> In this alone rejoice with awe
> Thy mighty grasp of me.[22]

Nor do we realize the awesome truth of God's reach to us more keenly than when we get off on the wrong trail. We agonize in guilt and remorse. We sink into bleak despair. After a time we may give up, and grow lazy, even forget God. Yet "even there shall thy hand lead me and thy right hand shall hold me."[23] We may think we can run away, willfully whisking ourselves at speed through space, or busying ourselves with multitudinous trivia. Even so, the tug of the Eternal is there, like the moon's pull on the tides.

For God seeks from us response, "he seeketh such to

worship him." He gives us our role to play, as he does more than his part: this is the covenant relation. We are bidden to turn toward him, to ask, seek, knock, hunger, thirst. Flowers blossom into what they were created to become, by following the sun with their faces. For the little we do, how *much* is done for us! For the little "apertures" we hold up (as Evelyn Underhill says),[24] how *much* light!

> Revelation's not so much
> The light or voice; the clue
> Is just the very fact you've stopped
> And God's caught up with you.[25]

As we look out over the ocean, we know that beyond the farthest horizon we can see, it stretches on and on, deep, full. So,

> We can see only a little of God's loving,
> Just a few rich treasures from his mighty store,
> But out there, far beyond our mind's horizon,
> There's more, immeasurably more.[26]

Steps or Stages in Personal Prayer

Much research nowadays is on "communication"—how people first began to talk and then write; how much is conveyed through gestures; what can be expressed or suggested through arts. Actually, though persons have tried since time began, no doubt, to "get across" meanings to each other, we as yet know but little; but we sense, through our common daily efforts and research, enough to know that there must be underlying laws or principles.[27]

The entire Bible, and garnered aids from the great ones of

all ages, teach us much about ways of communicating with one another and with God. Special insight is found in Isaiah 6:1–8 and in the prayer Jesus taught, Luke 11:1–4, and in the prayer Jesus prayed, John 17:1–26, for his friends. We may compare the "stages" described in these with stages or steps of experience that take place when we meet and converse with a human friend:

Suppose you are walking down the street. You look up, and see a friend approaching. He is one whose friendship you value highly; it is of *worth* . . . You are glad to see this friend.

As you meet, you exchange greetings. You may wish to thank your friend for some communication or gift, or simply to express joy in the friendship. But you think of something you have done or failed to do that must have hurt. You feel guilty, remorseful. It is hard now for you to look your friend in the eye. But this friendship means so much to you that you do not wish to lose it. You gather courage and express your regret and sorrow. To your amazement, though you know you are undeserving of such a response, he smiles and through his hurt and perhaps tears offers you genuine forgiveness. Now you wish more than ever to do something for this friend, to live up to what he hopes in you, to help him know how grateful you are for what he has done for you. You express sincere desire to please him henceforward. You part in mutual "covenant," and deeper understanding.[28]

As we have said, any human analogy is weak; all we can do is to think outward from our human friendships to the

infinitely greater communication with God. As Isaiah suggests (in Chapter 6), we find ourselves going through
natural steps:

Personal need, and inner readiness—6:1
Recognition of the Presence of the Lord—6:1, 2
Joining in glorious praise—6:3, 4
Sense of sinfulness and confession—6:5
Cleansing and renewal—6:6, 7
Challenge and call to service—6:8
Answering dedication—6:8

We do not mean that *every* time we pray or worship we
experience *all* these steps. Sometimes our experience may be
primarily that of confession and cleansing. Sometimes we
may make of our prayer-time a praise-time, thinking of many
things for which we are thankful and using psalms or hymns
of praise. But for full-rounded depth of worship or prayer we
need, to summarize the steps in a pattern, the *Upreach*, the
Inward Look and Confession, and the *Outreach* in Dedication. Or, we may use the terms *Recognition* of God, *Renewal*
from God, and *Response* in God's love toward others.

Similarly, we may chart the steps or stages in the prayer
Jesus taught the disciples. Have we become so familiar with
the words of the Lord's Prayer that we do not *think* it anew
each time we pray? And do we always strive to *pray* it and
not merely *say* it?

Along with it, we may read afresh the prayer of Jesus for
those disciples whom he had been training, and with whom
he was leaving his trust and terrific tasks, the prayer in John
17.

A young girl "wrote out" her own thoughts as she tried to pray:

> I was lost . . . all alone . . .
> One night I began to pray.
> I asked God to help me—
> Help me forget myself and think of others.
>
> I asked God to forgive me—
> It was hard for me to admit my faults to the Infinite.
>
> I asked God to lead me—
> Lead me on the right paths of service.
> Again I asked forgiveness—
> Forgiveness because I did not always follow obediently.
>
> I prayed for my friends and enemies—
> Friends and enemies who also need strength, tolerance, guidance.
>
> I prayed for our leaders—
> Leaders who need strength which only God can give.
> My request: God's forgiveness—
> Forgiveness for their shortcomings.
>
> I asked him to take me as I was with my few talents and many faults.
> To use and control me as his will commands.[29]

Can you trace the inward steps of spirit, in this story of one young person's experience?

A group of young people who lived by the seashore worked out a description of stages of prayer, using the analogy of swimming:

Relaxation and trust. "Let go . . . let God." When one is trying to learn to swim, one is tempted to try to make oneself stay afloat, and to thrash wildly about in the water. This causes one to sink. One must first lie quietly on the water, surrendering to the mysterious laws of gravitation in the water, and getting the feel of being borne up by something bigger than oneself. "Underneath are the everlasting arms." When we pray, we let go our own selfish striving. We try to let go, even, of the frantic concerns we may wish to pray about. We may repeat to ourselves great verses of Scripture that remind us that God cares, is our refuge and strength, and that we are in his unceasing love and Plan. It is one thing to remind ourselves mentally that "our times are in God's hands,"[30] and that around our incompleteness and need is his wholeness and sufficiency. It is a step of courage of spirit to "let him take over." Kierkegaard, the Danish writer, spoke of "risking" ourselves with a leap of courage over 70,000 fathoms, open only to God.[31]

Breathing in. As fresh air quickens and renews our bodies, so quiet, deep breathing in of great thoughts of God and his love and goodness supplies our enfeebled spirits. We may at this stage recall passages of Scripture, hymns, or poetry that move our spirits to wonder and awe. We may read devotional aids with fresh eagerness, concentrating our powers of imagination upon meanings we find. But we turn beyond all such helps, and open the windows and doors to God himself. With thoughts attuned, like arrows strung to the mark, we seek. We affirm his Presence, knowing that he is the Father Jesus revealed, and knowing that he is even now answering our inmost prayers and needs—even those which lie beneath the level of conscious will.

As we practice devotions, we grow in the habit of "recognition." We see in beauties of nature, not mere symmetry or color aesthetically, but evidence of a Creative Planner, and we thank him for eyes to see and hearts to grow aware. We recognize God at work in persons, whatever their color or nation or creed. In a crowded store or on a busy street corner, we look at tense faces as belonging to our brothers and sisters in God's one family and we breathe a prayer for them in his love. We pause to count blessings and realize with awe how measureless is his Providence to us. We realize anew each time we pray that God the Father loves each of us individually with "all the love there is," and that "everything the living God can do for us, he is doing."[32]

> Breathe on me, breath of God,
> Fill me with life anew,
> That I may love what thou dost love
> And do what thou wouldst do.[33]

Breathing out. As God has planned that we may breathe out the poisonous carbon dioxide and breathe in life-giving oxygen anew, so when we make confession in sincerity of sins and shortcomings for which we are in "true and hearty repentance," God's mercy and forgiveness reach to the depths and take away the wrongdoing, creating within us cleaner hearts and renewing a "right" spirit within us. We are not supposed to brood morbidly over our sins and weaknesses, nor yet are we supposed to take them lightly. Rather, we must face them in utter honesty, in all their horror. We must be really sorry. We must want, with our whole hearts and not just a part of ourselves, to be transformed and led to a level beyond such behavior or even such thoughts. We must purpose, God helping us, to try to lead a new life.

Because we fail and fall into sin each day—some of which sins we may know consciously, and some we may not know but they have become a part of us through evils in society and general selfishness and greed—we need ever and again to make confession. We need to examine our lives in the light of the Presence, sternly and earnestly and obediently.

But having confessed we need then to *trust* God anew. We do not need, as did Pilgrim in Bunyan's story, to pick up the heavy burden of sin again after having prayed. We need so to let God's forgiving power operate within that we become led even to that difficult step of forgiving and accepting ourselves (when we know we are "unacceptable")[34] because God's love now enfolds. Thereby we gain courage to take timid steps forward, now not in our own strength and pride, but seeking his. We pray, "God keep a clean wind blowing through my heart night and day."[35] We echo, from deep personal realization,

> There's a wideness in God's mercy
> Like the wideness of the sea.[36]

Preparation for action. Thus renewed, we seek attuning, that we may "love whom God loves," and be led to do what he would have us do. Such listening spirit is not merely passive; it is vibrantly active. We continue to try to still our anxious petitions and problems, to wait for diviner light. If we are still unsure as to which way to turn, we wait humbly or take tentatively the next step before our feet, not rushing willfully on in our own light.

The Spirit's operation within may cause painful stretching, bidding us let go of prejudiced attitudes, opening our eyes to needs unnoticed before. We may be called to tasks distasteful or harder than we think we can bear.

Intercessory prayer rises naturally and eagerly. We are thankful for the privilege of praying for others. Differences are made in never-ending circle: differences in us when we are prayed for, and when we pray for others, differences in others when they are prayed for and when they pray for us. Jean Frederic Oberlin would slip from his horse and onto his knees as he neared the village Ban de la Roche, tears streaming down his cheeks as he agonized in prayer for his needy people; then he would go on, somehow nerved and guided, for the problems and calls ahead. Catherine of Siena prayed the night through for the souls of persons in high office dealing with destinies of multitudes. Daily she tended embittered lepers, and went to the execution block with doomed prisoners.

How can we slide glibly over our intercession with a "Bless all for whom it is our duty to pray?" Just whom do we mean? Name one. Is prayer "duty" or "privilege"? Should we not stop, think, and focus on individuals, groups, national, and international leaders, and "aim" our prayers through God's love constantly reaching toward all these all along? Some adopt a prayer calendar of persons for whom to pray each day, each week. Love is generated within us as we pray, and guidance for acting. Some day we may understand more about how these mysterious laws of the spirit work.

> The weary ones had rest, the sad had joy that day,
> And wondered how.

A workman whistling at his work had prayed,
"Lord, bless them now."

Away in foreign lands they wondered how
Their feeble words had power.
At home the Christians, two and three, had met
To pray an hour.[37]

Before rising from our personal prayer, we may think back through these questions . . .

"What single act or stand has my faith demanded of me lately, or might today's events call for?"

"To what insistent call have I tried to turn a deaf ear?"

"As Isaiah heard his particular assignment, am I sensing mine?"

"Can I follow what I feel God would have me do, not with a resentful sense of duty, but with eagerness, continuing to pray, 'Make thy will my wish'?"

II. RELATING WORSHIP WITH
   ALL LIFE

ᴇᴇᵹ

Wʜᴇʀᴇ ᴀs ᴍᴀɴʏ ᴀs ᴛᴡᴏ or three are gathered together, there
a Presence may be in the midst. The "group" may be a newly
married couple, dedicating their life-purposes and initiating
the holy habit of shared prayer-time. Or it may be a large
congregation meeting weekly for worship, or a conference
which will offer a once-in-a-lifetime inspiration to the dele-
gates. Most of the groups of which most of us are members,
however, are fairly small—classes in the Sunday church
school or departments or divisions; women's circles or socie-
ties; men's groups; adult fellowships; youth fellowships; clubs
or other gatherings where the central purpose is to seek and
to follow God's will and way.

For such gatherings—and many more, of which these are
but examples—worship services or devotions are often
planned; and usually the members themselves do the planning and participating rather than looking to a professional
leader such as the minister, whose responsibility is the congregational worship service of the church. We have thought
how important it is that not only the planners or leaders, but

all the members of such groups have some training in worship meanings and ways of entering actively into the meetings as worshipers.

But over and above formal, planned times are those rare, high, and unforgettable moments when in gathered fellowship a sense of reverence begins to steal over the group—

When Worship Comes Unbidden

We cannot describe or define such times, nor can we say ahead just when they might "come." But all in the group "know."

Each such time is unique. The background of experiences leading up to it will affect what is felt, and what expression will be made. No rules can be laid down as to how to recognize such moments or what to do when they come. We must simply keep alert, limber, and responsive.

The wind blows where it will, and you hear the sound but cannot tell from whence it comes or where it goes. So is everyone who is born of the Spirit.[1]

The more sincerely the group members have entered into the planned-for times of devotion, and the more at ease they have grown with one another, the more likely it will be that they will respond to "winds of the Spirit" at other times.

Families in the Fellowship of Worship

Members of a family know one another well. As they share glad or sad news, happy aspirations or perplexing problems, they share *religion,* for religion has to do with all of life. Perhaps two basic types of experience lead us in our families to spontaneous prayer: (1) crisis times when we realize we are beyond our depth, and as a family need divine help in some special way; (2) glad times when hearts are made thankful, in some special sense, beyond the gratitude we express in grace at meals.

All of us are aware that our families know us at our worst; hence we may feel acutely self-conscious and even embarrassed when we attempt to phrase a prayer or meditation. This creates a barrier that in some families paralyzes the expression of spontaneous thoughts or prayers. This may be overcome only by honesty of confession, and in all relationships; only then is the spirit of each one freed to come forth with what he feels. Only in an "accepting" atmosphere where we take one another for what we are, "without one plea," can any of us venture out of our shells to reveal to each other and to God our sorrows, our remorse, our need.

Special occasions in families call for celebration or serious observance: the birthday of one, the death of a pet, a scholarship won, a musical instrument long saved for and at last purchased, the occasion of starting out on a vacation trip or returning safely, decisions about moving or choice of college or job or investment—regarding little problems and big ones, a family that prays together not only tends the more to stay together, but each member then can face his problems more secure in strength from Above and from all the other members of the family backing him up. Surely the young people going out from such families will continue to turn to God, and will always know that the family's prayers and confidence go with them . . . and in turn, they will bring such a spirit into the homes they themselves will found.

There are times and possibilities for *planned* worship in families also. Grace at meals can be made a habit from earliest years. But it should not become mere routine with the same words each time. All in the family, even to the youngest, can contribute. All may bring new songs, prayers, and thoughts, gathered from camps, conferences, or "made up" for the family. In some homes, a longer period for sharing and worship is allowed after one of the meals when all will be unhurried (if that is possible—at least sometimes).

Children and young people often enjoy preparing settings in their homes, using flowers or foliage or other aids from nature or pictures or symbols for which they will explain the meaning. Around these the family may gather for a silent moment or for quiet sharing. Particularly do the great seasons of the church year offer happy occasions for family worship. The denominations suggest special helps for making these seasons meaningful in the family. In some of the denominational periodicals is found guidance for family quiet times.

Worship at Camps and Other Outdoor Occasions

Healing comes to tired, anxious lives as wider horizons stretch and "unwind" us, and far vistas beckon us to "come up higher." Getting into old clothes, leaving behind time clocks and telephones, traffic and television, we give our spirits more chance to blossom and breathe in God's good air. Camping may be in a formal, organized setup (such as junior high, senior, adult, older adult), or one or more families may decide to "take a camping trip" together. Perceiving and enjoying together nature's gifts along the way may lead almost imperceptibly to thankfulness to the Giver. Nature, too, gets rough at times; facing hazards together may lead us to prayers for help, or prayers of forgiveness for getting edgy and ornery with each other. Many young people, if asked to describe occasions when they *knew* through experience what worship means, will tell of "a morning quiet time in camp, with the whole world still and a mist rising from the lake" or "a walk to the hilltop with a counselor in silence." For increasing numbers of adults (including those of the golden age), similar experiences have led to growing worship life.

For campers of any age, there is the charm of the campfire, hallowed down the centuries since our Hebrew nomad ancestors told in the flickering firelight the great old stories of the Faith and of the faithful. Sitting around the fire in the growing dark, with the welcome coolness descending and the embers burning low, we look up at the stars and know at the deepest levels of our being a kinship with the whole universe. And as embers burn low and singing moves from the rollicking fun to quiet folk-melodies and haunting spirituals, we look at one another in a new, more hallowed light and marvel at the comforting closeness of being there in the circle together.

There is no need for words to label or to take away from the fresh, unique vitality of each such experience. And there is no need for other, more formal materials (quotations, stories, hymns, meditations) to be used. The universe is the setting. Each one's thoughts supply the aids. As faces look skyward, hearts become more open to the Creator. The clay of our lives, grown crusty and distorted, becomes responsive in a new way to God's creative touch.

Worship Times in the Daily Round

One girl tells of a bus-load of students returning to campus after a victorious game in a neighboring community. After the shouting and singing, the mood could have turned to a raw hilarity, the telling of slightly off-color jokes, and such like. But someone in the back of the bus quietly started singing Malotte's "The Lord's Prayer." Soon others were joining in. Then different ones started favorite familiar hymns. "It was so different from our usual trips," this girl remarked. "Somehow we all felt cleaner."

Adults know such occasions also—although perhaps by adulthood we become more self-conscious about *starting* a song or prayer. In the everyday contacts of all of us, once in a while there come special moments that call for hallowing. Announcement may come of a catastrophe somewhere. Or something may happen to someone we know. Even though the persons around us may be of differing backgrounds, it may be fitting for someone to suggest quietly and naturally (certainly avoiding any pious tone), "Perhaps we need a moment of silence . . ." Or, one may bow his head in silent prayer and others may follow. Usually at such times we can trust silent communication.

Worship Related with Recreation

Spirits mellowed by laughter are easily attuned to One who gives life abundant. Who of us does not remember a closing fellowship-circle, campfire, or open fireplace where we wanted to hold forever the inexpressible sense of belonging? After refreshments someone starts a folk song, and then in a little while a spiritual. A quieting steals over all. Whether or not there is a formal prayer or overt expression, surely thankfulness to the Giver wells up—for the fun, for being alive, and for hope for the future. Young people have said that out of such times, rather than at more formal worship services, they began to feel a call upon their lives to serve God with their energies to bring more abundant life to others of his children who might not know this fun.

Worship as We Give and Serve

Probably most, if not all, of our classes, clubs, and groups of youth or adults adopt plans for sharing with others in some way—through direct contacts and helpfulness personally administered (as through nurses' aides, caring for children and aged, assisting with work-loads, calling), or through giving our money that others may express personally the concern we feel vicariously.

Do we sometimes wax so enthusiastic about this or that plan that we may forget to pray? Perhaps we need guidance lest we fail to be sensitive to ways in which even our best projects may hurt the feelings of the very ones we are trying to help. Perhaps we need to confess our steelheartedness or our laziness or our passing by on the other side. Perhaps we need to pray to be delivered from temptation to give or serve for our own (or our group's) pride and glory. We are called to serve and give, if we would follow our Master who gave his daily life. Yet to venture to serve and give is a frightening responsibility (implying response-ability). St. Vincent de Paul taught his little nurses to "give so that the poor can forgive the hand that gives to them."

Misunderstandings, barriers, and tensions may exist in our groups regarding where and how we should give and serve. In a men's brotherhood some spoke enthusiastically about raising the pledge for missions. But others repeated that "our first job is at home." Argument, or even attempted persuasion, would probably fail. But "devotional" approaches might help: times for quiet meditation; constant exposure to the Life of him who teaches love and wholesome methods for serving and giving; and the impact of radiant selfless personalities now engaged in missions work.

One group, eager to make a "Christian witness" in the area of race relations, was about to rush out impulsively with an ill-advised project that could have entrenched resistance and caused harm to the long-range cause. We may thank God and pray for some of the great leaders of different races who show vision, courage to endure, steadfast commitment to high purposes, tolerance toward intolerance, and creative nonviolent methods more productive of mutual good will than most methods used in the past. Local groups can consult with such leaders in person or through correspondence, seeking not merely vision as to *what* to do but insights as to *how* to act—for wrongheaded methods may destroy good goals. One young man mused, "I wonder what might happen if each week all church groups such as classes or fellowships would pray sincerely for guidance from God on the race question . . ." Do we thus pray? Dare we?

Immediately you think of other crying areas for Christian concern, giving, and action: The class or caste systems becoming more rigidly entrenched in cities particularly; labor and employment; a sound nuclear policy; movements for peace. With thoughts baptized through prayer, who knows what new and more creative ideas might spring forth? And who knows what wells of courage for action would be tapped?

Once we feel deep *concerns* laid upon our hearts . . . once we hear in the night the whimpering cries of hungry children over the world . . . we can never again go back to selfish complacency. Moving out, perhaps fearfully, uncertainly, tentatively, we realize—in a way we could never have known back in our downy beds and warm tents—that *we are not alone*. Only as we launch forth into tasks too great for us do we experience power. How can we pray for "peace" or "power" while we sit back encased in warm cocoons of self-interest? Only as we *give* do we *find*. The God who calls nerves us for whatever difficulties lie ahead.

God gives power only to men who need it. He does not waste power. He gives it to those who have tackled something so big, so overwhelming, that their own resources are quite insufficient. . . . Such a tackling of a task too big for human power is the opening of the door through which comes the rushing of a mighty wind of power.[2]

The test is that tasks adopted, projects planned, activities engaged in be motivated by love. Prayer together in our groups, every step of the way, will help us to find and practice the methods as well as goals of love; then power and joy come . . . not of our seeking. Once we experience this, once we have tried to follow Christ into some area of human need or some evil of society, and realize how mightily the power of God avails, the more courage we gain for tackling in his name and spirit ever harder tasks. Nothing less than this is meant by "following."

Worship at Times of Catastrophe or Confusion

One of the group's members may be hurt in an accident, or one may suffer unmitigated remorse for having caused an accident. A formerly active member who long since dropped out may have drifted into bad company and serious trouble. What should be the group's attitude and action?

A sudden sorrow falls heavily on the group.

A call of need comes that seems to call for more time, money, or wisdom than members feel equal to. How shall we answer it?

To the group comes a new person of a different background culturally, economically, nationally, or racially. What will be the attitudes?

So long as classes, fellowships, and other religious groups are *awake* to problems, there is hope. The saddest situation is with those who exult, "We have no problem!"

Unless we struggle to translate the high, glorious meanings of Christianity into daily realities "on the street where we live," why bother to continue to hold our regular meetings? Of what avail? Unless such problems are *faced, prayed about,* and *dealt with as best we feel led of the Spirit,* our groups—yes, even our church groups—may drift farther into back inlets of smug satisfaction, away from the living course of Christian history where God makes his mighty moves!

Worship When Community or World Situations Are in Crisis

Breaking into our routine "lessons for today" in our groups may come shocking headlines or newscasts, calling for prayer and meditation. In children's, youth, and adult groups surely the habit should be formed of lifting these concerns in prayer. We cannot shunt them off as "secular," or "not on the lesson." If we follow biblical concepts, *nothing* is secular, apart from the realm of religion. *All* life is under God. Only through attuning minds and hearts shall we give God instruments for research into better methods for settling disputes than old jungle ways.

From a young adult class in the church school came a young man who decided, after discussion and prayer about civic reform, to give his life to city government. Another young man took up the long, arduous study of international law, hoping thus to make a contribution toward peace. From the earnest discussions and worship times in her youth fellowship, a young girl stood unflinchingly almost alone in a time of turbulence in her town. We take time in our worship services to remember in intercessory prayer persons suffering anywhere in the world. We ask guidance for leaders of governments. We seek to forge out, through mental and spiritual struggle, Christian views on current questions—

following in the line of the great prophets of the Old Testament, and the Young and Fearless Prophet of the New. In such an atmosphere, sparks may be kindled in youth or adults to take stands and to work locally, or perhaps to prepare for Christian vocations as statesmen, diplomats, economics advisers, technicians, missionaries, journalists, "emcees," actors, dramatists, linguists, and such like—dedicated and skillful instruments of the Kingdom.

Worship in Business Sessions

We gather in council or committee. Agenda are passed around. The chairman says, "Let's begin with a word of prayer." Just a *word*? A quick gesture, before "getting down to business"? If minister or other professional leader is present, the chairman may nod to him to lead. Are we all but crowding God out, in our zest for efficiency?

Decisions the group makes may help or hurt persons, may thwart or open the way for kingdom work. No matter how brief the group's time, no matter how crowded the slate, would not a full-hearted, unhurried, well-planned time of prayer help to impress upon all present that "this is the Lord's work we're here to think about, not ours"?

Humanly, we often tend to maximize unimportant matters, and minimize what matters most. Paul's word to the Philippians was, "I pray God that he may give you a sense of what is vital."[3]

At the close of business or planning meetings, rather than breaking up with a sigh of relief to have the work done, might we take again a brief pause—to dedicate energies anew, and to ask continued guidance in following out the duties envisioned. Might we not go out from such meetings feeling "called" . . . taking up our tasks as "vocation?"

Worship in Situations of Study and Learning

Most of our classes and groups spend perhaps a major part of their time dealing with topics on which members learn more information, or seek to solve problems. Denominations provide curriculum units for each age-level for Sunday church school classes, youth fellowships, special electives, and so on. Some of these are about worship and prayer, some on Bible, church history, and the Christian heritage. Some units will offer challenge to follow out Bible teaching in problem solving of current personal, community, and world issues.

Time is precious. We dare not squander it by aimless "reading of parts" in a poorly chosen, unprepared "program." The groups may study their needs, and *choose* from the recommended denominational offerings. They will find that these units are not for mere spectator "learning about," but for direct, personal-encounter "coming to grips." Each is for a *verdict*. This is a more vital, profound, and exciting approach to our classes, our meetings, our fellowships. Such learning experiences involve our whole selves: mind, emotion, will. Each unit presents a crossroads and a call, "Choose you this day whom ye will serve." "See there, God's signpost on the way?"[4] Scripture is more than a repository of verses for memorizing or stories for half-listening: it speaks and reverberates—nay, thunders—in the heart. The impact of the lives of Christian great of the ages is more than biographical:

it is existential. "What about you in your day?" "Are ye able?"[5]

Worship has a place at any point in such a unit-process: at the beginning of a new unit that will stretch over a series of meetings, when the group seeks clarity of mind and fellowship in discussion; part-way through when perhaps the group is "bogged down" and needs to start up a fresh trail; at that crucial point when the terrific challenge of the Christian way becomes more clear, yet temptation is strong to back away; as the unit draws to a climax and we need leading from Above to make specific dedication in this particular area, and impartation of nerve for trying as best we can to "practice." Thankfulness should have a large part in our prayer and worship together: for the very privilege of thinking and discussing, for the call to dedicated living, and for the Example we have.

Worship at Times of Misunderstandings or Conflict

In what live group or class do there not come tensions or difficulties, nay, even arguments? As Paul reminded his young churchmen, a test of our Christianity is the way we face difficulties.

Surely at such a time the agenda or "lesson" may be suspended temporarily. Should we, for efficiency's sake, push through plans, projects, or votes when we lack harmonious spirit? Are we not guilty of "trying to do Christian work in un-Christian ways"[6] when we send people out torn-to-pieces inwardly? Might it not be better to remain longer in prayer, than to have a majority ride roughshod over a minority, or otherwise accomplish *things* at the hurt of *persons?*

In one hot, tired, argumentative group a girl ventured timidly, "It seems to me that an Unseen Member has not been heard from lately in our discussion . . . might I suggest our taking five minutes for silence, for listening?" Astonishingly, after the shock and silence, when discussion resumed, voices were pitched in lower key. Kindly humor crept in. Almost immediately a fresh solution, of which no one up to then had thought, came forth!

It takes honesty to look at ourselves, and courage to admit what is happening to us. Then it takes will power to hush our talkative busy-ness, and let ourselves be lifted and our thoughts set right in the Great Perspectives of God.

When any group at a time of great awareness of need or tension pauses to draw upon the resources of God, the inevitable results are clarified vision, deepened insight and strengthened purpose. Such moments are productive of religious experience of a high order, experience wherein one gains a new awareness of the power of prayer.[7]

Worship at High, Holy Times

Beyond our usual experiences of learning and worshiping, we all need high, special times. We may call them times of "illumination," "mountaintop experiences," "magnificent moments," when somehow we knew our souls to be strangely attuned and we saw all life with more meaning.

To groups as well as to lone individuals come times of poignant awareness, heart-rending concerns, deep dedication, and perhaps the "rush of mighty winds" of the Spirit. Such memories hallow all our other days, and all the group's other activities.

The great Jewish festivals, as recounted in our Bibles, gave lift to the people's years and cement to the community. In the high seasons of the Christian year are challenges to plan reverently: Thanksgiving, Christmas, Watch Night, New Year's, Easter, and other special or related observances. Simplicity and sincerity should be in the planning, for many find these occasions a time of personal rush and overload. One group decided *not* to give a Christmas play that year, for members were too busy for memorizing parts and making costumes. Instead, they provided quiet meditative music in the church sanctuary at twilight times when tired shoppers could drop in for meditation.

The very experience of planning, as well as participating in any worship observance should itself be a holy experience, not a harried, hurried one.

Religious groups have their own special times during the church year: reception of new members, promotion days, installations of officers and members, pledge making, appointment and dedication of committees, initiating new units of study or service projects, dedicating gifts to home or foreign missions, farewell to members going away to college or to camp or to families moving out of the city, dedication of new or remodeled room-space or equipment, revision of the group's constitution, election of officers, invitation of guests to special meetings . . . the list could go on.

Especially vital may be "retreats" where members go apart to a woodsy spot, with quiet and unhurried schedule through afternoon and evening or week end, and plan ahead. Such retreats should *not* be for officers only. All members should be in on all planning and on the depth-dimension experiences that come from camping and struggling, working and playing together. Officers are but servants to carry out the total group's wishes, not a select group to *do* the work for the group-of-the-whole. If the membership is large, a few may go at a time, but all should have whatever retreat times are possible. All planning is by and for all. Some groups work out rituals and insignia, and invest pictures or symbols and symbolic acts with meaning particularly pertinent to the group's purposes. Some plan their own traditional high times, such as candlelight services.

Worship in Enlarging Fellowships

All Christians—in whatever remote hamlet we live on this globe, and in whatever small group we associate habitually in our worship—need to realize that we are a part of a world-wide movement. In the time of The Acts when Christian churches were spreading, like flame touching to flame, if one were a member anywhere, one would belong everywhere. One joined, not just the home church, but Christian church life wherever it was found.

Many and difficult are the differences abounding today. Yet we should *know* about ecumenical councils, and *use* materials coming from worshiping friends all over the world. We may all join in contrition over our separations, sacramentally, ecclesiastically, nationally, racially, and in any other way.

Wherever any of us have the opportunity, we should welcome the chance to worship with persons of other denominations or faiths, other races or classes, other nationalities or languages. Have you ever experienced the thrill of hearing a familiar hymn or prayer in a different language? Have you ever participated in a service in another tongue? You might be surprised how real the meaning that comes through despite what would appear to be a barrier of language. What now look like other barriers may be steppingstones. The more richly we can acquaint ourselves with the worship heritage of fellow groups, the deeper may grow our own worship thoughts and the more readily we can join before the same God, in spreading the message to unreached persons and lands and combating rampant evils by joining together. "Let us break bread together on our knees."

Worship a Means of Strengthening the Individual Person

We do not give up being ourselves when we form a body for corporate worship. We become *more* ourselves. New thoughts may come to us while we are gathered, such as we might never have had alone. No "rights of personality" are sacrificed. Each is enlarged, enriched, exalted, illumined. Personal problems and needs become *focused*. We may be made more acutely aware of our failures, our self-centering, our greediness, our hate-habits, our propensities to prejudice; and through the group-tide as lifted by God and the gathered prayers and purposes of all, we are made better, given vision to perceive our brothers, made firm in larger convictions.

This is not our doing: "This was the Lord's doing, and it is marvelous in our eyes."[8]

Joy and zest are awakened. Praise is fuller sung together. Our prayers are broadened in scope, lengthened in depth. Scripture "strikes home." Through the pages of church history are exciting stories of persons "shocked awake" in worship services who went out to give God's influence a new "break-through" into their world.

No one of us ever goes out from worship quite the same. Choices we may have lacked courage to make alone can now be faced: "the hard right against the easy wrong." As one timid person goes out from a worshiping group into the cross-currents of his daily life, he gains strength from knowing that all in the group are facing similar problems and holding true, from remembering shared moments of aspiration and dedication. Perhaps each is remembering the others in prayer.

Problems on which we may have been grappling alone may flash into clarity in a worshiping group. Surprisingly, as we sit in a group thinking of personal problems that cannot be shared, light and help may come to us though not a word be said.

A high school boy related what one service had meant to him, and as we read each of us will re-enter our own secret inner chapel of memories and thank God for similar times:

One of the most outstanding experiences of worship that I have ever enjoyed, was at one of our evening youth fellowship meetings where there were a hundred and fifty youth present. I think that this service was real to the members of our group, because it was a service altogether more meaningful, and less crowded and rushed. . . . This worship experience will linger in my heart always, because I experienced a new light in my life, and then and there, I took time out to think what it meant when the minister said: "Ye that do truly and earnestly repent of your sins, and are in love and charity with your neighbors, and intend to lead a new life, following the commandments of God, and walking from henceforth in his holy ways; draw near with faith . . ."[9]

Here is a man who has to make a difficult decision in his office on the morrow. He bows in prayer and rises with radiant face. He is able to make his stand firmly yet with tact and kindly spirit. How? Not in his own strength but through only that power that comes from Above, and that operates not only within the person who prays but mysteriously within others involved also. Words are not big enough to explain, if our puny minds could comprehend. But the reality is there.

Here is a young person who knows that cheating is wrong, but whose buddies are the crowd who do it and their arguments at times sound attractive. He wants to count with this group which he regards as the prestige group. To take a stand alone would be hard, as it always is for insecure youth. Through his youth fellowship's worship service, he is lifted and helped where even his own private prayers seemed to him too weak. He takes his stand. The way is *not* easy. But, with the anchorage of that worship experience, "having done all" he *stands*.

Here is a woman who finds courage to say to another that she is truly sorry for having said unkind things. Here is a person who forgives another with generous gesture and genuine willingness to forget (which is the test of true forgiveness).

Here is a young person gifted with many talents, who is enabled to decide to use them in service with the lowly rather than for financial goals.

Here is a man who speaks a kindly word about persons of another race in conversation with his business associates many of whom hold prejudices and who have power to hurt his business. He is enabled to speak not in self-righteous tone but quite casually as if taking a Christian view were "second nature." Such "witness" under fire, made gracefully, *costs*.

Here is a young adult who, in his first important job, is asked by his superior to slightly falsify a product. He surrenders his golden opportunity and starts over again at the bottom. But he and his wife are radiantly happy, though poor.

—And so on. "God doesn't need much of a man but he needs all there is of him" . . . and "God plus one is majority."

Worship a Means of Stretching Horizons

From vital worship, a group takes on a finer, more sensitized team spirit—whether it be a small class or fellowship, a club, a congregation, a large conference. Can you recall a time when, after prayer, your discussion took on a friendlier, easier mood and you "got somewhere" creatively? Surely a group that has shared a high vesper hour on a mountainside could not split into selfish cliques. When in a meeting we have prayed for forgiveness, can we go out hardhearted toward one who has hurt us? The New Testament word for what happens within us is *koinonia*: fellowship, plus.

Reverence is the source of this cohesion. We do not in our strength draw near to one another. We love each other in God and God in each other. George Fox spoke of "that of God" in each man, however low, however high in the world's ways. God's *gift* is this sensitizing of spirit. But so long as we remain in individual sealed-in egos, inner hurts burrow deep. But when we dare venture out, *wanting* to find God and to let the sunlight of his Love find us, we let go of self-pride and self-preoccupation. Such humbling and mellowing of spirit before God *enables* fellowship among men.

Here each is visited with a sense that he, in his need, is one and only one among other needy ones; that he is one among the many who have come to offer up their adoration and aspiration; that he is responsible for all and can never wrench loose from that responsibility.[10]

This is more than human creation . . . here is enacted anew upon the face of the earth a fresh God-creation, each time we gather to plan, praise, and pray. When our motive is sincere, meeting can become a group-aperture for divine visitation. Love reaches into our personal and group need as sunlight into darkness. As we learn to accept ourselves in this Love, we learn to accept others as they are. Through worship "the imagination is kindled, the heart made catholic in sympathy and good will is fortified . . . if men were to cease to worship God, the greatest incentive to fraternal ways among men would be withdrawn."[11]

Our responding is to God in one another and to one another in God. In gathered worship we bring our unique individual skills and expectations, and readiness to follow customs meaningful to all; we are like players in a great orchestra awaiting the Conductor's downbeat!

When a congregation prays in solid array, we have the same conditions . . . the Book of Acts says, "When the day of Pentecost was come, they were all with one accord in one place. . . . And they, continuing daily with one accord in the temple, and breaking bread from house to house, did eat their meat with gladness and singleness of heart." Somebody could make a wonderful study of the manifestations of the Holy Spirit in the last 2000 years of the Christian church. He would, I think, find this . . . true: "The Holy Spirit is ever eager to break through, but fails, except where he finds loving, joyous unity in prayer."[12]

Worship a Test for Individuals and Groups

The disciples were facing their "examination time." For long Jesus had been with them. His daily life had taught them the Way of Love, and how to pray and live in that spirit. His life-impact had been to communicate the almost unimaginable truth: God cares!

Now he must know if these companions, so dear and near to him, were *understanding*—both what God is like, and what they themselves must do. "Do you love me?" Jesus asked. Peter, often spokesman for the group, fell all over himself protesting that of course he did! Again the question. Again the urgent assurance in *words*. And again.

Then Jesus, who must have been looking deep into the eyes of Peter . . . and perhaps of any others near . . . begged, "Feed my sheep."

How do *we* come to know what God is like? To endeavor to follow the Living Lord? Not just through thinking, feeling, even praying, in words. Only as with a loving heart we commit our ways to God, and go forth to find and minister to whatever "sheep" are in our orbit (and we must all let God stretch the orbits of our love as we pray and seek his will). The ones to whom we may be called to bring God's abundance may be as unattractive (and often ungrateful) as were those whom Jesus, in such lowly ways, served. "Come, worship," is only half the call; the other half is "Go, serve," . . . to give, as Jesus did, our *daily* lives.

III. FINDING AN INNER ORDER
OF SPIRIT IN OUR WORSHIP
WITH OTHERS

❧

IF AS INDIVIDUALS we are observing daily devotions, and growing in our prayer life, why should we need to gather with others for worship?

Why do so many over the world join with their fellows in groups for celebrations, ceremonials, rituals, dramas, singing? Does something happen when we worship together, beyond what happens when we worship alone?

Corporate Worship, When "Something Greater"
Happens

Sharing experiences deepens meanings. A glad surprise comes to us. Immediately we want to tell others, that they may enjoy our good news, too. When we suffer, the clasp of some-one's hand helps more than words can say. In Jesus' parables of the lost coin, lost sheep, and lost son, the occasion of the finding called for celebrating with others.[1] Did you ever stop to think how hollow an experience it would be to sit as a lone spectator at a ball game, doing all the cheering all by yourself?

When we join in worship together sincerely before God, there is a "Plus" somehow, something happening beyond the sum-total of what each individual worshiper brings. We are created for fellowship with one another and with God. Never are we nearer one another than when we are with God. Never are we nearer God than when we are in fellowship with one another. We are most truly ourselves when we are in brotherly relation before God. Only in this relation do we help others to be more truly and fully themselves.

All of us need both levels of worshiping and praying: *alone* for the more intimate private concerns; and *together* for the fuller tides of the Spirit and for guidance into action.

Private and group worship are alike in that both are based on faith in a God who cares and who has created us for response. We use the same aids in both: our Bibles, hymnals, prayers, meditations, poetry, settings, nature, the arts, silence.

But when we come together to worship, our individual needs give over to larger group needs. We let ourselves become members of a company. This means that when we pray, we try to think not just of ourselves but of all, and we do our part with the others to lift all before the throne of grace. When we sing, we blend our voices in harmony. When Scriptures are read or when a message is given, we let our thoughts be carried on the larger tide. When we meditate together, through the spoken word or through arts or in silence, we no longer enclose ourselves in a private shell, but we let God "lead our spirits out" into vaster concerns.

Whether or not this "something greater" happens when

we join together in worship depends in large part upon the worship life of each individual. We have each, no doubt, experienced the guilty realization that wrong attitudes on our part or failure to enter in may have shut out some of the meaning of worship to ourselves. Without realizing it, perhaps, too, we failed to "conduct" the contagion of worship unto others. Persons may be in the same room, and may even go through the same customs such as the singing of hymns, but not be sharing together in spirit. We call this a "collective" group.

But when they enter in, each seeking to take the others into his thoughts and prayers, the worshipers become led of the Spirit as one body. Read Paul's description of this high quality of fellowship in I Corinthians 12, 13, 14. Worship then is "corporate" (from the Latin *corpus*, body). "Sincere and true thoughts of God are the strongest known bond between man and man." Thomas Kelly said, "Persons in the Fellowship are related to one another through Him, as all mountains go down into the same earth."[2]

Corporate worship is the approach of a group to their God, to whom they have the access of a friend and before whom they yet humble themselves in adoration and devotion. Through tested forms or newmade devices, they express appreciation, their sense of need, their resolution to do his will, and their confidence in him in whom they believe. . . . From this act of devotion they expect immediate joy or satisfaction. They hope also to derive direction, wisdom and strength, individually and as a social fellowship, for controlled and purposeful living.[3]

One who speaks from sensitive awareness of what worship has meant to her, both as lay worshiper and as minister, describes worship as "the reverent, receptive opening of the soul to God in company with others of kindred intention."[4]

Worship as the "Drama" of the Soul

Sören Kierkegaard, Danish spiritual leader, suggested that worship may be regarded as the greatest of all dramas. Church attenders, he said, have wrongly interpreted this drama, however, when they look upon the sanctuary as if it were a theater, themselves as if they were critical "audience" there to judge or enjoy, and minister and choir as if they and they alone were chief "performers." This, said Kierkegaard, is squarely backward.

Where persons have found real relation with God, the reverse situation is experienced. Drama is there—magnificent drama—the greatest dramatic plots in the world: human souls before God. The stage is there. But now each living worshiper is himself "chief actor." He plays the part that only he can play. The stage for each is his life-span. The Audience? Almighty God! Minister, choir, and other helpers are but "prompters from the wings," who "cue in" the actors that each may the more acceptably play his own part before the Greatest Audience.[5]

Suppose now, you are on a committee responsible for planning for a brief service of worship in your women's society, or men's brotherhood, or club, or youth fellowship. You are keeping in mind this "each-one-before-God" concept, rather than thinking of yourself as performer before an audience. Your purpose is not to "put on a program," or to impress. Rather, your prayer is that whatever plans you make, whatever materials you use, and whatever you do as "prompters" may somehow enable worshipers the more readily to reach up to put their hands into the Hand of God.[6] You pray that the group may not so much be conscious of you as leaders or committee, but move forward in fellowship with One Greater.

Worshipers, too, can be helped to catch this view (see Chapter IV for suggestions for guidance and worship training). Worship then becomes for each, not a mere sitting and listening, but a fresh, ever-new Adventure. When one is not merely depending upon human leaders or aids to carry one along, one rises to enter in as *active participant*. One plays a responsible part, not only for one's own sake, but to seek to usher one another into the Holy Presence. By mysterious spiritual laws, of which we have but touched the fringes, one finds oneself growing in responsiveness, both to God and to others.

Outward Order Reflecting Inward Movement of Spirit

How can we know, in planning for worship in our small groups or in the larger congregation, what "order" is best? Is there any one "order" acceptable and helpful under all circumstances? Usually we think of using such aids as Scripture, prayer, hymns, possibly spoken thoughts. In what sequence should they come? Or, if worship be the drama of the individual soul before God, do we *need* any order?

On rare, wonderful occasions in intimate, close-knit groups or between friends or lovers, there may come an almost telepathic communication of spirit, so that together they move forward in a mutually understood "order" of expressing thoughts without pre-planning. A brilliant jazz combo, or a group of Negro singers gifted in empathetic feeling may improvise as they go.

But for most of us, most of the time, some guidance is needed. Dr. A. W. Palmer says that for groups, "worship must practically always be something prepared and planned."[7] The worshipers themselves, and not alone the minister or other leaders, need to be in on the "plot," to know clearly in what progression of steps the drama unfolds—so that each may play his part well, and in harmony or unison with the others.

On the one hand, the answer is not in easygoing formlessness, with no one (save perhaps the leader who may be "playing it by ear") knowing what is to come next, or indeed why they are now doing what they are doing. Imagine a ball game with each player making up his own rules as he goes along, irrespective of what the others are doing. Little meaning, less fun! When leaders rebel against all forms and orders and speak of keeping worship "free," they may (with however good intentions) impose their own personal whims in patterns more rigid, or leave the group floundering meaninglessly.

The answer, since true worship involves every individual actively, is not for minister or leader to "take the ball and run with it," whether with much form or little. Neither depth fellowship nor true worship is engendered when the situation is that of minister or leader over against group, *giving* directions, *deciding* for the group, *telling* members what to do. Group worship is not one person's achievement in getting others to do as he wishes (as in a military march). It is a mutual creation of all the members, using whatever helps (or overcoming whatever hindrances) the leaders offer, remembering always with humility that God is the most active One. His amazing grace "gets through" in spite of our weak (and sometimes ego-centered) ways.

Nor do we find answer as to the "plot" or "inside story" of worship in following mechanically a sequence laid down in books, or handed down through tradition. Much that has come to us, filtered through the experiences of thousands of worshipers, and preserved in the accepted books of worship of the denominations and faiths, speaks as deeply and truly of our contemporary spiritual needs as when first uttered. But from time to time all of us need to re-examine our customs, sequences, forms, materials, aids—in order to be sure that we are not following from habit or rote. When we look anew at such a familiar aid as the Lord's Prayer, vital meaning may flash forth. Too, we would in no wise want to fall upon certain orders as a crutch for spiritual laziness. We would in no wise want to use any words, customs, or forms as a cloak for hypocrisy.

Rather, worshipers together with their ministers or leaders (and *not* these latter alone) in prayer and discussion together ask themselves seriously what *inward movement of spirit* they are experiencing. Then, with honesty, simplicity, humility, and charity, they chart tentatively the outward steps or "order."

Worship is not like a television show where scenes and sound-tracks were made long before and now played over. It is "alive" in all the thrilling senses of that word!

Each time of worship together is a new enterprise, for never before was any individual at just this stage in his spiritual need and capacity. Never before was the group at just this point of readiness and expectancy.

That is why each worshiper needs guidance and training, along with those asked to lead—for worship is not "put on" for a group. Each, inescapably, is "leader." Each brings his utter uniqueness of personality, his secret yearnings known only to God. Each must strive to focus his thoughts, to "hunger and thirst," to hold himself in readiness for the God-response. There is a decorum of worshiping together, where each guards against wandering off to pick spiritual flowers alone, because he feels "knit" with the others, answerable to them and God. As, gathered together, each of us then does his part to express the music of the spirit, it becomes "concert." We find ourselves lifted beyond what any one of us might experience in prayer alone; for to each, in God's generous Plan, is given the awesome privilege to help "conduct" to others and to receive from them, as together we all receive from our great Conductor.

Public worship is the outward, dramatic expression of what is actually happening in the soul of the worshiper. That is why . . . we use a form patterned after this inward drama, as it has been lived and re-lived in the souls and lives of the saints of the ages.[8]

"Order," "ritual," "liturgy," "sacraments," "ordinances," then, are not something our worship leaders do for us, or put us through. If we as worshipers enter in wholeheartedly, whether the customs be centuries-hallowed or creatively new, we move forward together, praying to catch step and to match any outward expression with inner sincerity.

> Here, O my Lord, I see thee face to face;
> Here would I touch and handle things unseen,
> Here grasp with firmer hand eternal grace,
> And all my weariness upon thee lean.[9]

The simple procedures by which we rise to praise God together in a hymn, and bow to pray in confession—or the more elaborate procedures in a great church congregation—become sacramental when we as worshipers experience a touch of the Living Presence through them, and when we seek with all our hearts. As said by Augustine and repeated by Calvin: that which is said or done outwardly becomes, then, "a visible sign of invisible grace."

A simple beginning "order" of steps we may take together in worship is (1) *The Holy Presence, and our recognition and praise*; (2) *our confession and divine forgiveness and renewal*; (3) *God's call and our response.*

Always we remember the miracle-way by which, for our every puny, human gesture in worship, God does far more. Keeping this in mind, we may use the three short terms, *Recognition, Renewal,* and *Response* as guide words. In more elaborate liturgies, each of these steps may be broken down into several more. For all groups, small or large, whether informal or formal, the three steps are minimal.

THE HOLY PRESENCE, AND OUR RECOGNITION AND PRAISE

Before we approach a service, we should make prior preparation of spirit, coming "to find God and be found of him."

As we enter the place of worship, we may bow for silent and intercessory prayer. If music is played in prelude, we let our expectancy grow in glad faith. If there is a printed order of worship, a few "bidding" words may suggest preparatory thoughts. Groups may work out for themselves customs, such as Calls to Worship, with leader and group in antiphonal response. Some youth groups work out special customs, such as having a member move forward quietly to light a candle; the light becomes a signal that as a total group, members think of the *Living Presence*. There are many Scripture passages which would be particularly appropriate as ringing calls to us to lift our thoughts to the One Most High. In small groups, carefully prepared settings or pictures may help members still their anxious thoughts and prepare to worship.

Our next inward step, one that wells up spontaneously yet naturally, is that of *praise* to God. What could be more humbling, yet breath-takingly reassuring than that the God of the universe should, in seeking us, move our hearts to seek him! Our most exultant, and perhaps our universal, way of expressing praise, joy, awe, gratitude is through song. All can join thus together.

Doxologies offer a glorious vehicle of praise, as do many of the psalms and other passages of Scripture. Young people sometimes prepare special litanies or other expressions of praise, through music, words, or symbolic action.

As a further expression of our *recognition* of the Presence, we may join in affirmations of belief. The custom is for all of us to stand as we recite the Creed of our faith. Some small groups find it an intensely meaningful experience to discuss beliefs together, or perhaps have a unit or series on backgrounds of their faith, and then to put into their own words their personal statements. If one is used in a period of worship, the participation should be reverent, sincere. The expression of belief should call for ever-new heart searching and thinking. Shall we "say" a creed or mean it? And if we mean it, how shall we speak? Surely not in mere mumbling!

You don't really believe your creed until you want to say it standing at spiritual attention with the roll of drums in your ears, the light of love dazzling your eyes, and all the music of a splendid world crashing out a prelude to its truth.[10]

OUR CONFESSION, AND DIVINE FORGIVENESS AND RENEWAL

This suggests (following Isaiah's realization of his own unworthiness in such a Holy Presence) our own sharpened awareness of our uncleanness, our selfishness, our sinfulness, our unreadiness to stand before such unfathomable, undeserved love.

We engage in soul searching, preparatory to *confession*. We may be prompted in this inner act by queries, such as the Friends use. A leader may "bid" us to make, in the secret of our own hearts, the act of confession, through a few well-chosen general words, quietly given. A wealth of aids may lead us to contrition—Scripture, incidents from past or present, films, dramas, units of study, panels or discussions, current events. We see ourselves in all our sinfulness and need before God; we experience sorrow for the general evil and hurtfulness in society multiplied every hour.

We know that there must be in us no unforgiveness of spirit, either toward God who created us (no resentment for his having put us here in the midst of sin, or, if our theology prompts, sin in the midst of us), or toward our neighbors (for any specific hurts they may have caused us or for their alienating of us in cold indifference). We must surrender our tendency to put self in the center, if the operation of God's *forgiveness* may accomplish its miracle work.

The ways in which we express our confession outwardly may vary (from silence, to unison prayers, to prayer-hymns, to individually spoken words). That we each make this step in the inwardness of our own secret lives is the important thing. The great collects of the church of the ages express in brief word-rhythms, simple yet powerful statements of confession, so that—while joining voices in the same words— each of us will be stirred to think into the words a confession for our own sins. Together we confess for each other and for all. A prayer may be spoken for all by a leader. A hymn may be sung. "All we like sheep have gone astray."

For *renewal* we but wait, in faith yet holy awe. For we cannot achieve it of ourselves, by our much working or wishing, our much speaking or praying. Any "creating within us of a clean spirit" comes from Above. It is miracle.

Assurance is sometimes expressed by the worship leader in such words as, "He that confesses his sin, the Lord is faithful and just to forgive and to remove all unrighteousness from him," or "So far as the east is from the west, so far has he removed our transgression from us."

At this point, we may wish to express through some medium of thanksgiving, our joyful *receiving* of the renewal given.

GOD'S CALL AND OUR RESPONSE

This involves, now, our openness, in renewed state of sharpened sensitivities, to the calls upon us of others' needs; or to *God's call*—to ways our Maker may be prodding us to give ourselves more lovingly and unstintedly, or challenging us to surrender selfish tendencies, or arousing in us new purposes to engage more strenuously in disciplines of discipleship.

Prior to the step of renewal we would not have been made ready for hearing a "call" to serving and giving. Now, our consciences should be more alert to problems in society and in ourselves that face us as Christians' unfinished tasks.

The particular ways in which challenges come to us may vary from the spoken message (minister, worship leader, panel, discussion) to story, to picture of need, to drama. Questions may prompt us to realize that we face crossroads where choices are called for. Units of study may have prepared us, made us more open for challenge!

How remiss we often are—we in our complacency, indifference, self-centeredness. How often we tend to go our way with scarcely a thought of others near or far. What of someone's deep, secret need for friendliness, understanding, good will? What of another's desperate plea for life-essentials: food, shelter, warmth, clothing? Many walk a lonely road, clinging to a last tattered shred of hope.

Dedication is more than sentiment or emotion. With hearts made responsive by the Father's forgiving love so unmerited by us, we are moved to let our prayers reach forth, beginning with ones nearest us and moving on out.

Until in our groups we first learn to *pray* for others, how can we learn to serve and give with sensitive love and selflessness? Pastoral prayers usually include a time for intercession. But what of our prayers in smaller groups such as adult or youth fellowships, or classes?

Reading about Jesus directly from the Gospels (with eyes fresh and eager, as if we were hearing for the first time) shows that he said (though others later said differently *about* him) that he came to earth to live (not die), to give life abundant, to be God's anointed one to help blind, lame, imprisoned, lonely, hurt ones—the last, the lowest, the least, the lost! This (holding all our dogmas in abeyance for a moment) is what Jesus did! *He gave his daily life!* What greater miracle? What could be more redemptive, more like the very heart of God the Father?

In the *response* stage of our worship, presenting our tithes and offerings symbolizes our total self-giving in Jesus' spirit and footsteps, and in thankfulness for what is given us. Money is but "coined energy"—our own lifeblood minted for larger service.

Thus dedication or response is of self: time, talents, possessions, to be used as God may see fit in showing concern and care. After a sermon, the congregation or conference should seek to make dedication specifically in terms of the issues that have been raised then and there. Perhaps too often our expression of dedication is vague, abstract, sentimental— when, to nerve us for following through, we need to focus upon definite purposes, perhaps specific immediate steps that seem at the time to be God's "leading forth." To be sure, there are great turning points in our lives when we make full, eager dedication of our total selves. Then, this is given practical implementation as, through worship services and personal prayer, we "put feet" to the high covenant made.

Through what outward means may inward dedication be expressed? Moments of silence may be given after the sermon or message (which may be in film, drama, through discussion). A hymn of dedication may be sung thoughtfully, heads and hearts bowed. A prayer of dedication may be expressed by one or by several or in unison. When appropriate, suggestion may be given by the leader that individuals wishing to come to the altar to kneel for their dedicatory prayer may do so unhurriedly, lingering as they feel the need.

Benedictions are, as one junior high boy said, a way of "asking God to go home with you." They do not mark the *end* of worship, but the transition into one's personal arena of daily living from the gathered fellowship. How are benedictions expressed? Usually a minister or leader expresses a benedictory thought, perhaps taken from Paul's eloquent words found at the closing of various letters. The worship leader may extend his hand over the group in token that the "great cloak" of God's care continues over all. Music, psalms, special benedictions as chosen or created by the group, may impart assurance. In some groups (such as youth fellowships) there are "official" benedictions which all speak together. Let *not* the leader speak of "repeating" the benediction; even though familiar phrases are used, they can be freshly prayed. As the group is divided into two halves, all standing facing one another, they may pray looking into the eyes of those opposite, "The Lord be with you." One has a strange awareness of belonging, of being prayed for, as one leaves such a group.

Chimes may be played after the postbenediction silence. Gradually congregations and groups can be trained not to rush to put hymnals in racks, struggle into coats, gloves, and rubbers during the closing moments. As a full-rounding of dedication, the benediction is the climax of the service. If the fellowship with God and with each other has been real, we may wish to "linger in the sanctuary." Persons should respect others' need to remain in the pew or meeting place for quiet prayer; the rush of conversation should wait until all have left the sanctuary. Some may have special problems, some may wish to think back over the experience and (as St. François de Sales quaintly suggested) "gather little nosegays" of memory to take into the rush of every day.

In Summary

Some books of worship of various denominations and faiths suggest a far longer series of inward steps, to be matched by a more elaborate order of worship. We have here sought a "common denominator," a simple beginning such as may guide planners in small-group worship, and from which those who wish can grow. One might see in the step of *recognition* the upward look, in the step of *renewal* the inward look, and in the step of *response* the outward look.

Some would suggest that the beginning point for group worship should be *confession*. In the theologies of some, the fact of our human sinfulness and unworthiness is uppermost. These would say that we dare not attempt to approach God in worship without first confessing. They may be right. But one can center introspectively upon one's own state to such an extent that one fails to look courageously toward the Sun of Righteousness! One can grovel in one's dark apartness from God until one resists, unwittingly, the tropism of his Love! Our suggestion here, in beginning with the step of *recognition* is that only as we have first become aware of the holy greatness and love of God can we sense the true depth of our own sin, and do we stand in the presence of One to whom we would confess.

Some use formal phrases in mapping the steps of worship, such as "Act I, Service of Confession," "Act II, Service of The Word," "Act III, Service of Dedication," or whatever may be the preferred wording or order. If an entire congregation, or if the members of the worshiping group, have been so trained and guided that phrases have *meaning,* then such may have a place. For resilient worship-spirit and readiness to be "led along" by the Author of all our worship impulses, we must not become chained to patterns so rigidly that we cannot be limberly responsive. We must not mouth pet words or phrases as if these in and of themselves possessed some magic key. We must guard against making any patterns or forms ends in themselves, or becoming dependent upon any one way.

Not all services will have these three steps, or in this order! Some may be devoted entirely to praise. Some may be devoted entirely to confession. When individuals and groups are ready, some high and holy services may be devoted entirely to dedication.

A group of senior high young people had been discussing

and discovering more about worship for several sessions; out of their experiences in this unit, they wrote their thoughts—beginning (as perhaps most of us do before we have grown more mature spiritually) with *feeling*, then moving to the use of *reason* and *insights*, growing through the fellowship of *talking over* with kindred minds, on to the higher levels of *direct praise* and *service*.

WORSHIP IS—

- The feeling of awe as we see beauty and realize it is God expressing his love to us.
- The feeling of reverence or respect as we think with our whole beings about God and know that he is bigger than we are.
- The feeling of need for help because the world is too big and has too many problems to have us solve them alone.

WORSHIP IS—

- Searching for a better understanding of God, realizing our smallness and his greatness.
- Talking each in his own way to God of how we feel, to get peace of mind and forgiveness for our sins.
- Praising and thanking him as we are aware of him in all his creation.

WORSHIP IS—

- Working with God to make the world more Christian, beginning with us.[11]

IV. AIDS FOR PLANNING AND PARTICIPATING IN WORSHIP

◈

WHETHER WE ARE ALONE or with others, our turning to God in prayer and worship is not dependent upon any external aids: upon anything we see or hear or touch or smell, or upon any rituals or ceremonies we might devise. Plotinus said centuries before: Worship is the flight of the alone to the Alone.

We all know this. When we want deeply enough to pray, we do. We can pray, in private and quiet, in crowds or in bedlam. The mark of sincerity and intensity in prayer is not external but internal. The test is whether in our thoughts we truly seek—to find, and to be found.

But human history through the ages and our own personal life-stories show that our inward readinesses and responses are helped along by such aids as music, surroundings, words, symbols, pictures, symbolic acts and materials, and particularly by "holy habits." Certain aids are for the purpose of *preparing* us to make our acts of worship; other aids offer us a way of *expressing* what is being experienced inwardly. Perhaps few have lived who could dispense entirely with all aids. But in history and in our own life-ways, perhaps as we grow more mature spiritually we depend less upon the outward, in growing inner concentration and consecration.

The Leadership of the Spirit

That sacred word—pointing beyond itself to the Infinitely Holy, the Inexpressible. "The Spirit itself bears witness with our spirit"[1]: promise awesome in magnificence, tender in compassion upon our wistfulness and need; hope that fresh winds from out eternal spaces may move over our little weak, needy lives as winds blow over the wheat fields.

The Function of Aids in Spirit-Led Worship

Why use aids at all, if the Spirit is the Mover? First, God knows we need aids. He gives us myriads of them richly to enjoy. Look at Nature's changing pageantry, every moment. The contagion of others' spirit of joy, of reverence, of friendliness moves us to be thankful, humble, responsive. Let it be clear that to consider in worship the marvelous works of God is *not* to imply pantheism. Surely to let ourselves be reminded of the Creator by his creation is far removed from belief in no God save the diffusion of spirit through nature. In our worship, let us simply dedicate to the God who is creating still, any thoughts inspired by his world—storms, mountains, seas, lakes, rivers, flowers, deserts; and let us explore with zest yet awe the newer revelations to which we of this age are heir for the first time in all ages: pictures of deep-sea life, camera-through-telescope-windows into outer space, microscopic patterns marvelous in intricacy hinting of other "universes" still smaller as yet unseen even with cameras!

Second, psychology helps us to understand a bit more clearly our human needs: what we respond to, what enhances our moods. This does not mean that we can use psychology to manipulate worship (that would be impossible, for true worship is Spirit-led and voluntary, "from the inside . . . out" in the worshiper's intent). An egoistic speaker who wants to sway crowds may use hypnotic tones or paraphernalia. Perhaps many may be moved, even thousands. The test question is whether the center in their focus is this leader, or whether long since they have forgotten him in moving Godward. Again, as with Nature, we are called to use such insights as come through psychology about our needs and moods, and dedicate them in the service of God, that he may do with us and our knowledge as he will.

Third, worshipers everywhere through all ages, have used aids. From their own inner fires, they have passed on much to us. Through centuries of praying and worshiping, they found what customs, prayers, settings, music, words, and other helps really *helped*; they sloughed off what hindered. They simplified and made strong and vital as living stuff these "holy habits."

Our Scriptures are monuments to meditative moments of unknown many, as tremblingly they "felt God near." Devotional classics from early centuries of the faith (including ones who gave their lives for the faith bequeathed to us), hold and transmit a luminous reality, expressed in powerful clearness.

Denominational books of worship garner treasured writings, customs, liturgies, rituals, hallowed by use of thousands of worshipers.

Symbols tell a story of spiritual wonder and creative effort to communicate what could never be encased in mere words.

Sacraments and procedures help worshipers to identify spiritually with founders and heroes of the faith and with all who have in fellowship partaken.

Criteria for Choice and Use of Aids

When you hold in your hand your hymnal or book of worship or your Bible or devotional writings from some saint of long ago, *tremble* . . . take off your shoes! For the spot whereon you stand is holy ground. What you hold here is capsuled flame. What seem to you words of print on paper are immeasurably more: eager aspirations, tormenting strugglings, midnight toilings upward through meanings to faith, agonizing prayer through dark nights of the soul, high hilltop awarenesses when these souls knew themselves addressed from Beyond. Because these materials were in varying degrees "inspired," in them is imprisoned flame, capable when used sincerely of helping to light new sparks. What first came as "revelation" in someone's thoughts (made available to us now through words or arts) in turn leads within us to new "revelation." *Our* experience is not necessarily the same as, or even similar to, the original one's experiencing; for what God has to bring forth now, in our ongoing responses, may go beyond that which was said of old . . . Or through us as instrument, making some meaningful aid available, the Spirit may speak in some new way to some other life and he in turn may be moved with a message for others . . .

Choosing aids in terms of the age-level, experience range, and thought-forms of those who will be in the group.

All who work with young children—parents and *other* teachers—discover how easily and naturally a child moves from laughter to prayer to play, and how spontaneous children are in their expressions "from the inside . . . out." As grownups, we can learn much about worship from children. We can let them lead us by the hand, for how surely they know the ways to a God who is Love. Worship is "response." And how wholeheartedly responsive little people are! If gladness at God's good gifts makes them want to praise and thank, they jump up and down and their faces glow with smiles or even laughter! (The Eastern Orthodox worship which has maintained this poetic, intuitive response-spirit has a place in its ritual for "paschal laughter.") How fateful for routine-bound adults to begin to force children into their more artificial "patterns" of separating worship or devotions from all other activities; or to demand of children certain "set" ways or phrases. A visitor in a certain home was sharing the good-night prayer time with the family, and was thrilled with the spontaneity of the little girl as she expressed to God her gladness about special things she had seen and done that day. But impatiently the mother's voice broke in, "Hush all that now and *say your prayer*" (meaning, of course, a "set" one which this mother apparently regarded as more "real" or perhaps a more appropriate vehicle for showing off before the visitor). The resiliency of little children's thoughts, their warm affection, the eagerness for surprise, their intense responsiveness, their fresh creativities—are not all these precious in the life of the spirit, and of utmost worth to carry on through all years? The mark of spiritual growing is *not* a hardening into routines or verbalisms, but continuing to "give the fullest spirit play!" Only such aids should be used with any age child as "let the light through," of what that child himself means.

Camping, retreats, and such informal, outdoor occasions help keep us all "limbered up," and responsive to God and one another. Camping is for all age-levels, and there are aids for leading toward those high moments in camping when expressions of worship and prayer may come forth. In youth groups, it is advisable that not only the leaders but all the young people themselves "store up" within their memories, along with happy associations from camps and retreats, songs and spirituals, special verses from Scripture, stanzas of hymns that have held special meaning; these in turn "touch off" further spontaneous expression when used at moments of high meaning. Thus youth create aids.

Adults, perhaps especially, need to use a far wider variety of helpful aids in their worship: prayers and thoughts from the great devotional leaders of the ages, profound rather than piously sentimental; songs and spirituals such as youth use, which would be similarly meaningful in kindling adults' prayer-times; the aids from nature, experienced firsthand on retreats and through color pictures.

Remembering, as we choose and use aids, the differing needs of persons even within the same age-group. Psychologically and spiritually, our varying personalities call for using different aids at different times. What helps one, may leave another cold. What speaks to us this day, may leave us needy tomorrow. Why? Because we may have grown "a-ways"!

Never let us freeze or deaden our procedures at any given point. Suppose a person says, "Symphonies are beyond me." But if led gradually to hear beautiful symphonic music with a bit of interpretation now and then until familiar themes become like old friends, this person might find the majestic music leading his thoughts to vaster realms and opening up a "whole new world" of experience to him. Thus it is with worship. Do we not all need to be nudged to stretch and reach, to be introduced to that which is higher and holier, perhaps, than what we have yet apprehended but which calls to us, "Climb ever higher"? Else might we not remain, year after year, on the same low, weary levels?

Some persons say they are helped by worship forms and materials that move quietly. Others thrill to the exuberant. The moods of the Spirit, say the saints of the ages, are like the rainbow: adoration, confession, thanksgiving, supplication, submission. In some denominations and faiths, traditionally customs veer to the solemn, in others to the ecstatic. Maybe devotees in each type need a bit of the other to "round out" their worship life.

Probably most of us in our rushing, noisome, superstimulated ways today, need quieting aids as we perhaps take longer to "unwind and prepare" to worship than did our forebears who were already "of a mind to worship." Then perhaps, having begun to achieve that inward stilling and focusing, we may need such aids as glorious music and Scripture rendered with stirring meaning, to help move our latent, lazy spirits into Godward intent!

At all times, choosing and using aids that are felt to be worship-worthy. As we begin to plan for a devotional service in our group, we would *not* ask, "What would impress?" Or, "What would be startling and new?" Or, "What would be easiest for us to get by with—maybe something we can just read?" Rather, we would search for some thought, some hymn, some idea, perhaps some prayer or picture or other aid that *speaks forth*; for if we the planners feel "addressed, spoken to unmistakably," the chances are that the others of our group will be addressed, too. Further, when the "bell rings" inside us—as we read some phrase of Scripture, or read over the words of some hymn, or examine some poem or meditation—we cannot then, when we use this in our group, speak it lazily or crudely or unthinkingly. If it has moved us, will not our very voices ring? Will not that mysterious contagion through "nonverbal communication" move through the others also?

Here is our criterion: we should not use that which is uninteresting, unmeaningful—just to "get up something," to "fill up the time," or to "have a program"! Better cancel the meeting. We should never "read a prayer," unless first our own spirits have been moved mightily so that it *prays* through us! We should not announce a hymn unless first we have let its message reverberate mightily through us, and even as we suggest the number, or read the first line to help the group catch the mood and meaning, our prayer is that through the singing all may be ushered into fresh, vital under-standings!

If such indeed be our prayer, not only about hymns, but about any worship aids used, how dangerously important it becomes *what* we as planners select and use!

We would rule out all stuff that caters to ego-centeredness, that calls for play acting or that makes casual and glib that which should be hesitant and holy. We would rule out cheap pageantry. We would rule out attention-getting devices (like the skeleton a group placed on a table they called a "worship center"). We would rule out songs which deal merely with human states-of-feeling, or which fall short of great and glorious ideas of God. We would rule out casual speakers who slide too simply over our human need and predicament and make out God as a somewhat doting grand-fatherly being upstairs. We would rule out any piece of material that implies that the path of spiritual living, of prayer, and of service to others is a sensate "sweet-peace," "rosy-glow" introspective orgy. Much that has been produced in so-called programs suggests, perhaps, a too easy view of worship—as if it were a smooth program to be moved through graciously and impressively, rather than a dynamic, life-changing, possibly foundations-shaking inner process!

We should try to overcome temptations to lean too heavily upon aids, lest we clutch them too tightly as ends in themselves. When we become overly interested in any aid as such (a certain kind of setting, certain types of meditative materials, certain songs, certain rituals) are we not like lame people, depending on crutches, afraid to try to take a step alone? One spiritually anaemic churchman says, "I cannot worship where there is a divided chancel." Another, equally anaemic, says that he cannot worship where there is not one. The high formality that one person "dotes on," another calls "frigid." In a country church, the leading laymen gathered the carefully mimeographed "orders of worship" a new minister had prepared, and burned them angrily. In another church, members read their bulletins avidly, perhaps at times getting so wrapped up in following what is there that they might just miss the spiritual inwardness of the service.

These extremes reveal how "culturally conditioned" we become, how habit-bound. Let us remember humbly that any aids such as those mentioned are man-made and man-chosen, though perhaps originally inspired. We as worshipers should strive always to be open toward God, letting our spirits remain leadable. If there are means that sincerely used merely as aids, not ends in themselves, will help us to draw near the throne of grace, let us not shut ourselves out from using them. But let us never idolize any method, custom, or material as an end in itself.

Some persons tend to gravitate ever toward the familiar. In a hymn well-known, a custom well-used, is warm security. But wait! This sense of ease must not be confused with live God-communication! To be sure, at times he imparts security and assurance when he feels we need it. Let us not clutch at it, this side of God's giving, through aids imparting "pseudo-security." At times God may indeed be trying to break through this cloudbank of our lives, to jog us out of our comfort loving, that he may set our feet toward higher ground!

Some worshipers exult in the beautiful—in settings, music, art. Surely the crude, the poor in craftsmanship, the ill-prepared, is not worthy in the service of the Most High. But let us not as worshipers confuse the natural aesthetic thrill and joy with God-response. He gives beauty. He creates the awareness within us. But God is not synonymous with beauty. We may use it as a vestibule to venture through, on to the Meeting.

We can worship in forest cathedrals or charred ruins, among majestic hills or on barren deserts, in ordered surroundings or chaos. We can say, "Yes, I am thankful for aids, for at times my own spirit's wings are heavy." But we can say, too, "I will endeavor to keep free lest any one pattern become so important of itself as to cage me from God's surprise!"

Ways of Training Individuals and Groups

Why continue in a deadly dull routine? Why keep on having "devotions" or "programs" that—for lack of preparation or reverence, or *because of ignorance*—fail to "get off the ground?" At a retreat out in a camping spot, or in an unhurried meeting of the whole group, might we not view ourselves in a mirror? The "group" may be small or large: an adult or youth fellowship, club, even representatives of the church congregation. (We trust that what is in this book may prove helpful as a mirror, and that you will find here something that will inspire you to further aspiring and growing! Move forward—and "God go with you, Great-Hearts!"—and venture beyond anything here . . .)

Mirroring our worship needs, we would consider *orderliness* (the way we arrange space around us and aids for the eyes) and *order* (the way we arrange the time-sequence of steps in our worship together, and aids for the ears). For example, from certain youth and adult groups, who were considering "hindrances" to their devotions, came the following:

"Late arrivals—both teachers and pupils."

"Ages too varied—old and young together in the same room."

"Few willing to lead or take part."

"Laziness, lethargy. Wrong attitudes—often people do not find God because they do not look for him."

"Programs too long—too much like church services—too many talks and sermonettes."

"Unnecessary noise and interruptions—trivialities."

"Singing poor—no seeming enjoyment. Music cheap. Piano needs tuning."

"Unclear purpose, poor planning and preparation."[2]

Might not such problems explain (a) why many who come to youth and adult meetings fail to find the spiritual strength their souls cry for; and (b) why many stop coming?

Let us face it: to label such meetings "devotions" or "worship" and yet not to try earnestly and reverently to plan *as if we expected a meeting to take place between God and ourselves* is unworthy of Christianity, our great heritage, our church, our time. Would it not be ever so much better *not* to hold such meetings? For every time we "go through motions" (in a prayer, a hymn, sitting in a service) and do not *mean from the heart* what we are doing (either as "leaders" or as "members), we are *deepening the habit-groove of hypocrisy!* What we "learn" is not to worship God—but to pretend. And the more we practice this, the surer the learning, the harder the unlearning! That is why it is so difficult to win back some persons who drifted off as youth or adults. That is why it is so hard to "win" to vital, expectant, participating *worship* many who keep coming but who do not enter in.

Whatever our group, can we not set up standards to aspire to?

First, we might begin at the heart of the matter by encouraging habits of personal devotions in the members. (What is in Chapter I is offered here for personal reading and discussion in interested groups and prayer fellowships.) We would not argue with members about why their devotional habits are so important. (Who of us does not realize that there might be vast sources of spiritual help, joy, power, challenge spread out before us if we only took the time and gave ourselves to the great venture!) Rather, we would make some simple aids available to individuals—guidance as to ways of beginning, some prayers and meditations to "light the spark," some helps on using the Bible. We would provide times when persons might talk over with one another their problems and discoveries (this is the simple meaning of a "prayer fellowship").

Likewise, we would encourage our fellowship members to participate—reverently, expectantly, wholeheartedly—in the congregational worship services of their faith or denomination. Again, arguing or exhorting for attendance is valueless, even harmful. Some need to have the steps in the service interpreted to them; all ministers should count it a central phase of their task to help *each member* in their parish grow in learning how to pray and worship; far more important to the lives of people than mere sermons is this guidance in helping them learn to worship God the great Teacher. If the minister lacks training, or cannot teach well, let him learn and let resource helpers be brought in. Some ministers, fearful for numbers in their congregational services, may demur with, "If the church school worship services in the departments and other group worship is made more vital, will people tend to stay away from 'church'?" *All* times of meeting, in small groups or large, under church auspices, are "church." Often worship may be far more deeply real in these intimate fellowships than in large congregations. It is all "church," and when worship is *real*, the more eagerly will we seek further living fellowship with God in other services and meetings!

We could develop in the church a continual voluntary group-in-training: persons willing to read, think, discuss, and prepare to help others, particularly in the age-groups of children and youth. Christian education has been pathetically inept in not providing worship-helpers alongside all teachers, whose particular training and insights would enable them to aid the teachers, children, and other helpers. Often the task of "getting up the worship" in a department has devolved by default on the "superintendent," an administrator already busy and often one untrained. No wonder a "depth dimension" has often been lacking in Sunday church school and youth fellowships. The gradual training (it may take years) of a group of lay persons in deeper understanding of worship, and then of methods of integrating worship guidance with all that is done with age-levels may be the most significant step forward a church could take! These persons should be winsomely Christian, humble, and growing.

In our particular group (adult or youth, for instance) we could set for ourselves a standard that we would not use any aid or go through any procedures without endeavoring, "God being our helper," to let what we do outwardly come honestly from within. We would not sing a hymn "while others are coming in," or to cover up noise, or as an excuse to stand up. Meditations, messages, stories, dramas, or other aids would be approached receptively, not as "special speakers," "special music," or otherwise entertainment.

We would be careful *not* to have prayer unless we were prepared to mean it. Honesty before God and one another is foundational in Christianity. Dr. Allan Knight Chalmers tells of a meeting of women, where tension over business matters had created an atmosphere not conducive to fellowship *or* to prayer. Dismissal time came, and the leader announced, "Dr. Chalmers will lead us in prayer." "That I will not," he replied; then he suggested that a few minutes of silent thought might help them get ready to pray.

Definite times should be charted into the group's calendar for the year, to train and guide all the members in ways of worshiping more reverently together. Where can you find a group that *takes time* to do this? Habitually, do we not hurry to "get up" something for the next meeting? Year after year, do we not remain on misty flats, having progressed but little

—for all our hymn-Scripture-prayer-talk "programs?" What of congregations? One of Protestantism's major tragedies is the appalling lack of training, or even rudimentary interpretation, given churches. "The hungry sheep look up and are not fed!" If ministers are unwilling to give up any sermon time for such guidance (or perhaps, sadly, are untrained for such guidance), in the groups of adults and youth, prayer fellowships, and the like, surely time can be given. Here the Reformation remains unfinished! The clarion is for multitudes who, through deeply vital worship, become more committed to the Greater Will and who go out in all walks of life as spring harbingers, for Christianity must *grow*—or be lost.

Let us look at some possible times for worship training.

The morning worship service of the congregation. One minister made his "sermon" a helpful teaching-time about ways of worshiping. He had thought one such period would be sufficient. So overwhelming was the response, so eager the questions that he kept on in a series of six. Out of this grew more earnest response.

Units of study in the curriculum for youth groups, adult groups. In most denominations too little is offered; the units are sometimes brief, and teachers (having not been trained to see the high seriousness of these studies) do not always guide well. We can make the most of these, with each age-level in turn, and add much, much more for adults than is usually offered.

Charting of introductory "worship preparation" periods of five-to-ten minutes before the devotional periods in our groups. Instead of wasting time, beginning late, or having poor "devotions," we can start early, when two have arrived (soon others will be coming early); we can interpret hymns; discuss symbols, creeds, and other aids; deepen our understandings of inner "order" of worship; prepare for sincere prayer. In the age-level departments of the church school (including adult), after such "preparation," perhaps for true worship all we might then need would be a period of prayer and perhaps one glorious hymn of praise! (This might be far more real than the incipient habit of half-hour ramblings.)

Coaching all who are to plan and take part in worship services: youth committees, women's circle chairmen, spiritual life advisers, men's leaders, and the like. These in turn can coach others. Instead of saying, "Your class will 'get up' the devotions for next Sunday," plans would be charted months ahead; meanwhile, *all* should have coaching. Participants need to take their tasks with frightening seriousness. One who is to read Scripture should practice, look up pronunciations, pray that the meaning may "come through." Those helping with music should not regard themselves as "special" (or be so announced). Music is in the *service* of worship, a means of immeasurable helpfulness when dedicated.

No matter how brief the service being planned, each one who is to help in any way (including those who prepare the setting and give out hymnals) should know its purposes; let all gather for prayer before beginning.

Never should the possible worship experience of an entire

group be sacrificed merely to provide "training" for one in speaking, or playing an instrument, or whatever. In many *other* phases of a group's activity (business meetings, parties, discussions, workshops) practice is received. *Only* those ready to do their parts especially well, and reverently, should ever be asked to guide in worship. Meanwhile, the others would have a higher example to aspire to!

In contrast, sometimes "leaders" wait until the last minute, "give out parts," say, "This won't take much time." Better *not* have such services, and certainly not call them "worship"! In one youth group a girl was listlessly reading aloud, but evidently felt that something was wrong. She looked up at the adviser to ask, "Is this where I am supposed to read?" How far from worship can you get!

Ways of Planning for Group Worship Services

A committee, or you as an individual, will be preparing for a certain time of worship—perhaps for the Sunday church school hour, or evening fellowship, or vespers, or camp.

What might the result be? That persons will say, "An interesting program"? Or, "We enjoyed it"? Or, "Don't ask that speaker again"? Or, "Next time, choose a familiar hymn"?

Or, might the result be that by something said or done, some help conveyed through setting or surroundings, or from listening-time in silence, members came into fellowship with . . . God?

Begin plans with prayer, nurture plans with prayer, evaluate with prayer afterward. If those initiating and guiding the service be not spiritually attuned, poised, sensitized, how can they expect others to respond? Tremble . . . for it is a fearsome task to lead others to the threshold of the Most High—and then, as helpers yourselves, to withdraw out of the way, out of His way, that the members may approach for themselves.

Consider particular purposes for this *service, in relation to the members' needs, and in relation to the group's total plans.* Each time we worship together, let there be *focus,* direction, goal. From this will come any "theme." Basically, of course, all services have only *one* real theme: to find God and be found of him. But each service may have its special path, its focal thought.

Use aids in setting and surroundings. In a church room, simple settings may be provided to "remind" or "call" thoughts of worshipers, from the moment they enter the room. Let these not be cluttered. One tall chaste white taper may lead aspiration upward. Fresh greens laid on a white-spread table may remind of the Plan for growing, evidenced all around. Pictures should be used sparingly and chosen with utmost care. Taylor's "When I Survey Thy Heavens" shows one lone shepherd looking into the night sky; one tends to "enter" the picture alongside the shepherd. Cheap reposeful pictures of Jesus, overused, may become like glib clichés, almost meaningless; let such be balanced by vital, strong pictures of him in motion. Care and taste should be shown in framing or draping. All settings should be prepared with dedicated, exquisite care. Drapery material (over table-tops, chalkboards, or easels) should be of rich, dark fabric carefully ironed. On Easter or at times of installations white may be used, and then only.

Whatever is used should "lead Godward." The garish, the bizarre, or the merely clever has *no* place. (Note that for "learning situations" various attention-getting aids may be fitting, but worship settings should have an atmosphere of the holy.)

In the out-of-doors, let Nature provide the setting and do not use anything artificial or that belongs indoors. A spot may be chosen looking toward the horizon or by a lakeside or in the shadows of hills; let seating provide for comfort and hearing (or in large groups, use speaker system). A "silence trail" may encourage all to grow quiet as they walk toward the spot, and to come in anticipation. The violin may give a call to worship. Voices humming together create an organ effect as prelude.

Let music, in its myriad forms, be used appropriately as a means of praise, prayer, meditation, and dedication. In "ushering" us into reverent spirit, music seems to reach us on a level below the conscious, "calling from the deeps." As we recognize the Presence, through psalms and hymns, or perhaps through choral reading or anthems or symbolic motion, music gives wings to our adoration and aspiration. As the service proceeds, quiet themeless music may help us to search our souls for making confession. As we sense a "call" upon us to serve and give, music may enable us to sing forth from our hearts our dedication when emotions are too deep for mere words. Music, of all forms of worship, is universal and unitemporal, from the groaning psalms of confession in ancient Jewish tradition, "Out of the depths have I cried unto thee," . . . to the sky-piercing exultation of Van Dyke's words and Beethoven's Ninth Symphony theme in

"Joyful, joyful, we adore thee!" as sung by a great group that loves to praise its Lord!

For guiding groups in learning great hymns, responses, chorales, and the like, the *best possible* musicians should be found, in church or community! Worship is too sacred to have a poorly skilled, inept, untrained pianist or leader whose limited repertoire might cripple a group's experience! Good organists can put accompaniments on tape for groups to use; recordings can be secured with which a group can learn and sing. Only the *best*, the most glorious, the most God-centered music should have a place. (A mere "song" is a jingly self-centered or emotions-describing piece; a real hymn is about God or addressed to him!)

Increasingly, youth and adult groups go to camps, or on retreats. Persons responsible for music can make or break the mood. Fortunate is the group with one who feels music in his soul and can catch the contagion of a group's growing reverence and be one step ahead in helping to mold and guide . . . one who can sit in the group and quietly start (without accompaniment or even pitch pipe) just the right spiritual or hymn at just the right moment without intrusion. This is "leading from within," and it requires high spiritual attunement, stern self-discipline not to intrude or do too much, and a loving, gracious attitude.

Let the spoken word be not obtrusive, calling attention to itself, but used sparingly and ever prayerfully as "instrument" of a diviner voice.

If one is to "lead" the service, what may his opening words be? Surely *not*, "Let's all get a hymnal and turn to Number X." Surely *not*, "I didn't have much time to prepare." Surely *not,* "I'm reminded of a little joke. . . ." Surely *not,* "I like to hear loud singing—ring 'er out!" Surely *not,* "Pray for me that I may speak golden words to your ears." (Who of us have not heard such expressions? But how *far* from worship, and maybe even from humility!)

Let there be a quiet moment after the leader arises (his praying should have helped him become poised, God-centered previously). Let the words be lifting toward God— "The earth is the Lord's and the fullness thereof, and our fellowship gathered here . . ."; "The Lord is in his holy temple—of the listening earth, and even now, of our waiting hearts. . . ." A "Call to Worship" is really a response we make to God who has been calling us. After such opening words let there be a moment of quietness for such great meanings to sink in! Too often, we say or read something profound, something magnificent, from Scripture or other aids—and then rush on as if nothing of moment had been uttered!

Where there are printed guides or bulletin boards for services, numbers do not have to be announced for hymns; but where they are announced, let the central point of emphasis be on the *thought* of the hymn, whether it is for praise or confession or dedication or what. A reading of the first two lines (or more) may help the group prepare to *mean* the singing. Rather than, "Turn to Number X," it is better to say, "You will find this hymn numbered X." Let all stanzas be sung wherever possible! (Did you ever notice how often the third stanzas contain some of the most meaningful messages?)

Scripture reading should be *prepared!* The one to read

should have practiced until he will not stumble, until he has each word including names clear, and until the thrilling *message* speaks through him. Actually, in a service, the moment when the Scripture is to be read is the high point: all should look forward with breathless awe . . . the Word of God, preserved, translated, and now commended to us! Allow for at least a moment of quiet for the message to "go home."

What of meditations, stories, poems, and other aids prepared by others—whether of long ago, or of more recent times? Use only what is needed, when needed, and in the manner needed. In the pages following are some aids, most of them brief. Select from here (and from other recommended anthologies and references) with care and prayer. Use about half the items you are tempted at first to use. We build for worship, not by stringing many pieces together on a theme, but by seeking to be led of the Spirit, and using what seems not only "right" but illumined . . . then use that deeply. Better one hymn sung with thought than twenty without. Better one brief, clear, ringing thought than a long profusion. Use only what gives wings to your thoughts as planners. If you have felt "spoken to" by some bit, probably you *cannot* use this in a service listlessly—the resonance of your own sincerity will "come through." Pray that you may be a clear window through which worshipers will come to a greater View.

What of messages for brief services in small groups, or sermons? The same considerations apply. Certainly the holy period of God-centered worship is no time for argumentation, haranguing, tear-jerking or other antics (the source of which is usually ego). Any messages, including sermons, which we prepare should be humbly wrought forth from the depths, with dedication of our utmost craftsmanship in making the wording right and economical, that we may be but window. With human progress in understanding communication, and with developments in use of dramatic, choral, and other aids along with music, the time may come when people generally will be led Godward through more symphonic methods, and there will be less dependence upon long messages or sermons—but perhaps far greater depth of experiencing, as each worshiper is challenged more fully to enter in, and as gradually more lay persons who become ready are enabled to share in their own sincere ways.

Particularly is dedicated creativity needed for use of media of mass communications—radio and television. Rather than starting with the old patterns such as focusing on face speaking, these media give far wider range for use of sound and visual helps—and, if used well, may lead into new ranges of worship experience.

Encourage all to participate actively as worshipers and use helpers in various phases of the services. Note again the suggested "core" or minimum steps one may take inwardly in corporate worship (see Chapter III): *recognition, renewal, response.* Printed guidance or quietly spoken "cues" from the leaders may help the worshipers to "know what they are doing" more clearly and thus to move forward meaningfully.

At various points in a service, there may be active participation by all—not only through corporate hymn singing but through responses, joining in refrains after the leader says his part, prayers in unison, and such like. The worship aids in this book offer varied examples where group response would help create a diastole-systole leader-group movement of thought. Where printed guidance is available the group can read together; where it is not available the leader may suggest, before beginning a simple litany, the words of the group's refrain, which in turn would be given after each section.

In denominational worship books have come liturgies from earlier times, made strong and deep by the use of thousands. As we participate in small group or large congregation or conference, let us seek to catch the stately rhythms, letting them swing our own souls into motion, and let us strive to identify with all who have gone before as with those now with whose voices we blend ours.

In addition to participating through music and the spoken word, we do so through *acts*. We bow, symbolizing our fealty —our utmost to the Highest. We kneel at the altar. We partake of sacraments and ordinances. Through the use of visual symbols, symbols handled by leaders or by ourselves, and through symbolic acts we express (and are impressed by) meanings far deeper than words. As youth in our day have revived symbolic motion, or rhythmic dance interpreting great hymns, Scripture, or aspiring thoughts, they join with worshipers of all ages who have thus sought to express reverence with their total selves.

There is a "liturgical revival" in many faiths, like fresh winds of the Spirit. To the extent that profoundly meaningful prayers, rituals, customs, "come alive" today from of old, our worship is given dimension. To the extent that the use of heavily patterned, intricate, elaborate "orders" and the like becomes escape or fad or emblem of pseudosophistication, they may lead us afar from true worship, which must ever be humble. Let us remember, in all liturgy—both that created of old and that created anew now—that the worshipers themselves, and not merely the so-called "leaders" must be helped to use any medium meaningfully, else they are being manipulated or made to pretend. Too, in our day with streamlined language, and short rhythms the cumbersome sentence-structures and phraseologies of some old writings weight down and confuse—until one gets so busy trying to follow or make sense, that he forgets to worship. Whatever we use should *free*, not freeze, the spirit of worshipers.

Let prayer rise "as incense." There are myriads of *ways* of expressing prayer, one essence or inner God-reaching. If this reality is being experienced, the outward forms do not so much matter—whether they be the whispered prayers of many in a pre-service prayer-time, simultaneously like wind through pines; or a decorous unison prayer from of old, as a communion collect; or a prayer-litany; or a hymn sung with hearts if not heads bowed; or a period for silent meditation and querying; or a led prayer when the one speaking aloud is trying to sense and give voice to the prayer-thoughts of the many gathered; or a fellowship of prayer in an intimate group where each feels free to let his prayer come forth aloud or lift silently as the Spirit leads; or a fellowship where "word-prayers" may come, each speaking aloud but one word, but somehow all "filling in" in vicarious interaction;

or prayer as one sings, or as many sing, and thanksgiving or petition rise as the notes ascend.

Shared silence, in prayer and meditation, brings its own special Plus, beyond what silence would give of healing and help to each one. Young people who at camps and conferences have observed "Benedictine silence" from the closing campfire until after the next morning's watch, testify that this is not *blank* time (as some at first tend to fear) but intensely positive, and that new adventures, thoughts, realizations come as come in no other way . . . "For the first time," they will say, "I *listened*."

Silence . . . is prayer gathering itself into an intensity of concentration in which it lays firmer hold on God, and on that for which it intercedes. The prayer of words is prayer of movement. It passes on from thought to thought. . . . The prayer of Silence is free to halt before a single need. . . . Silence enables imagination and memory to do their work of quickening into actuality and power the love and faith that underlie all intercession.[3]

Trust! Having planned, we put our trust not in our plans, materials, settings, ourselves. We "take the risk," to be guided by the Pilot, for to worship is more than an enterprise on a horizontal, human level. We reach up our little "apertures" or windows as Evelyn Underhill suggests,[4] in glad confidence:

It is not so much the thing we do as the fact we do something to express our faith—that is acceptable to God. On the one hand, nothing we can ever do can express love; on the other hand, in doing many things we establish two-way traffic for love. The simple acts of song, prayer, Scripture, sermon, offering and rite, when used in the service sincerely and reverently and gratefully, do create a recognizable pathway between the soul and God.[5]

Keep open to the winds of the spirit! We may be led farther than we had dared to dream . . . for only when we launch forth to "do business in great waters" do we see the wonders of the Lord! Can we echo the spiritual, "I'm gonna sing when the Spirit says 'Sing!'"? Is our response wholehearted? We who get so excited over such insignificant matters as a shopping spree or party must learn to make our worship more than halfway, lukewarm, hesitant! Let long-dormant aspirations, near-buried in our overconcern for *things*, waken as to spring rain, and let us say once more,

> By so many roots as the marsh-grass sends into the sod,
> I will heartily lay me a-hold on the greatness of God.[6]

Tempted to take a supine, spectator role in worship as in many other aspects of life, we need to hear God say as to Ezekiel, "Son of man, stand upon thy feet, and I will speak to thee!"[7] In our swift rushing after pseudosecurities, we need to decide upon life's quest of utmost seriousness, to dare "the courage to be,"[8] to "let go, let God,"[9] to keep on hungering and thirsting, asking, seeking, knocking—

> But my one unchanged obsession, whereso'er my feet have trod
> Is this one enormous, haunting, never-sated thirst for God.[10]

For on beyond all our preparations, settings, messages or anything, God may have something to say, a new breakthrough! Thus, all plans . . . and all facets of our lives . . .

need to be "open-ended," for our Leader says, "Behold, I make all things new." True worship breathes into our spirits what von Hügel calls *perennial freshness*, "a quality of being able to become more humble, true, and loving . . . marks of apostleship."[11]

PART TWO

Resources for Planning

1. CALLS TO WORSHIP, OFFERTORY SENTENCES, BENEDICTIONS

~§

Calls to Worship

We are met in fellowship in this holy meeting-place.
This is God's house.
This is none other than the gate of heaven.
Need we implore his presence with us?
Nay! Rather, we are his guests.

He bids us open wide our hearts to receive his blessing, and
to be at home in his fellowship.
For we are of God's one family in the whole wide earth.
At this hour when we are met in fellowship, Christians
around the world are meeting, in their own places in their
own ways.
Mighty tides of prayer are rising.
Let us lift our hearts to worship the God, the Father of all,
in spirit and in truth, in fellowship and in love.[1]

*   *   *

O God of love, whose spirit wakes in every human breast,
Whom love, and love alone, can know, in whom all hearts
find rest,

127

Help us to spread thy gracious reign till greed and hate shall
cease,
And kindness dwell in human hearts and all the earth find
peace![2]

*   *   *

Lift up the curtain! For an hour lift up
The veil that holds you prisoners in this world
Of coins and wires and motor-horns, this world
Of figures and of men who trust in facts,
This pitiable, hypocritic world
Where men with blinkered eyes and hobbled feet
Grope down a narrow gorge and call it life.[3]

*   *   *

O come to the altar of God and worship. Bow down your
heads in reverence and pray. Open your heart . . .
Let him heal your sorrows . . . Let your forebodings cease
. . .
Let him share with you the thunder and lightning of his
mighty dream,
That you may rise in glad, good partnership to bring the
world to him.[4]

*   *   *

Spirit of life and love, Come to us and fill us.
Spirit of truth and power, Change us and use us.
Spirit of growth and grace, Come like a wind and cleanse,
Come as a fire to burn, Stab us awake to reality.[5]

*   *   *

God does not sound trumpets before.
He comes as silent as a mist.
One does not hear him at the door,
To enter he does not insist.
But if the door is open wide,
So gladly will he come inside.[6]

*   *   *

The Lord is in his holy temple;
Let all the earth keep silence before him.
And heart, keep thou silence;
Gather up thy wandering thoughts,
Thy vain imaginings;
Hold thyself open to the mystic power
Just for this little hour.
Let all thy vexing cares,
Thy roving thoughts
Keep silence in his holy temple,
Where thy spirit now has entered,
To worship the Most High.[7]

*   *   *

Father, in thy mysterious presence kneeling,
Fain would our souls feel all thy kindling love;
For we are weak, and need some deep revealing
Of trust and strength and calmness from above.[8]

*   *   *

We pray that God will be with us in this place—
But God was here already, even before we came.
We pray that God will speak to us—

But God has already spoken and is continuing to speak in all life about us.

We pray that God may reveal his will to us—

But God's will cries to be known, even in the disorder, the lostness and loneliness in our earth today.

We wait in our meetings and services and devotionals for the soft voice of God—

But sometimes we do not hear anything,

For the voice of God is terrible,

And the thoughts of God are not man's thoughts,

And the will of God is not an easy path.

It is a dangerous thing for a group of people to come together and in the silences of their own hearts to seek to hear and to interpret God—

For in it there is no comfort . . . In it there is no security . . .

In it there is no rest; . . . In it there is no peace—save the deep peace of costly discipleship!

Yet we dare to come into this place today . . . seeking to affirm that God has spoken and speaks clearly to us, in our church, in our land, *in this hour*.[9]

*   *   *

Happy are they who, nerved by thee, set out on pilgrimage![10]

*   *   *

Come, O Lord, like morning sunlight,
Making all life new and free;
For the daily task and challenge
May we rise renewed in thee.[11]

*   *   *

Listen to the Voice of God—
Around you . . . Within you . . . Listen . . .
It calls you to grow,
To strengthen your mind with new knowledge,
To stretch your heart to include new friends,
To open your soul that God may fill it with hope and beauty
and love and great purposes . . .
Listen . . . to the Voice of God![12]

*   *   *

We praise thee, O God; we acknowledge thee to be the
Lord.
All the earth doth worship thee, the Father everlasting.
Hear now, O Holy God, the prayer that wells forth from
us, thine unworthy creatures; and let the awesome
Majesty of thy merciful presence come near us this hour.
Let the holy thought of thee fill our waiting thoughts, as
dawn greets the waking earth. Amen![13]

*   *   *

God is a Spirit. And the communication of Spirit is Love.
Limitless is this Love, beyond our farthest imaginings, yet
nearer than compassion's finest hour.
With reverent wonder, and with childlike trust, we come,
O God, to worship thee.[14]

*   *   *

Silently we wait in worship, God of goodness, God of love,
God of power, God of beauty, God of earth and skies above.
Fill us with thy loving spirit, Make us want the good and
true;

Lift our minds with thoughts of beauty, Give us power thy
work to do.[15]

Offertories

OFFERING DEDICATION

A part of ourselves, we give, O God;
    A part of ourselves we consecrate here.
Claim our whole selves, O God,
    Time, talents, all,
Till our surrendered lives,
    Thy plans fulfill. Amen.[16]

PRAYER

How little, O Lord, of what we use each day to sustain
life and to enjoy, is of ourselves; how immeasurably much is
given! We are fed and nurtured, and our lives enriched by
labors of innumerable others whom we know not. And all our
efforts, and all materials with which we work, all our energies,
and our very life-breath, are from thee—gifts from thy holy
love. Therefore, may we, catching a bit of this love, in turn
make our gifts (of money, of time, of energies, of concern),
for to give is joy. Amen.[17]

PRAYER

O Father, may it never be said of us who are thy stewards
that having come to an open door, we closed it, having come
to a lighted candle, we quenched it, having heard the voice

of the neighbor begging bread, we made denial, speaking of our own ease. . . . Rather may thy great gifts to us, both of means and of opportunity, work in us thy will . . . and may we become, for Jesus' sake, thy perfectly faithful stewards. Amen.[18]

GRACE

O Great God, Giver, as gladly we partake of the harvests of the good earth, enrich also the thoughts of our minds by thy truth and thy love. Keep us ever close to one another in the holy comradeship of bread; and kindle within us the desire to share with all in any kind of need. Draw the peoples of thy world closer around thy great family board. Be thou our Host, forevermore. Amen.[19]

BRING TO GOD YOUR GIFT

Bring to God your gift, my brother; he'll not need to call
      another—
   You will do.
He will add his blessing to it; and the two of you will do it—
   God and you.[20]

I WOULD BE GIVING, AND FORGET THE GIFT

(*Conversation-meditation about the meaning of giving in Christlike spirit*)

"I may distribute all I possess in charity, but if I have no love, I make nothing of it" (*Moffatt translation*).

(*Moment for quiet thinking; then spontaneous sharing as to practical implications, in consideration of such points as these:*)

• How may we *receive* in Christlike spirit? Are we receiving, as fully as we might, of God's good gifts to us daily (that is, are we being conscious of the gifts, and actually, definitely, specifically, *thankful*)? When others give to us, do we make genuine use of their gifts and let them know we have done so?

• Love springs voluntarily from the heart. It cannot be commanded. God implants the love-energy. We give it expression. There is such a thing as giving many gifts, but mechanically and without first loving from the heart. *People can usually tell* if the gesture is genuine. So can we, of gifts given us. What differences would it make, in the way we spend what money we have for gifts during a year, if we let Christlike love lead the way? (*Suggest sharing, followed by moments of prayer.*)[21]

HEART AND MIND, POSSESSIONS, LORD

Heart and mind, possessions, Lord, I offer unto thee;

All these were thine, Lord; thou didst give them all to me.

Wondrous are thy doings unto me. Plans and my thoughts
   and everything I ever do are dependent on thy will and
   love alone.

   I commit my spirit unto thee.

Heart and mind, possessions, Lord, I offer unto thee;

Thou art the Way, the Truth; thou art the Life.

Sinful, I commit myself to thee. Jesus Christ is filling all the heart of me. He can give me victory o'er all that threatens me. Jesus Christ is filling all my heart.[22]

WHO WOULD HAVE GUESSED?

That my money is really another pair of feet to walk today where Christ would walk if he were still a man on earth?

Or what is my money but another pair of hands to heal and feed and bless the desperate families of the earth?

What is my money but prayer of intercession suddenly crossing time and space to help answer its own petition in one swift, unselfish gesture?

What is my money but my Other Self—either hard and cold and metallic, like cash in a cash box—or warm and exciting and compassionate—tenderness in action.

It is my Christian Life![23]

Benedictions

All that we sing with our lips,
May we believe in our hearts;
All that we believe in our hearts,
May we practice with our lives.[24]

*   *   *

Father, give us peaceful hearts to spread peace;
Eager hearts to do thy will,
Friendly hearts for those who need us,
Clean hearts to allow no evil,
Understanding hearts to love our neighbors as ourselves.[25]

*   *   *

The Lord be with us as each day his blessings we receive:
His gift of peace on all we pray, before his courts we leave.
The Lord be with us as we walk along our homeward road;
In silent thought or friendly talk, our hearts be near to God.[26]

* * *

Take us on the Quest of Knowledge,
Clearest Thinker man has known;
Make our minds sincere and patient,
Satisfied by Truth alone.

Take us on the Quest of Service,
Kingly Servant of man's need,
Let us work with thee for others,
Anywhere thy purpose leads.

All along our Quest's far pathways,
Christ our Leader and our Guide,
Make us conscious of thy presence,
Walking always at our side.[27]

* * *

Grant, O Lord, that the ears which have heard the voice
of thy songs may be closed to the voice of clamor and dis-
pute; that the eyes which have seen thy great love may
behold also thy blessed hope; that the tongues which have
sung thy praise may ever speak the truth in love; that the
feet which have trod thy courts may walk henceforth in the
ways of righteousness and peace. Glory be to thee for thine
unspeakable gift. Amen.[28]

* * *

O God, who knowest us to be set in the midst of so many and great dangers, that by reason of the frailty of our nature, we cannot always stand upright, grant us such strength and protection as may support us in all dangers and carry us through all temptations; through Jesus Christ our Lord. Amen.[29]

*   *   *

O Thou who teachest the trees to grow strong and tall, who guidest the birds in their trackless homing way through limitless skies, who holdest the orbits of all universes in thy hand, bid me answer to thy ever-present call upon my life to truth, steadfast righteousness, and love. Knowing that my life is not isolated or alone, may I walk bravely forth into the unknown as thy child. Let thy wisdom direct me, thy understanding teach me tender concern, thy strength empower me, and thy vision call me up and out of self-centering, laziness, blindness, and sinfulness. Forgive all that is unworthy, as known consciously or as not fully known; and set my feet along the path thy larger will beckons. Amen.[30]

*   *   *

And now may the peace of God which passeth understanding, that peace which the world can neither give nor take away, be in our hearts and abide with us forever. Amen.[31]

*   *   *

O God of all the changing cycles and seasons of our lives, as the stars and planets in their majestic rhythms follow the leading of thy will, may I in my small way answer responsively to the tug of thy spirit upon mine.

As rays of dawn stir a waking world to purpose and motion, bid me to rise to love and work in ways harmonious to thy will.

As noontide brightness makes all things clear, help me to think truly, to perceive faithfully, that my mind may be led into wisdom and understanding.

As shadows gather around the earth in the evening, may I trust myself and all for whom I care to thy tender watchfulness.

As flood-tides from the ocean fill all tiny nooks and bays, may awareness of thy unbounded love fill my life and overflow into a glad spirit of service, until at last the final shadows lengthen and the light breaks into eternal day. Amen.[32]

*　　*　　*

Now unto the King Eternal, Immortal, Invisible, the only wise God, be honor and glory, forever.[33]

*　　*　　*

And now, O Father, as in this time of gathered worship we have paused to be directed by thee, in the steps we take as we move away from this place may we not move away from thee but continue in a spirit of fellowship and prayer, conscious ever of thy larger Presence around us, thy love enfolding us, thy guidance directing us, thy righteousness challenging us, thy dream for our lives and for our world beckoning us. As in fellowship we have knelt here, and broken the bread of life together, and blended our voices in singing and praying, may we move quietly out from this place with the same spirit of harmony, of compassion, of common creatureliness before thee, and may we each in our separate walks of life be instruments of thy peace. In the name of the Prince of Peace. Amen.[34]

* * *

Now unto him that is able to keep you from falling, and to present you faultless before the presence of his glory with exceeding joy, to the only wise God our Savior, be glory and majesty, dominion and power, both now and ever. Amen.[35]

2. GOD IN HIS GREATNESS
AND MAJESTY

وهي

THE MAJESTY OF GOD

Out in the desert of Sinai one crystal clear night a few
years ago, after our expedition camp had settled down for
rest preparatory to a day of exploring the ancient Egyptian
turquoise mines high on a ridge above, I wandered out into
the Wadi Serabit nearby. Keenly aware of the ancient drama
of Bible times, I sat down upon a rock to enjoy the thrill of
the grandest view of the universe I had ever been privileged
to see. Above me appeared heavenly bodies I had read about
but never before seen. The glorious panorama aroused within
my mind the words of the ancient Psalmist:

The heavens are telling the glory of God;
    and the firmament proclaims his handiwork.
Day to day pours forth speech, and night to night declares
    knowledge.
There is no speech, nor are there words;
    their voice is not heard;
yet their voice goes out through all the earth,
    and their words to the end of the world.

Here above me was the full meaning of the silent testimony to the glory of God. The silence that surrounded me in that Sinai valley is hard to conceive in our bustling Western world, but the voice of testimony was clear.

Then came the overwhelming meaning of those other lines:

> What is man that thou art mindful of him,
>> and the son of man that thou dost care for him?
> Yet thou hast made him little less than God . . .

In the presence of such majesty one feels infinitesimal. Only faith can bring relevance into such a contrast.

Then that silent testimony aroused a deeper thought. Those heavens above were far less great to the Psalmist than to me. He had no 100-inch or 200-inch telescope to give him evidences that stretched his imagination to inconceivable limits. He did not know that that patch of light called the Nebula in Andromeda, on the meridian, was another galaxy of stars like our Milky Way, but 800,000 light years away (light traveling at the rate of 186,000 miles per second). He did not know that the earth on which he lived was a mere speck in such a vast universe. The heavens for him were but a canopy covering a very limited, but central, world. But with his limited understanding, the silent testimony spoke of God and his handiwork, for his faith was large.

The lesson the Psalmist taught me that night had nothing to do with the structure of that great panorama, its design, or its size. He taught me the greatness of his faith. He taught me the relevance of my life in the presence of God. His universe was small, but his faith was great. He showed me that my vast universe was but a testimony of the greater faith that I must have, for the silent testimony is to a far greater God, whose majesty is beyond comprehension.

PRAYER: God, our Creator, teach us to listen for the silent testimony of the heavens that speak forth thy glory. Enlarge our faith to match the vastness of our universe. Lead us through the music of thy Word toward a deeper understanding of thyself, and draw us closer to thee. Amen.[1]

HOW GREAT GOD'S LOVE

How great God's love must be!

How deep God's love must be! It must be deeper than the deepest ocean.

How wide God's love must be! It must be wider than the horizon, the borders of which can never be found.

How everlasting God's love must be! It must be more everlasting than the space which surrounds the worlds. There is no end. That must be God's everlasting love.

How ever-present is God's love! It must be more ever-present than the black shades of night as they close the door of day. It must be more ever-present than the people and things around us, that continually irritate and upset us. It must surround us as a cloud, protecting and caring for us in every need.

How quiet is God's love! It must be as quiet as the purple violet; something beautiful and perfect—waiting for me to pluck it and carry it away in my bosom to keep forever.

Dear God, may we unlovely creatures realize the depth and

width of thy ever-present love. We pray that thy love will become a part of us. May we radiate the light and warmth of living in love. Amen.[2]

WONDERS OF GOD

God lets us see his wonders; great things he does, beyond our
    ken.
He bids the snow fall on the earth, also the heavy rains,
that keep men within doors—to let all mortals feel his power;
Storms blow out of the south, and cold comes from the north;
the ice forms at his breath, and freezes the broad water hard;
he loads a heavy cloud with hail, and from the clouds his
lightning scatters, darting here and there, turning as
he directs it, doing whate'er he bids it over all his world.
Listen to this, stand still, and think of the wonders of God.[3]

CAN YOU DISCOVER?

Can you discover the deep things of God?
    can you reach the Almighty's range of wisdom?
Higher it is than heaven—how can you match it?
    deeper than death—how can you measure it?
Its scope is vaster than the earth, and wider than the sea.
If you will turn your mind to God
    and stretch your hands to him,
if sin you banish from your life,
    and evil from your house,
then you can face him unashamed,
    you may be firm and fearless;

your life will rise more radiant than the noon,
you can have hope and feel secure.[4]

*   *   *

O God, thou art holy, like snow upon Mount Everest that climbers rarely reach. May we begin to reflect thy shining purity.

O God, thou art strong, like a mountain river moving irresistibly to the sea. May we let some of thy strength flow through us.

O God, thou art lovely, like clouds at sunset transfiguring the sky with unspeakable glory. May we be filled with joy and color, too.

O God, thou art true, like stars that never waver from their courses. May we hold firm and unyielding to that which is not real and true.

O God, thou art friendly, like the sun that warms the earth and brings forth growing things. May we be friendly, too.

O God, thou art compassionate, like the blood within our veins always removing poison, always healing wounds, always bringing health. May we bring thy healing and health to the world. Amen.[5]

*   *   *

Like summer seas that lave with silent tides a lonely shore, like whispering winds that stir the tops of forest trees, like a still small voice that calls us in the watches of the night, like a child's hand that feels about a fast-closed door; gentle, unnoticed, and oft in vain; so is thy coming unto us, O God.

Like ships storm-driven into port, like starving souls that

seek the bread they once despised, like wanderers begging refuge from the whelming night, like prodigals that seek the father's home when all is spent; yet welcomed at the open door, arms outstretched and kisses for our shame; so is our coming unto thee, O God.

Like flowers uplifted to the sun, like trees that bend before the storm, like sleeping seas that mirror cloudless skies, like a harp to the hand, like an echo to a cry, like a song to the heart; for all our stubbornness, our failure and our sin; so would we have been to thee, O God. Amen.[6]

AN ACT OF ADORATION

LEADER suggests: "Let us praise God!"
(*After a moment of silence during which worshipers may prepare to praise by thinking of the greatness of God and his holy gifts, the leader instructs the group that after each section, he will give them the words of praise, which they in turn will repeat in response.*)

For the holy bread by which our bodies are nourished; for the opportunity and joy of creative labor; for our homes which shelter us from the blasts of nature and adversity; for all the physical goods which contribute to our effectiveness and pleasure in living,

RESPONSE: *God be praised for holy bread.*

Let us praise God for beauty by which our spirits are nourished; beauty of pictures and books and music, beauty of gardens and lakes and forests, beauty of great buildings whose towers shoulder the clouds.

RESPONSE: *God be praised for beauty.*

Let us praise God for love, for the deep abiding passion binding together a man and a woman in lifelong fellowship and joy; for the love of mother and child, father and son; for the love of friends and the greater love for mankind which a man may sometimes feel in his heart.

RESPONSE: *God be praised for love.*

Let us praise God for the Church, the home of the human spirit; the Body in which we find living union with Jesus Christ, our Lord; the arm of mercy which reaches out to bring the gospel to the poor, healing to the brokenhearted, deliverance to the captives, sight to the blind and liberty to them that are bruised.

RESPONSE: *God be praised for the Church.*

LEADER (*speaking*)

Glory be to the Father,
  and to the Son,
    and to the Holy Ghost—

GROUP (*singing the latter part of Gloria Patri*)

As it was in the beginning, is now and ever shall be, world without end. Amen, Amen.[7]

THERE'S A WIDENESS IN GOD'S MERCY

PRAYER, especially at the beginning of a service, may be exulting, after such manner as the following:

Thine, O Lord, is the greatness and the power and the glory and the beauty. Thine the loveliness of this new day;

thine the one certainty amid all the changes and chances of
life; thine the vital throbbing reality—towering above the
false and faltering dreams we try to grasp.

(*Moment of silence* that our thoughts may expand to a
greater awareness of the majesty and might of God—even as
a great telescope is adjusted to vaster skies.)

Response from all: We worship thee. We bless thee. We
lift our lives in gratitude to thee.

Continuing: Thou who madest the mighty clusters of the
stars hast also made our hearts to seek thee. Thou who rulest
over the destinies of nations and empires rulest also over the
tenderest hopes and desires of our inmost aspiration. (*Silence*)

Response: We seek thee. We still our thoughts that thy
will may be made known to us.

*Possible further response, using hymn, "There's a wideness
in God's mercy," through movement.* (*Members of group
may move apart so as to give space for arms to be raised. In
the first phrase about "wideness," let arms be extended
slowly, then brought forward to the word "sea"; upward,
hands together as if forming a cup to receive the "kindness
in his justice," and then in turn expressing as if to the whole
world this kindness by extending arms on "liberty."*)

Reminder: "They that wait upon the Lord shall renew
their strength. They shall mount up with wings as eagles."[8]

IN TOUCH WITH RADIANT FORCES

Prayer is putting ourselves in touch with radiant forces,
"like hanging up one's stocking to God." "Prayer," said a
holy nun, "draws the great God down into the little heart,
and raises the hungry soul to God who holds all things."

Prayer means opening every channel of our lives to the "deep health" and "quiet glory" of God . . . being still that we may know that the Eternal God is alive and ready to meet us in holy fellowship. Where God is there is clearness of mind.

Where God is, there is confidence in living. In the words of one who perceived deeply, "All the natural quiet confidence of God's earth and its manifold life surges up to give us strength and courage."

Where God is, there is joy—joy as manifest in all the young, growing creatures of nature, joy as felt in the human spirit's high adventure.

Where God is, there is renewal, restoration—tension relaxing, tiredness disappearing, guilt forgiven, inward self made clean and refreshed and whole again.

"Be still and know . . ."

Let his great, sweeping strength flow through you . . .

Let his joy refresh you . . .

Let his beauty thrill you . . .

Let his love bring you peace . . .

Let your whole being meet him with a song—

"Glory be to the Father, and to the Son, and to the Holy Spirit."[9]

WHAT IS WORSHIP?

LEADER: What is worship?

VOICE 1: It is praising God; it is recognizing his presence in everything about us; it is giving thanks for all that he is and does.

LEADER: What is worship?

VOICE 2: It is admitting that we have not always done our best, that we have been too easily satisfied; it is asking God's forgiveness.

LEADER: What is worship?

VOICE 3: It is trying to discover what is God's will for us, what he wants us as young people to do now; it is seeking to know how we fit into God's plans.

LEADER: What is worship?

VOICE 4: It is a new starting point; it is a new agreement with God and with ourselves that we are going to try even harder to live up to the best that we know.

LEADER: What is worship?

VOICES 1, 2, 3, 4: Worship is praise and thanksgiving; worship is confession; worship is seeking; worship is rededication.

LEADER: Come, then, let us worship.

HYMN: "O Worship the King."

MEDITATION: "Isaiah's Worship, and Ours."

LEADER: Men and women have always worshiped. From the earliest accounts we have of human history right down to last Sunday in church, they have tried to express their deepest feelings to God.

The prophet Isaiah, who lived some 2700 years ago, worshiped in ways which are very similar to ours. The manner in which he described his worship experience is not how we would describe our church service, but our ideas are much the same.

For Isaiah, worship was praise.

VOICE 1: Isaiah 6:1–4.

LEADER: Few of us have had such visions as Isaiah had, yet we too need to praise God and give thanks. Let each of us pause to remember some of the many things for which we should be thankful. (*Moment of quiet*)

For Isaiah, worship was confession and forgiveness.

VOICE 2: Isaiah 6:5–7.

LEADER: Our language will be different, but we also need to use worship as a time of confession. Let us pause to remember and to ask forgiveness for our shortcomings. (*Moment of quiet*)

For Isaiah, worship was seeking.

VOICE 3: Isaiah 6:8.

LEADER: We too must seek. In a time of quiet, let us think of some of the new ways in which we can serve God more completely. (*Moment of quiet*)

For Isaiah, worship was rededication.

VOICE 4: Isaiah 6:8, through verse 9, "And he said, Go . . ."

LEADER: Let us also dedicate ourselves to the tasks which God shall give us to do. (*Moment of quiet*)

LEADER AND VOICES 1, 2, 3, 4: May the words of our mouths, the meditations of our hearts, and the quality of our daily living be acceptable to thee, O Lord our strength and our redeemer. Amen.[10]

"AND THE GLORY OF THE LORD SHALL BE REVEALED"

(Note: *The selections below from the Bible are arranged for "choral" reading. Form a speaking choir of "light," "dark," and "medium" voices, by evaluating the timbre of the natural speaking tones, whether deeply rich and resonant or light and lilting. If desired, "light" parts may be taken by women and "dark" parts by men. Note that often the questions are by "light" voices; let these queries be given briskly, eagerly. Affirmations may be by "dark" voices or by all; let these be spoken slowly, surely, powerfully. Let selections for solo voices be made. Then let all read the entire selection in unison first, to get the great rhythms and the sense of the passage; after that, break into parts and rehearse.*)

PSALM 24

ALL: The earth is the Lord's, and the fulness thereof; the world, and they that dwell therein. For he hath founded it upon the seas, and established it upon the floods.

LIGHT: Who shall ascend into the hill of the Lord?
Or who shall stand in his holy place?

MEDIUM: He that hath clean hands, and a pure heart; who hath not lifted up his soul unto vanity, nor sworn deceitfully.

ALL: He shall receive the blessing from the Lord, and righteousness from the God of his salvation.

DARK: This is the generation of them that seek him, that seek thy face, O Lord of hosts.

LIGHT: Lift up your heads, O ye gates.

MEDIUM: And be ye lifted up, ye everlasting doors.

ALL: And the King of glory shall come in.

LIGHT: Who is this King of glory?

DARK: The Lord, strong and mighty, the Lord mighty in battle.

MEDIUM: Lift up your heads, O ye gates; even lift them up, ye everlasting doors.

DARK: And the King of glory shall come in.

LIGHT: Who is this King of glory?

ALL: The Lord of hosts, He is the King of glory.

ISAIAH 40:1–11FF.

SOLO (*ringing voice, resonant with compassion and concern*):
Comfort ye, comfort ye my people, saith your God. . . .

ALL (*quietly*): The voice of him that crieth in the wilderness:

CRYING VOICE: Prepare ye the way of the Lord, make straight in the desert a highway for our God.

THREE VOICES: Every valley shall be exalted, and every mountain and hill shall be made low; and the crooked shall be made straight, and the rough places plain.

SIX VOICES: And the glory of the Lord shall be revealed, and all flesh shall see it together: for the mouth of the Lord hath spoken it. . . .

CRYING VOICE: Behold, the Lord God will come with strong hand, and his arm shall rule for him: behold, his reward is with him, and his work before him.

THREE VOICES (*quietly, somewhat slowly*): He shall feed his flock like a shepherd: he shall gather the lambs with his arm, and carry them in his bosom, and shall gently lead those that are with young.

SOLO: Who hath measured the waters in the hollow of his hand, and meted out the heaven with the span, and comprehended the dust of the earth in a measure, and weighed the mountains in scales, and the hills in a balance? . . .

ALL: Sing unto the Lord a new song, and his praise from the end of the earth, ye that go down to the sea, and all that is therein; the isles and the inhabitants thereof. Let the wilderness and the cities thereof lift up their voice . . . let them shout from the top of the mountains.
Let them give glory unto the Lord.[11]

* * *

Thou, Lord Almighty,
hast created all things for the sake of thy name
and hast given food and drink for men to enjoy,
that they may give thanks to thee;

but to us thou hast vouchsafed spiritual food
and drink and eternal life
Through Jesus, thy Servant.[12]

* * *

Glory to thee, glory to thee, glory to thee, God, Christ, the King, only begotten word of the Father, that thou hast counted us, thy sinful and unworthy servants, worthy to enjoy thy pure mysteries for the remission of sins, and for the life everlasting. Glory to thee.[13]

* * *

Great art thou, O Lord, and greatly to be praised; great is thy power, and of thy wisdom there is no end. And man being a part of thy creation desires to praise thee . . . Thou hast formed us for thyself, and our hearts are restless till they find rest in thee.[14]

* * *

We give thee thanks, yea, more than thanks, O Lord our God, the father of our Lord and God and Savior Jesus Christ, for all thy goodness at all times and in all places, because thou hast shielded, rescued, helped, and guided us all the days of our lives, and brought us into this hour, permitting us again to stand before thee in thy holy place, that we may implore forgiveness of our sins and propitiation to all thy people.[15]

* * *

We praise thee, O God, we acknowledge thee to be the Lord. All the earth doth worship thee, the Father everlasting.

To thee all angels cry aloud, the heavens and all the Powers
   therein
To thee Cherubim and Seraphim continually do cry,
Holy, Holy, Holy, Lord God of Sabaoth.
Heaven and earth are full of the Majesty of thy Glory.
The glorious company of the Apostles praise thee.
The goodly fellowship of the Prophets praise thee.
The noble army of the Martyrs praise thee.
The holy church throughout all the world doth acknowledge
   thee . . .
Day by day we magnify thee
And we worship thy name ever, world without end.[16]

*(Example of writings from between third and fifth century,
showing wholehearted praise and affirmation. This is both
like a song and like a creed, and was used to help people not
only to praise God from their hearts, but also to keep their
faith, though tempted by doubts and heresies.)*

*   *   *

And thou shalt know in thine heart that the Lord thy God
he is God in heaven above, and on Earth Beneath, and
there is none other besides thee: for there is no God besides
thee alone, there is none holy besides thee, the Lord, the God
of knowledge, the God of the saints . . .[17]

PARAPHRASE OF THE TWENTY-THIRD PSALM

God is my guide,
He is all that I need,

He takes me out where the fields are green and open,
He is with me where the water is still and cool.
I think of him in the beauty of his World
And my tiredness leaves.
Sometimes I walk into unlovely places,
Where people are afraid and where death is,
I shall not be afraid because I shall remember
That God is God.
He prepares food for me to share with others,
He makes me care for people and all living things—
He makes me feel forever at home in his world.[18]

A PSALM OF HEALTH

(*Read Psalm 27.*)

"*The Lord is my light and my salvation; whom shall I fear?*
"*The Lord is the strength of my life: of whom shall I be afraid?*"

In the full vigor of my youth there was strength in my body and courage in my heart;

When I was young, my head was unbowed and I looked upon the brave new world with a brave new heart.

The Lord was my Creator, my God and my Master:

My breast was unscathed and my spirit was free from suffering.

I feared no one, for the Lord was my light and in him was my salvation;

Whom should I fear? The Lord had blessed me and put strength within me; I was unafraid.

With a song upon my lips and laughter in my eyes, with confidence and hope, I went forth into the world.

> *"One thing have I desired of the Lord, that will I seek after;*
>
> *That I may dwell in the house of the Lord all the days of my life,*
>
> *To behold the beauty of the Lord, and to inquire in his temple."*

One thing, and only one, have I given my attention, in the cool of the morning and in the evening's quiet.

While the strength of my youth was upon me, and the courage of unhurt pride surged through me:

That I might dwell in the house of the Lord all the days of my life;

One thing, and one thing only, did I desire—that I might drink deeply of the beauty around me and pray within his temple . . .

> *"For in the time of trouble he shall hide me in his pavilion . . ."*

This I believed, and I went forth, forth to sadness and destruction, to sickness and disease, to suffering and to hurt.

Trouble overtook me and I went down before its onslaught, down into despair and loneliness; darkness closed over me, and my spirit broke under it.

I sought the rock of the Lord and did not find it; I cried out in my despair, but my voice came back an empty echo.

I prayed, but I heard no answer. I sought the courts of the Lord, the place of my rejoicing, but found them not.

The hope of my youth and the trust of my heart forsook
me;

My youth flowed from me, and strong words laid hold upon
my tongue.

"*I . . . fainted*":

I cursed the Lord and waited . . . I poured out my con-
tempt and waited,

Waited for the thrust of death to claim me, for God's anger
to destroy me.

"*Wait on the Lord.*"

I no longer waited, nor believed, nor sang his goodness.

I drank bitterness and departed . . . But I did not die.

Slowly my body was renewed; slowly my health returned and
strength flowed into me.

My youth had passed, but the tasks of manhood laid hold
upon me;

Strong faith in the Lord had passed, but understanding
claimed me;

Slowly, like the passing of a storm, like the building of a
city, God renewed me,

Renewed me in courage and in hope, in trusting and in
patience.

God laid hold upon me and led me, led me in a plain path
of knowing;

When my eyes were clouded and my mind confused,

When I cried out, I could not wait.

I could not see the courts of God which surrounded me, nor
the pavilion of the Lord in which he hid me.

Now I say, "Wait . . . wait on the Lord."

Not with words and empty phrases, not with idle song and
   praises—
Wait with quiet determination; wait with hope and consecration;
Wait upon the Lord with gladness—wait with patience and
   with gladness . . . "Wait, I say, on the Lord."[19]

3. GOD AS CREATOR

◄§

THE STORY OF CREATION

With amazed wonder and profound reverence, the long-ago Hebrew people wrote the way they thought the earth and life came to be. They used ideas and language familiar to them. In their beautiful poem which appears in Genesis 1 and 2 are found three great thoughts: (1) that God was "in the beginning" before ever there was an earth or world or life; (2) that He created, according to a marvelous Plan; and (3) that human life is not merely His highest creation, but in some strange mysterious way "in His Image," and that persons can somehow experience communication with God.

In our day, with the help of many thousands of dedicated scientists who have discovered important secrets about the universe, the same amazed wonder and profound reverence that was in the early Hebrews can be in our hearts. If we were writing the story, using our ideas and language of now, we might phrase it somewhat like this (but it would be the same prayerful poem, aware of God at work with a Mighty Plan, and of persons as made in his Image for communicating with him):

(May be given as choral reading, with voices coming in, as suggested below—or may be read reverently by one.)

ALL VOICES TOGETHER: In . . . the beginning . . . God was creating the heavens and the earth, and the world was without form or light. Through boundless spaces there wandered tiny electric particles, separate and solitary. And there was chaos and night.
(Silence)
And God said,

VOICE FOR GOD: Let there be island universes.

VOICE 1: And the Spirit of the Eternal moved upon chaos. Through unmeasured spaces here and there, the electric particles gathered together, masses that turned on themselves and formed into spirals, mothers of suns yet to be . . .

ALL VOICES: And it was evening and morning, the first age. *(Pause)* And God said,

VOICE FOR GOD: Let there be stars.

VOICE 2: And the island universes broke into star clusters, and shaped themselves into stars. The electric particles were drawn together in ever-closer union, in fierce turmoil and inconceivable heat; the suns shone forth, and there was light.

ALL VOICES: And it was evening and morning, the second age. *(Pause)* And God said,

VOICE FOR GOD: Let there be planets.

VOICE 3: And it came to pass that one great sun in its course swept near another. From that other it drew forth a great tidal wave of flaming matter. From this wave, great jets spurted forth, and started on their separate orbits around the sun. And the planets were born, and the earth planet.

ALL VOICES: And it was evening and morning, the third age. (*Pause*) And God said,

VOICE FOR GOD: Let there be atoms and elements.

VOICE 4: Out of electric chaos in a myriad suns the atoms appeared. In the cooling Earth planet the ninety-two elements were shaped. And out of the elements were formed earth and air and water and the countless physical structures of the world.

ALL VOICES: And it was evening and morning, the fourth age. (*Pause*) And God said,

VOICE FOR GOD: Let there be life!

VOICE 5: And God took the elements that he had made; and God shaped the living cell and the forms of lesser life and higher, of life—vegetable and animal—simple but ever more complex, moving slowly upward through ascending levels.

ALL VOICES: And it was evening and morning, the fifth age. (*Pause*) And God said,

VOICE FOR GOD: Let there be man.

VOICE 6: And God chose one of the lesser creatures of earth. And God bade him walk erect, with hands set free to shape tools and rule his world, with eyes that could look forward and upward. And God touched his lips that he might speak and so have fellowship with other men in love and toil, and hand on greater treasures for a later greater race. And God quickened into life the soul of man that he might know the meaning of life, that he might set high goals and rule himself, that he might hunger for the Infinite, that he might commune with the Eternal.

ALL VOICES: And it was evening and morning, the sixth age. (*Pause*) And God saw everything that he had made. (*Pause*) And God said,

VOICE FOR GOD: It is not yet finished . . .

ALL VOICES: And God rested not from his labors. And God called man to know the purpose of the Eternal, and to enter upon the fellowship of creative love, and to know that his labor was not in vain in the Lord. And it was the morning of the seventh age . . .[1]

OUR GOD CREATING STILL

There are many parts of our Bible which we should not read with cold literalness as if we were reading a mathematical equation, but only with hushed, prayerful spirits, humble "tuning" toward vaster, deeper truths than mere words can hold. We pause before the holy magnificence of the two Genesis accounts of creation, until the depth-thought comes through to us: "In the beginning, *God*." Holding that thought reverently in the center of our minds, we read then all we can about what scientists tell us of beginnings. There can be no conflict. Human words are inadequate. We feel the truth pulsing beyond and in and through: "In the beginning, God." He is creating even now . . . this very minute . . . in the rhythm of blood-circulation in our bodies . . . in the moving planets and all the vast systems in their orbits . . . in the seasons' cycles . . . in the evaporation-condensation of moisture . . . in our thoughts contemplating such wonders . . .

(*Different members of group may suggest present-day evidences of God's hand at work now.*)

We ourselves know what joy sings in our hearts when we make something with our hands, or write a poem, or compose a tune, or paint a picture, or take part well in a drama. A gardener or farmer thrills with the fine response of plants peeping up from the ground, knowing full well that to God's ongoing creativity is coupled his own: that somehow, tingling through his own fingertips, is something of God's dream, too. The human hand and mind directing can bring to glad reality a dream once hid in the secret recesses of the soul. All that has ever been created of beauty and helpfulness on earth was first an idea in someone's dream. God's dreams reach on into a future as yet unbuilt. Our thinking and working with him couples our God-given creativity to his, and lo! something new that never was before. "My Father worketh," said Jesus, "and I work."

What may be the "secret plan" (to use Kagawa's beautiful thought) hid in our hand by an ever-creative God?

(Moments for silent thought. It may be suggested that each look at his right hand.)[2]

THE MIRACLE IN THE FACT

The important thing is not the fact of miracles: it's the miracle in the fact.

The people passing down the street, the stars in the sky we forget to lift our eyes to, are both parts of the same miracle. Astronomers analyzing light rays know that the materials in the most distant reaches of the stellar universe are no different from the elements of our own bodies.

And green grass, leaves, our life itself—things accepted in a blur of taken-for-grantedness—are interdependent parts of another miracle. Rutherford Platt, businessman, botanist, and a genius with the camera, tells us: "If any man invented a machine which would run by the power of sunlight and make food out of water and air he would be considered a genius."[a] And he adds, "wasting his time." Green leaves have been doing the job a long while. Their patent, chlorophyll, was invented before animal life could exist. They put chlorophyll to work so well they created a food surplus, from which animal life could be sustained. "Animals, including ourselves, have never found any other way of getting food. We are entirely dependent on green leaves."[b]

The greater the man of science, the more unashamed and spontaneous his wonder before the miracle in the fact. It is Einstein who affirms: "The most beautiful thing we can experience is the mysterious . . . the source of all true art

and science. He . . . who can no longer pause to wonder
. . . is as good as dead; his eyes are closed."[c]

Any day's dullness is neither life's nor the world's: it is our
own.[3]

A PLAN COME TRUE

From an early beginning
God fashioned by his will
The spaces high
The distance far
The reaches deep
The seasons true
The sun and moon
The sea and land
The stars and flowers
   And
The Universe was born.
His Plan began.

In the course of the ages
God created for his glory
The single cell
The growing tissue
Little bits of life—
Fishes in the sea
Birds of the air
The chattering ape
The crouching human
The growing spirit

Sons of God
  And
The Universe continues,
His Plan fulfilling.[4]

THE HAND THAT MADE US IS DIVINE

Joseph Addison in his poem (which was made a hymn) paraphrasing the 19th Psalm, pictures all the planets in their turn and in fact all of creation, coming in like instruments in a grand orchestra until all attuned are singing, "The hand that made us is divine."

But sometimes we forget that . . . or willfully persuade ourselves that however we may have arrived here on this planet, we're merely mechanisms giving off energy for the food we take in. But surely a brief look, even at the mechanism of the human body, leads us to marvel at the intricate planning that gave us life and *keeps us alive!*

Suppose you take ten pennies and mark them from 1 to 10. Put them in your pocket and give them a good shake. Now try to draw them out in sequence from 1 to 10, putting each coin back in your pocket after each draw.

Your chance of drawing No. 1 is 1 to 10. Your chance of drawing 1 and 2 in succession would be 1 to 100 . . . your chance of drawing from No. 1 to No. 10 in succession would reach the unbelievable figure of one chance in 10 billion.

So many essential conditions are necessary for life to exist on our earth that it is mathematically impossible that all of them could exist in proper relationship by chance on any one earth at one time. The existence of a Supreme Being is demonstrated by infinite adjustments, without which life itself would be impossible. Man's presence on earth and the magnificent demonstrations of his intellect are part of a program being carried out by the Supreme Intelligence.

How much in God's wider creation conspires together to make it possible for human life to *be*: forces of gravity, gases in the air, contents of topsoils growing our food, temperatures, seasons—what if any of these had been different, even in slightest degree? We would not be here! Says a prominent scientist, "There is . . . not one chance in millions that they should be at one time all on one planet in the proper proportions for life."

What proof of a divine plan!

Read Ecclesiastes 3:11; Psalms 19:2; Isaiah 40:29–31.[5]

PROVIDENCE

If ice were engineered so that it would sink instead of floating, the many rivers and lakes would turn to solid ice in winter. Because ice is lighter than water, the layer of ice on top serves to insulate a river or lake. So the lower levels remain liquid, permitting the survival of fish and plant life in the water.

No scientist, regardless of his learning, understands why ice floats. All he can do is to describe the reactions that take place. He does not know why water is made in such a fashion that it becomes lighter when it turns to the solid form, ice.

We can never hope to understand all the wonders of God. But we can take our personal problems to the God whose glories we discover in the world that he created.

SCRIPTURE: Psalm 8.

A LITANY (*to be read responsively by selected readers*):

How beautiful are the rivers and the oceans of Earth, O Lord.

They testify to thy providence.

How marvelous is the design of a snowflake, our God.

All our engineering skill is child's play in thy sight.

How fearful are the north winds, the storm clouds, and the icebergs, great Jehovah.

They remind us to acknowledge our ignorance and our weaknesses.

How glorious are fleecy clouds against blue skies, promising rain to water the thirsty earth.

They call us to prayer and praise, rejoicing that thou dost love us.

PRAYER: God of majesty and of might, we see how very small we are when we measure ourselves by thee. Keep us mindful of our limitations, we pray. Help us remain vividly aware of our need for help, so may we turn to thee in certainty. Amen.[6]

MESSAGES FROM GOD IN SPACE

One who professionally served as navigator on commercial intercontinental flights tells of his thoughts of wonder up there in higher space . . . his remembering that the rainbow which he sees up there momentarily is possibly for God's eyes completely—a "covenant of color" between God and man, as when God spoke with Noah . . . The navigator writes:

"This revelation of the covenant appears ofttimes before

me at the close of summer rain. No matter where I fly over sea or land I feel its colors haunting me like the eternal melodies of David. For frequently and quite literally I take his 'wings of the morning' and dwell in the outermost skirts of the sky, and even there the hues of the covenant reach warmly forth to bolster me.

"Am I wrong in supposing divine revelations to be written in just such figures in the heavens? Is not the sunset a message from its heavenly creator, and the courting of eagles a code for the human spirit? Could the fivefold rainbow be any less than a hint of the supreme glory beyond?

"If the shepherds of the earth have gleaned something of the message of the stars, should not we watchers in the pastures of the clouds see even deeper into ultimate truth? What is gravity to the fly inside a bottle being waved about by a flight engineer in an airplane? How does the problem of navigation feel to the least mole? . . . You are just beginning to learn perspective when you discover that it is not alone the railroad train that moves, that the track moves also . . . when a man tastes a potato, the potato also tastes the man. Or if to the flower the bee is a messenger of love, to the bee the flower is a fountain of life. In the Lord's house are many mansions . . ."[7]

FIRST THE DREAM AND THEN THE DOING

Infinitely beyond all our human imaginings or analogies are the ways of God our Creator. But perhaps through the lenses of our own experiences we come to sense some faint glimmerings of what he is like and of how he works. James Weldon Johnson, in his perceptive poem picturing the creation, describes the personal God stepping out upon space with the glad dream, "I'll make me a world!" From there, step by step the vision is worked into reality, until at last: man!

Surely this tingling eagerness within us to fashion mud pies or kites, poems or symphonies, pictures or dramas, better working relations among peoples, good will instead of hate— surely this need within us to make, to do, to improve, to express is God-given, a kind of echo of the divine creativity. Then, let us take it gladly and rejoice. But let us take it with a prayer, that always this creative urge and skill be dedicated to his greater will, to peace on earth and good will to man!

Before man ever stepped forth into a little dugout canoe and began learning how to paddle through the water, he had to dream. Then, step by step he learned how to build bigger ships and to venture into deeper waters. Then came the dream of flying. And step by step ways were found of airship building, working always with God's great laws of outer space. May we learn to *live* bravely, creatively, as we have learned to sail and to fly!

> Hear now the eager throbbing of wings,
> Steel-nerved and eagle-swift in their flight,
> Reined by the steady hands of a soul
> That needs must be going on![8]

*   *   *

O God, we thank thee for this universe, our great home; for its vastness and its riches, and for the manifoldness of the life which teems upon it and of which we are a part. We praise thee for the arching sky and the blessed winds, for the driving clouds and the constellations on high. We praise thee for the salt sea and the running waters, for the grass under our feet. We thank thee for our senses, by which we can see the splendor of the morning and hear the jubilant songs of love and smell the breath of the springtime. Grant us, we pray thee, a heart wide open to all this joy and beauty, and save our souls from being so steeped in care or so darkened by passion that we pass heedless and unseeing when even the thorn bush by the wayside is aflame with the glory of God. Amen.[9]

*   *   *

O God, whose laws will never change,
We thank thee for these things we know:
That after rain the sun will shine,
That after darkness light appears,
That after sleep we wake again;
That life goes on, and love remains,
And life and love can never die.[10]

CLUES TO GOD

I sit alone in the fading light near a vast lake and think. And I search . . . I search for God.

A cool breeze lazily passes by, blowing my hair and pinching my face. The nearby trees stand tall and straight and all but reach the heavens. The sky is a canopy of many colors. It seems that an unknown artist has dipped his brush into many different colors and then flung that brush into space creating a beautiful velvety sky. The breeze moves through the grass causing it to sway as if caressed by an unknown hand.

Birds in the distant trees are all that break in upon the stillness. But yet, they do not break in, they seem to be a part of this lovely scene.

The lake dances in the last rays of sunlight. It seems as if millions of tiny feet, light and gracious, have heard the song of the birds and are doing their part to create beauty.

But God? Can he be here?

Yes, he has been here all the time, but I have been too busy with other things to find him. I have been too busy worrying about the threats upon the world to see its beauty.

Upon the evening breeze coming from afar, I hear his words, "Be still and know that I am God."

PSALM 46.

PRAYER: Father, open my eyes. Amen.[11]

4. JESUS THE CHRIST

ﻭﺝ

JESUS THE YOUTH—SHARING THE
HIGH DREAM

To the young man Jesus came the long-anticipated trip to
Jerusalem. Every good Jewish boy looked forward eagerly
to seeing the Temple, and worshiping there; through age-old
ritual he would then "belong" with the men. The long
journey, usually on foot, would be lightened by the thrill,
and by fellowship with many other pilgrims. Probably before long, Jesus would be known throughout the company—
for his strong arm in cuddling a sick child or helping an aged
man, for his help in making camp at nightfall, for his story-
telling and his song. Being much amongst people, his
parents might not miss him at first on the return trip.

> Did Jesus come singing over the hill
>   In his thirteenth spring in Palestine?
> Did his shout, like a rain from heaven, fill
>   The boughs of orchards of olive and pine?
>
> Did the Temple burst on his boyish view
>   Like a marble flower on history's stem
> As his vision loosened its wing and flew
>   O'er the roofs and walls of Jerusalem?

Did his feet go racing down the slope,
  As his glad eyes burned toward an open gate?
Was his young heart charged with a boundless hope?
  Did his thoughts leap, eager and passionate?[1]

We do know that he felt "at home" in the great Temple—his Father's house. His keen mind asked searching questions. His Father's work was now to *think*, and work out new answers along lines of God's love. With heart aflame, he went back now with a job to do: to live and then teach a way of love. Perhaps his steps were surer, more grown-up as he returned. Every idea must first be *lived*, tested out wholly; then he would share. He had found God's mighty dream for his life: he would *give his daily life.*

MEDITATION ON THE DREAM

(*After a few moments of meditation in silence about Jesus' giving of his daily life, let a query be directed to the group:*)

"How earnestly are we *seeking* to find God's dream for our lives?" "Have we sometimes been so busy dreaming of greatness in faraway places with strange-sounding names, that we fail to see the everyday opportunities of daily life-giving *now?*" "In what ways is our school life now a 'vocation'?"

"If Jesus were a senior high or older youth in our school or living in our community, in what specific ways might he show God's concerned love for people?" "What next steps may we take?" "In thinking of our vocational choices, have we sometimes erred in focusing mainly on the jobs rather than keeping our commitment always central to the living Christ . . . and letting the actual job-path open?" "Are we ever aware that any worthy task, no matter how humble, can be a 'calling' and done with Christian love?"

It is a daring thing, almost a frightening thing, to adopt a purpose. There it is. Startling in its immensity. Gripping in its challenge. Let us fall to our knees. To feel *needed*— needed, just as we are, we with our particular individual name and face—needed by Almighty God to live daily lives for him! In our calendar of time. On this earth! O Father, we thank thee![2]

JESUS—UNIVERSAL

LET US WORSHIP: "So this is not a time for confidence, nor is it a time for despair; it is the time to turn to God."

UNISON PRAYER: Our Father, God, in whose love we find meaning for life, in whose truth we find light for our world, and in whose presence we are made whole, we come now to the altar of thy love. We know that we stand among a people who worship other gods; we know that the sins of our society reflect our own imperfect ways. From the depths of our hearts we repent and seek thy outreaching spirit anew. Thy love alone can save us. Thy forgiveness alone can make us whole. Thy power alone can give us direction for right living. For us thine *is* the kingdom, and the power, and the glory forever and ever. Amen.

SCRIPTURE: Isaiah 6.

RESPONSIVE READING

LEADER: Now at this dim-out hour the world waits the coming of one who is universal.

ALL: There *is* one whose life and word are true for all men and all times.

LEADER: Jesus always spoke and lived in world terms. He did not say, "I am the light of Asia." He said, "I am the light of the world."

ALL: He might have said, "Ye are the salt of Palestine," but he didn't. He said, "Ye are the salt of the earth."

LEADER: He might have said, "God so loved the Jews," but he didn't. He said, "God so loved the world."

ALL: Man's experience with Jesus proclaims that in him there is neither Greek nor Jew, slave nor free. All are one in him.

LEADER: Jesus belongs in all the world. He is, like no other person or force or plan, universally meaningful in men's lives and in the life of mankind. His life spirit speaks to every area of human experience. In Christ there is no East nor West, no dividing lines, no curtains of hostility.

ALL: Our Father, grant that we may begin to know and love thy Son, the Christ universal soon enough and well enough. Amen.

HYMN: "All Hail the Power of Jesus' Name"[3]

*   *   *

I saw myself, in a dream, a youth, almost a boy, in a low-pitched wooden church. The slim wax candles gleamed, spots of red, before the old pictures of the saints.

A ring of colored light encircled each tiny flame. Dark and dim it was in the church. . . . But there stood before me many people. All fair-haired, peasant heads. From time to time they began swaying, falling, rising again, like the ripe ears of wheat, when the wind of summer passes in slow undulation over them.

All at once some man came up from behind and stood beside me.

I did not turn toward him; but at once I felt that this man was Christ.

Emotion, curiosity, awe overmastered me suddenly. I made an effort . . . and looked at my neighbor.

A face like every one's, a face like all men's faces. The eyes looked a little upwards, quietly and intently. The lips closed, but not compressed; the upper lip, as it were, resting on the lower; a small beard parted in two. The hands folded and still. And the clothes on him like every one's.

"What sort of Christ is this?" I thought. "Such an ordinary, ordinary man! It can't be!"

I turned away. But I had hardly turned my eyes away from this ordinary man when I felt again that it really was none other than Christ standing beside me.

Again I made an effort over myself . . . And again the same face, like all men's faces, the same everyday though unknown features.

And suddenly my heart sank, and I came to myself. Only

then I realized that just such a face—a face like all men's faces—is the face of Christ.[4]

JESUS THE MAN—WE TOUCH HIM IN LIFE'S THRONG AND PRESS

We look up from the Gospel we are reading. The centuries seem to fall away. We're *there*, in the scenes. He starts answering somebody's question; others press closer to hear, still others; we ourselves draw near on the outskirts of the crowd. How ringing with sureness his voice, yet how kindly! Now he smiles, as a powerful truth hits home, and he looks yearningly into the very heart of the asker, as if to say, "Won't you see?"

We're drawn to look at his eyes . . . eyes such as we have never seen before. Now they flash fire, as a trick question of a Pharisee is met with swift insight and living truth! In the depth-look from those eyes is hint of long hours of meditation looking out over vistas stretching far.

But we're struck most with the kindly, compassionate look in those eyes—as if the very heart-love of the Father God were looking forth: to this harassed cripple comes assurance that he is loved, that his life and his suffering are not in vain; to this anxious mother comes peace; to this tottering old man comes new strength. And to one who has erred yet who seeks the way back comes forgiveness; and shoulders straighten, and breath comes deep and strong once more.

Silently, those eyes come to rest upon us . . . and we feel cleansed, made new and tenderhearted that we may care for others, too. Whatever the burden, it is as if the eyes of Jesus assure, "God understands. He cares."

But look! The crinkles at the corners of his eyes! And the heavenly glints as he laughs now merrily with a young man at a pun they've thought of together. This is no shallow laughter, but from the heart, bubbling up from wellsprings of joy. He was to say later, "I came that your joy might be full."[5]

HIS LIFE AND OURS

(*For this meditation, a good strong picture of Jesus may be central—one showing him in motion, not in repose; if a slide is available, the picture may be projected on the wall above the participants; though it be dim, the impression will be there, and perhaps more meaningful than if clear. The Reader stands to one side, holding an open Bible. The Leader is opposite, perhaps holding a picture of a modern church: even the one in which you are worshiping.*)

LEADER: Why do we have churches today? Not simply for our own benefit, to give ourselves a place to worship and serve, and to enable us to meet new friends . . . Not simply to baptize us, or marry us, or bury us. We have churches today because a Man came and lived among people to show them what God's love was really like . . . and to show also what a joyful, understanding, loving *human* life could be like.

He had just started, really, when they took him to a hill and . . . you know the rest of the story. But what about the "rest" of his story—the work he began? What tasks are still unfinished today?

He made it clear at the beginning of his ministry what he had come to do and why . . .

READER: Luke 4:16–21.

LEADER: And that is just what he began. He went about the streets of villages, healing sick ones, helping blind ones to see. He tried also to help people get over the spiritual blindness that comes from hate-curtains in the soul, and causes people not to see the good in others who may be different. He tried to show people that justice in actions must spring first from love in the heart. In the crowded ways in *our* towns and cities, people have exactly the same kinds of needs. What would he say are *our* unfinished tasks?

READER: Matthew 20:25–28. (*Silent thought*)

LEADER: Through little stories called parables, he showed exactly where responsibility rests.

READER: Matthew 25:31–40.

LEADER: We may be tempted to excuse ourselves by saying that we have racial and cultural divisions today. But in Jesus' day, did not the Jews and Samaritans have a cruel "curtain" of misunderstanding between them? Jesus knew no barrier. He told about one who overcame it. What peoples would he use for illustration today?

READER: John 4:6–15. (*Silent thought*)

LEADER: Jesus organized no church, built no building, set up no committees. But his life of unselfish service touched others to want to do likewise, His bands of followers, down through all the ages, have stood for kindliness to the suffering, courageous good will in difficult situations, love that melts barriers. People who set out to try to follow in these ways he lived, join together in a "church."

READER: John 15:8–15. (*Silent thought*)

LEADER: Our world today has multiplied problems, much sorrow. More than ever, the call goes out—who is willing to live again as he lived? For only through such lives can love replace hatred, good will replace war, and a new day of dawning brotherhood begin.

READER: Revelation 21:3 (*Silent thought, followed by prayer*)[6]:

MY PRAYER

Lord, help me to see
The beauty of a life
Made wholly thine.

Dear God, on bended knee,
My all to thee I give;
Make that life mine.[7]

THINKING TOGETHER ABOUT A PICTURE

(*Though everyone may not have a copy of even a small print of Zimmerman's "Christ and the Fishermen," the way the "study" is worked out indicates ways other pictures may be studied—the group sitting quietly before the picture for a few silent minutes, to "let" the picture speak forth, and then sharing in fellowship.*)

Zebedee was an old man but he was an agile fisherman. A day on the lake with his son James and his younger son John found him less tired than either of them.

It was toward evening, after a day of fishing, that Zebedee and his sons drew near the shore to find a young Rabbi walking along the sandy beach. The Rabbi was not a stranger in Galilee but never had Zebedee, James, and John been able to talk with him in the way they had long wanted to. Now they could talk with him all by themselves. No one was near; no crowds followed.

Zebedee dragged his nets, heavy with ropes and sinkers, from the boat. He would sit on the shore and mend while the attractive Rabbi talked with James and John.

As the Rabbi talked, his hands touched the hard, brown hands of the elder fisherman. The mending stopped, and strange words came from the young man's lips, "Love your enemies"; "The kingdom of God is within you"; "Turn the other cheek"; "Peace I leave with you"—was the young man crazy? He seemed to have forgotten the world in which they lived—the tribute money; the exploitation of the poor; the unfair advantage tax collectors take; the bargaining; the hatreds among races and classes of people. "It's a great idea," thought the old man, "but only a young visionary would dare say things like that."

"John thinks it's wonderful! He believes it, too! He would almost take up with this young dreamer!"

"James thinks he is good. He is leaning closer!"

"Yes, it's a great idea," and Zebedee felt the hand on his

hand. His skin was leathery and his clothes were worn but he felt important. New hope surged through his body. He was not through. He had a life before him, and other lives. "It's a great idea even though it cannot work in a world today— but I'm glad someone believes it! He has a right to think as he pleases. No one else would dare."

Zebedee looked at the Rabbi. The Rabbi looked at John who had already risen from the sandy beach. "Come. Go with me. I will help you to become a fisher of men." Not John, ah, no! He was too young, quick, and virile. He loved fishing, the sun and wind in his face. He loved people in the village and work with his hands.

"Come," the Rabbi said, "follow." And the old man's hand tightened in the net ropes as he heard John's whisper— "Master!"[8]

AND HE WENT AWAY

One day a bewildered youth came to the Master and said, "What must I do, good Master, to gain favor in your sight?"

"First, you should keep the commandments."

The youth looked puzzled. "Which commandments do you mean?"

"You shall not murder, commit adultery, steal or bear false witness. Honor your father and your mother; love your neighbor as yourself."

"But these things are just force of habit with me. I learned them when I first started to Sunday school and I've always just kept them. Is that all I have to do?"

"What else, my son, have you done toward living a Christian life?" asked the Master.

"Well, I do what I was always taught. I never murdered anyone. That's against the civil law, anyway, and so is stealing; and I honor my father and my mother, and I think I love my neighbor as myself. I go to church nearly every Sunday and I've read in the Bible. I try to help other people. But I don't feel I've succeeded."

The Master said, "My son, you must put your service to the church—your life as a Christian—above everything else. Everything else must be second."

The youth walked away sorrowfully, for he thought of all his school activities, his social affairs, the big party Saturday night, various clubs, and all the things asking for his time—things that were so important to him.[9]

IT IS NOT EASY

Jesus often withdrew from the crowd
Across the sea, to the mountain-top.
In a desert drear, or a garden green;
Withdrew to worship God, to meditate,
To make his vision clear, his purpose strong,
And thus, through prayer, to see the way to go.

. . . .

Did Jesus find it easy—
To apprehend God's will, to live God's way in such a world
    as this,
To trust in truth and simple love, to hold God's triumph
    sure,
To walk steadfastly to the cross while loving life?

. . . .

It is not easy—
To be in the world, but not of it; to break with its standards,
    not to conform;
To miss the martyr role, yet bear the outcast's scorn;
To be shunned, misunderstood, labeled crank, fanatic, all
Still loving men, co-operate with God, to build the wor
    anew.

It is not easy—
To be open-minded, free from prejudice,
To know our blind spots and our bonds of color, caste, and
    creed;
To seek release for all men—children, scholars, sinners, saints.

It is not easy—
To trust love and good will, when violence threatens;
To withhold the arm, to stay the blow;
To rely upon ideas, simply spoken—ideals, nobly lived—
Slowly to persuade—transforming enemy to friend.
To face the chaos man creates—the greed, the hate, the
    pettiness—
To think man more than robot-beast, to see beneath the
    sin-smirched front—the man who may like Christ become.

Yet if not easy, still it must be true—
There is no other way triumphantly to live, create,
To make life yield its richest gifts,
To bring the Kingdom nearer here on earth,
To have the joy of work and love,
Of fellowship and peace that has no end.[10]

PRESSURIZED CHRISTIANS

"Lo, I am with you always, even to the close of the age. . . . " (Matthew 28:20)

When you fly across the continent by way of one of the major airlines, the chances are that you are flying high in the stratosphere, where the air is thin, and where it would normally be impossible to breathe. To combat the rarified air, passengers on these planes travel in pressurized cabins.

Christians are being pressured on every hand to let down their scruples.

- Just one drink, says the world . . .
- Just one game of chance, says the world . . .
- Just one lowering of standards, the world calls to us . . .

But when we are consecrated Christian young men and young women, we are pressurized against the evils of the world. Such pressurization helps us to make wise choices when the forces of evil compel us to make decisions.

With the spirit of Christ, no pressure is too great, no temptation too large for us to overcome.

O God, open our hearts and open our lives to constant presence in our lives. Help us to make wise choices on this day. Amen.[11]

CHRIST OF THE INDIAN ROAD

Have you not heard about Him,
O my brothers?
Do you not know about Him,
O my sisters?

He was a carpenter.
The wood yielded to his hands.
His yokes were easy upon the ox's neck,
    and sweat was upon his brow.
He called Himself the Son of Man.

. . . .

He gives a dream that will not
    let a young man sleep.
He gives an adventure that will not
    let a young man rest.[12]

5. OUR BIBLE

ی

I AM YOUR BIBLE

I am your Bible.

I am a book of life.

I grew out of the experiences of people like you . . .

Through the hot struggles and the steady achievements of those whom you meet in my pages you can see the story of humanity on a vast and dramatic canvas.

In that story you find yourselves revealed . . .

Your struggles for a better life and the response of God to that effort are there.

Your living over again the heroic experiences of mankind is also in me.

Your love for heroes whom you can worship I can satisfy.

Your need to learn from the mistakes of others I can supply.

The ways of God in his tender dealings with a sinful or an aspiring soul I make clear.

All of these gifts of mine are mediated to your growing lives through those people who are called of God . . .

I am your Bible.[1]

THE BIBLE—A LIVING BOOK
FOR A LIVING AGE

The Bible is alive because it comes out of life. You always hear voices whenever you go near the Bible. Sometimes you hear men talking with eager zest. Sometimes you hear them pleading. Sometimes you hear them praying. Sometimes you hear them weeping. Sometimes you hear them singing. But you always hear them. Armies are marching. Workers are laboring. Judges are hearing complaints. Kings are ruling. People are busy about all the interests of life. There is stir and movement everywhere. And above all the human voices is the high command of that great voice which speaks with the authenticity which comes from the Master of life himself. In the Bible human life becomes articulate. And deeper than that, in the Bible God becomes articulate, speaking in the language of men.

"There goes a Bible character," said a shrewd observer, as the saint of the village passed down the street. "How do you get him inside the Bible?" queried a bystander. "I thought Abraham and Moses and Paul were the Bible characters." "I don't get him inside the Bible," was the quick reply. "I get the Bible inside of him. Bible characters are not merely people the Bible tells about. They are the people the Bible makes."

It is this power of making people which is the deepest basis for our calling the Bible a living book. It has life in it. It sends life out of it. It masters men's minds and rules their thoughts. It masters their bodies and keeps them clean. It masters their hearts and determines their feelings. It masters their wills and rules their actions. And this it does not as a book of rules to which men submit mechanically. Its supreme power is exerted by a strange ability to get a vital grip on the inner motives of men, and from within to work out. So it becomes bone of a man's bone, flesh of a man's flesh, and life of a man's life.

Of course, mere white pages with black marks on them do not do this. The Bible is not a book of magical formulas. It is not a god to worship. It is not a shrine before which to kneel.

It is the adequate expression of a message which grips men and changes them and lifts them to a new quality of experience and activity. It is the message in the Bible which makes the Bible a living book.[2]

LISTEN!

It is as if in the theater, where I am hugely enjoying an aesthetic view of life, God interrupts the show with a stentorian announcement: "Is John Smith in the house?" And I am John Smith. And the interruption continues: "Report immediately . . . for a task intended for you alone!"

—That is the way it is as we read our Bibles. God is apt to stop the show and put us into the act . . .[3]

LITANY OF LOYALTY TO THE STORY THE BIBLE TELLS

To the sacred truth revealed to holy men of old and transmitted to us by the sacred Scriptures,

O God, help us to be loyal.

To their questing spirit which ever sought to know thee better and understand thy will more fully,

O God, help us to be loyal.

To their high integrity which maintained the truth even at the cost of pain and death,

O God, help us to be loyal.

To that glorious company of faithful souls who have recorded the message, conserved the truth, and transmitted it unto us,

O God, help us to be loyal.

To all who have loved thy word, rejoiced in service, and so enriched the stream of human life,

Help us, O God, ever to be loyal. Amen.[4]

6. THE CHURCH

৵

THE CHURCH FOR YOU DOTH WAIT

Rise up, O youth of God!
The church for you doth wait—
Her strength unequal to her task,
Rise up and make her great!

YOU,

YOU, at this moment, have the honor to belong to a generation whose lips are touched by fire . . . The human race now passes through one of its great crises. New ideas, new issues—a new call for men to carry on the work of righteousness, of charity, of courage, of patience, and of loyalty!

But why the urgency now? Down through history, when crises have come, has there not always appeared a "man to match the hour?"

NO! At times, to be sure, when the need was urgent, someone has appeared, God-led to give leverage to the world toward better ways. But think of the times when surely God must have been calling, calling—and people were too busy, or preoccupied with other things, or lazy, or unconcerned, or

193

worshiping other gods. A few more faithful might have been used of God to prevent the destruction of Sodom and Gomorrah; to have convinced the Turkish Sultan, with St. Francis' help, that God loved him—and had he believed, how different subsequent history might have been! What of times just past—had more answered God's call for missions in China, Africa, all over the world, how much farther might humanity have come along in response to the Creator's Mighty Plan. And what of now? If we fail, God the Invincible will work on through aeons and other lives. But how sad to miss our cue, in this our hour of life! "The Master is come and calleth for thee!"[1]

TODAY I JOINED THE CHURCH

Lord of the earth, today I was received as a member into the fellowship of thy church on the earth.

To the sound of music, and with the words of my minister, and in the presence of my parents and my friends, I was received into the brotherhood of those who seek above all else to do thy will.

Burn the scenes of this day into my mind so that they can never be erased while time shall last.

Keep the words I have heard ever alive in my ears.

May the beauty of this morning be before my eyes forever.

When I would choose the selfish path, let this act of mine today remind me of him who said: He that loseth his life for others shall find it forever.

Help me always to remember that he is my Saviour and

Lord, and that I have chosen him as Master of my life. In his name. Amen.[2]

TODAY IN CHURCH

Pour out your heart before him (Psalm 62:8).

Read Psalm 62:5–8. What do you expect when you enter church to worship today?

Do you look forward to inspiring music and stirring hymns? Do you anticipate moments of silence in which those about you sit in hushed awe? Do you await a moving prayer in which the very richness of the words, or perhaps the simplicity of the delivery, brings conviction of the leader's earnestness? Do you expect to arise again, strengthened in your convictions, assured that this must be the way?

Is this all?

Or do you expect to meet God?

• To come face to face with the underlying reality of the universe that makes us see the shabbiness of most of our daily routine?

• To pass through the kind of experience that would drive the writer of Hebrews to say, "It is a fearful thing to fall into the hands of the living God?"

• To struggle with the moral darkness within your own soul as Jacob wrestled with the angel, and to arise a better person?

• To find at last that overwhelming love of God that brings assurance of divine forgiveness and sends us forth seeking incessantly to share that love with all mankind?

Father, today, let me meet thee in worship. Amen.[3]

ALL ONE BODY WE

(*Suggested setting: a globe of the world with an open Bible in front of the globe. A black cut-out of clasped hands on the wall above and behind the globe. A spotlight on the entire scene.*)

CALL TO WORSHIP: *I Corinthians 12:20, 25, 26.*

HYMN: "O Church of God, Divided."

VOICE PAGEANT: "ALL ONE BODY"

SEVERAL VOICES: All One Body We!

VOICE 1: You know, there are lots of churches.

VOICES 2 and 3: Big churches, little churches, country churches, city churches.

VOICE 4: There's the church at the crossroads in the country, with no town for miles, yet people worship there each Sunday.

VOICE 5: And they really worship, too.

VOICE 6: They sing with all their might, and no one complains, and God hears them.

VOICE 1: They have Sunday school in the same room before the morning worship . . .

VOICE 2: And teachers struggle,

VOICES 3, 4, 5: And children and adults learn great truths.

VOICE 6: Then there are the busy downtown churches in our big cities,

VOICE 1: Where people drive for many miles to worship,

VOICE 2: And parking places are hard to find;

VOICES 3 and 4: But many have had a perfect attendance record for years;

VOICE 5: Because they believe in their church as the tower of strength for their lives.

VOICE 6: And don't forget the neighborhood church at the corner of the block!

VOICE 1: Lots of the kids on our street go there, even though their parents sleep on.

VOICES 2, 3, 4: We pass the church each day on our way to school.

VOICE 5: It reminds me to take my faith into the classroom.

VOICE 6: It's a good church . . .

VOICES 1 and 2: It's God's church.

VOICES 1, 2, 3, 4: All churches are God's churches.

VOICE 5: We've just mentioned the locations of churches; what about their names?

VOICE 6: "As it is, there are many parts, yet one body."

VOICE 1: And each part has a name,

VOICE 2: And there are many names,

VOICES 3 and 4: Baptist, Methodist, Congregationalist,

VOICE 5: Lutheran, Quaker, Roman Catholic,

VOICE 6: Mormon, Adventist, Presbyterian,

VOICES 1 and 2: Episcopalian, Reformed,

VOICE 3: And just plain Christian.

VOICE 4: Each church has different ideas and different ways of doing things,

VOICES 5, 6, 1 and 2: And so do each of us, yet . . .

VOICE 3: We can all get along together.

VOICE 4: Let us join in a prayer of thanksgiving for all churches, and for their unique contributions to our Christian faith.

ALL VOICES: We thank thee, Lord, for—

VOICE 5: The Eastern Orthodox Church, with its secret treasure of mystic experience, its marvelous liturgy, its regard for the collective life, and its common will as a source of authority.

ALL VOICES: We thank thee, O God, for—

VOICE 6: The Roman Catholic Church, with its glorious traditions, its holiness, its worship, its noble company of martyrs and saints.

ALL VOICES: O Lord, we are grateful for—

VOICE 1: The great Protestant communions, for the Congregationalists and their concern for the independence of soul and group,

VOICE 2: For the Baptist stress upon the relation of the mature soul to its Lord;

VOICE 3: For the power of the Methodists and the Evangelicals to awaken the conscience of Christians to social evils, and for their emphasis upon the witness of personal experience and the power of the disciplined life.

ALL VOICES: O God, we thank thee for—

VOICE 4: The Presbyterian and Reformed reverence for the sovereignty of God, their sense of the moral law, and their confidence in God's faithfulness.

VOICE 5: For the witness to the presence of the Inner Light as stressed by the Friends, and their free prophetic ministry.

ALL VOICES: We thank thee, Lord, for—

VOICE 6: The Church of the Brethren, and their concern for unselfish sharing and compassion, and for their efficient service to all in need.

ALL VOICES: O Lord, we are grateful for—

VOICE 1: The Lutheran Church, for its devotion to the Word of God; for the Anglican Church, with its Catholic heritage and Protestant conscience, longing to be used as a house of reconciliation.

ALL VOICES: We thank thee, Lord, for all churches, that they may serve thee upon the earth. Amen.

VOICES 2 and 3: As it is, there are many parts, yet one body.

LIGHT VOICES: One body in Christ, and individually members one of another.

DARK VOICES: All one body we.

HYMN: "Onward, Christian Soldiers."[4]

THERE ARE ALWAYS TWO CHURCHES

There are always two churches, that is, two kinds of churches. One kind turns its eyes inward, is primarily concerned about itself as an organization, tests its success mainly by increases in membership. The other kind turns its eyes outward, is primarily concerned about the life of the community, tests its success mainly by the contribution it can make to the growth of brotherhood.

For lack of brotherhood, the whole world is in a bad way. We have great riches, but many are poor. Our granaries are bursting with surplus food, but many are hungry. We boast about our technical skill, but many are homeless. We talk much about peace, but every day we walk fearfully on the edge of war.

In this frustrated world, it is clear that the Christian churches must do more than *proclaim* the gospel that in the sight of God all men are brothers: they must *demonstrate* that gospel. The place for the churches to begin to demonstrate is in their own communities. Rich in things, but poor for want of brotherhood, our world does not need more churches half so much as it needs churches with a mind and a heart for the community . . .

Concerned Christian young people can help . . . to turn

the eyes of their congregations outward toward the community, and so give us greater hope, both for the future of the world and for the future of the church of Christ.[5]

FAILING THE CHURCH

Youth went to Church on Sunday,
Saw the empty pews,
Turned, walked away,
Wondered why the Church was
Doing nothing.

Down the street
He heard the beer glasses tinkle,
Saw the drunk stagger,
Heard a child's cry of hunger,
And a curse piercing the calm night.
Why doesn't the Church do something?
Thought he.

And God said to him,
"Why don't you?"
And then he knew
The Church was not failing him;
He was failing the Church.

Our Father, forgive us for the times we have shifted responsibility from ourselves to others, for being critical, for blaming others. Now we see that we are the Church. Thy work depends on us. I must do my part today. I begin by dedicating my time and energy for the next hour. Amen.[6]

"GIVE ME THY HAND"

The church I worship in,
The creed I speak by heart,
The hymns I sing or listen to—
Are these things my religion?

The language in which the minister prays,
My kneeling—or not kneeling—upon entering the sanctuary,
The noise or quiet that accompanies my worship—
Are these things my religion?

They must not be
For I have the knowledge that
Though my brother and I go separate ways,
We both are seeking one end.

Wisdom says that
Though I may seem to have the whole of truth,
Only the Eternal has the whole
And my brother, too, a part.

My religion is one that can say with John Wesley,
"Give me thy hand."
I do not mean you to be of my opinion.
I do not expect it or deserve it.

I do not mean embrace my modes of worship
Or I embrace yours . . .
Only
If thou love God and all mankind,
"Give me thy hand!"[7]

THOUGHTS OF A YOUNG CHURCHMAN

Thoughts of an average person:

We live in a dark and discouraging hour.

Evil is so prevalent that one life cannot possibly make a difference.

So many persons have wronged me, why should I not hate back?

Jesus' teachings might work in some far-off future, but not now.

Thoughts of a young Christian:

Jesus' time was tense and difficult, too, but love worked then.

Jesus kept always his boundless faith in God, and through prayer always found strength for each day.

Jesus prayed for those who wronged him . . . and kept loving them.

Jesus flung his whole self into living by the will of God, utterly regardless of consequences. There was no holding back.

Jesus bade his followers be—not halfway, or partly—but wholeheartedly perfect. He said nothing about giving in to the problems of the times.

Does my light shine strongly?

The legend of "the church of the lighted candles" reminds us that each one's light makes a difference. The little Alpine village church had no lights, until the people came, each bringing his own lantern—and then what radiance!

Church members today who fail to watch the quality of their daily lives, spread darkness rather than light: become stumbling blocks to others seeking the Way. (What about myself?)

Sometimes I ask anew the old question, "Does it pay to be good?" "Shall I hold to my idealism and reap censure, or shall I follow the gang and taste glory?" As a young churchman, I remind myself that if my life is on God's side I cannot be defeated. Money, prosperity, popularity may be taken away, even my life. But I shall still be victor, for I move with him who has overcome the world.

PRAYER: O God, draw me back from silly excuses and apologies, and grant me courage and wholeheartedness to live in my day by God's will, too. Give me faith to keep me going when things around me are cracking up. Give me trust to know that thy way is triumphant and teach me to walk confidently in thy way, daily. Amen.[8]

WHAT IS THE CHURCH?

The Church is man when his awed soul goes out
In reverence to a mystery that swathes him all about.
When any living man in awe gropes Godward in his search,
Then in that hour, that living man becomes the living
    Church;
Then though in wilderness or in waste, his soul is swept along
Down naves of prayer, through aisles of praise,
    up altar-stairs of song,
And when man fronts the mystery with spirit bowed in
    prayer,
There is the universal Church—the Church of God is there.[9]

7. OUR BELIEFS AND CREEDS

❧

STATEMENT OF FAITH

We believe in God, the Eternal Spirit, Father of our Lord
Jesus Christ and our Father, and to his deeds we testify:
   He calls the worlds into being,
      creates man in his own image
      and sets before him the ways of life and death.
   He seeks in holy love to save his people from aimlessness
      and sin.
   He judges men and nations by his righteous will
      declared through prophets and apostles.
   In Jesus Christ, the man of Nazareth, our crucified and
      risen Lord,
      he has come to us and shared our common lot,
      conquering sin and death and reconciling the world to
      himself.
   He bestows upon us his Holy Spirit,
      creating and renewing the Church of Jesus Christ,
      binding in covenant the faithful people of all ages,
      tongues, and races.
   He calls us into his Church
      to accept the cost and joy of discipleship,

to be his servants in the service of men,
to proclaim the gospel to all the world
and resist the powers of evil,
to share in Christ's baptism and eat at his table,
to join with him in his passion and victory.
He promises to all who trust him
forgiveness of sins and fullness of grace,
courage in the struggle for justice and peace,
his presence in trial and rejoicing,
and eternal life in his kingdom which has no end.
Blessing and honor, glory and power be unto him. Amen.[1]

WHAT IS A CHRISTIAN?

Am I "Christian?" Perhaps it's time I held a little conversation with myself. I usually think of myself as Christian—after all, I'm not Hindu or Jewish or Moslem. I live in a so-called Christian country. My parents have brought me up to go to church. I live a clean life. I am growing—proudly so, as a young person in my community. Am I a growing *Christian?*

What is a Christian? I take my dictionary and find the word. Here it says: "One who believes or *professes* or is *assumed* to believe, in Jesus Christ, and the truth as taught by him." Reading further, I find that, in the colloquial sense, a Christian is "a decent, civilized, or presentable person."

Surely I am that! But my blood begins to boil! I *must* be more than that. More than just "decent," "presentable." Furthermore, am I to be one who *says* he believes, or *is assumed* to believe? Maybe I should go to my Bible. I'll look for the word "Christian."

I find it only three times in the Bible!

In Acts 11:26, I find that "in Antioch the disciples were for the first time called Christians." Here the word was coined: made from the name of a Teacher called Christ. These disciples must have been so living that they *reminded* others of him! Does *my* life remind others of him? Would strangers think of me, "He must be a Christian," from the way I act?

A second time I find the word. Paul is pouring forth his wholehearted belief in God and His Son, when King Agrippa interrupts, "You almost persuade me to be a Christian!" (Acts 26:28, King James, adapted). Does *my* wholehearted-ness and joy in my faith help others to want it, too?

A third time I find the word: I Peter 4:16, as the Revised Standard Version has it: "yet if one suffers as a Christian, let him not be ashamed, but under that name let him glorify God." Here is the testing point. Would I be willing to suffer, now or in the future—pain, danger, unpopularity, whatever? *Would I?* Does following him who was called the Christ, and taking his name upon myself mean that much to me? What new meaning does my life, in turn, give the word?

(*After moments of quiet thought, one may start singing,* "Lord, I want to be a Christian in-a my heart," *continuing prayerfully with* "Lord, I want to be like Jesus.")[2]

BELIEVING

WORSHIP SETTING: *Place a cross and two white candles, un-lighted, on a table at the front of the room, with leaves around the base, or a plant.*

CHORAL CALL TO WORSHIP: *(by several seated on front seats)*

LIGHT VOICES: Open my eyes . . .

DARK VOICES: That I may behold wondrous things out of thy law.

LIGHT VOICES: Make me understand the way of thy precepts . . .

DARK VOICES: And I will meditate on thy wondrous works.

LIGHT VOICES: Teach me, O Lord, the way of thy statutes . . .

DARK VOICES: And I will keep it to the end.

ALL: My heart is ready, O God, my heart is ready.

LEADER *(standing before group at one side of table)*:
There are two words that we use many times each day, almost without thinking. These words are I BELIEVE. Over and over again we say such things as these:

READER *(standing at the other side of table opposite leader)*:
I believe I'll go to town today . . . I believe it's going to rain . . . I believe she's putting on an act . . .

LEADER: We have become so accustomed to this kind of expression that we seldom pause to think what we are saying. What does the word *believe* really mean?

READER: The dictionary says that the word *believe* means to have faith or confidence—usually *in* or *on*; as, to believe in a person. It also says that believe means to have convictions, and that a third meaning is to think or to judge, as, to believe meanly of one's neighbor.

LEADER: We all know that what we really believe makes a difference in the way we behave. For example, even when we say lightly, and perhaps incorrectly, "I believe I will go to town today," it means that we shall make some special effort to go to town.

When we say, "I believe it's going to rain," we know that such belief will probably determine a change in our actions. Maybe we shall try to get inside, or speed up a task so that it can be finished before the rain comes. Maybe we run for a raincoat or umbrella, or maybe just seek out a sheltered spot where we can watch the storm.

When we make such statements as "I believe she's putting on an act," our belief is certain to show in our attitude toward the person spoken of.

We may be able to hide what we really believe for a time, but eventually something in our lives gives us away. Do you agree?

READER: I think we shall all agree that what we believe makes a difference in what we do. If I believe that as a Christian I must be honest, then I cannot cheat on tomorrow's test. If I believe in Jesus' teaching that every person has worth as a child of God then I certainly shall not make fun of others or gossip about them.

LEADER: There are so many little everyday things that show what we believe. Sometimes, as Christians, it is good for us to put into words what we believe about God, about Jesus, and about the Christian life. It is good to restate or affirm what we believe. (*It would be appropri-*

*ate at this point to use the group's creed or affirmation of
faith. Reader then lights candles on table.)*

LEADER: The symbols we use in worship remind us of what
we believe. On the table there is a cross—a reminder of
our belief in Jesus Christ and his resurrection from death
upon the cross. The two candles burning beside the
cross remind us of our belief in God the Father, and
Jesus Christ, his Son. The greenery is symbolic of the
possibility of growth that is open to all Christians.

As our beliefs change or deepen with new knowledge
and understanding, so do our lives change—so do we
grow as Christians.

PRAYER: Our Father, strengthen us as we try to hold firmly
to our beliefs as Christians, and show us how we may express our beliefs more fully in everything we say and
do each day. Amen.[3]

HOW CAN YOU SIT THERE?

*For I tell you, unless your righteousness exceeds that of
the scribes and Pharisees, you will never enter the kingdom
of heaven* (Matthew 5:20). Read Matthew 5:38–48.

How can you people sit there and say, yes—I believe in
God—yes—I believe in a God of love? If you know there is
a God—a God of love, how can you just sit there? The whole
world is desperate to know that the God of love is a reality.
You should be proclaiming it from the heights to the
depths—there should be "one holy passion filling all your

frame." Your every act should bear witness to a living God.

How can you sit there—if you *know* there is a God!

If I could but have the assurance that God is a reality—the God of Christ—the God of love! It seems to me I could not contain my joy, if I were but to have such an assurance. But how can I when I can sense no reality?

And you—I see no assurance on your faces—no joy, no passion, no dedication. If you believe in a living God, I see no evidence—you show me nothing more than your brother atheist. You only sit there passively, as though if there were a God, he is dead.

If he is real, if he is living, how can you just sit there? And if you just sit there, how am I to know he is real?

PRAYER SUGGESTION: May God shock us out of our indifference. Ask for a new awakening to his will and way of life.[4]

THE SHADOW OF A MIGHTY ROCK

CALLS TO WORSHIP: Psalm 62:1, 7.

HYMN: "O God Our Help in Ages Past" (*suggest singing the first two stanzas with bowed heads, thinking of ways in which God has led his people through the dim distant centuries to now, our privilege of living in a land where we are free to worship God, and the times we can remember in our own lives when we have realized that through difficulties God's helping hand was there*).

SCRIPTURE: Psalm 18:1–6.

CONTINUING MEDITATION THROUGH THE HYMN: "O God Our Help in Ages Past" (*remainder, singing standing in affirma-*

tion. Let last stanza be sung slowly, in unison, making this our wholehearted prayer).

MEDITATION: All of us realize that our little human words are too small to express what *we* feel God is like—and we know, too, that all that we feel and think and know is but a minutely tiny reflection of his infinite greatness, goodness, creativity, lovingkindness. Our Scriptures abound in beautiful word-pictures about God, and his relationship with us his created family on earth. There are word-pictures expressing many moods of many people: rejoicing, agonizing prayer, wonder, even fear, confession, thanksgiving.

May we think quietly, searchingly, now about one of these word-pictures, God as "rock." In the Moffatt translation of Psalm 62:1–2 are these words: "leave it all quietly to God, my soul, my rescue comes from him alone; rock, rescue, refuge, he is all to me, never shall I be overthrown." You can imagine what possible circumstances may have led this person in the long ago to cry out for help, for rescue, for refuge. Maybe he has been on a long journey, over desolate land with scarcely a little hill lifting above the dead level; perhaps the hot sunlight causes a shimmering on the horizon before his eyes. He may be thirsty or hungry. He may have become separated, somehow, from others; or he may have had to take a perilous journey in a hurry alone because no one else could go with him. In the depths of his loneliness, in the merciless rays of the hot sun, he cries out. As he moves along, perchance he comes to a more rugged, rocky terrain, and against one great crag he leans and rests, feeling the strength and sureness of this rock, its comforting coolness. "God," he realizes in deep wonder, "is *there*, even as this rock is there for me to lean upon. God can be depended upon always and at all times. He is not like the shimmering mist on the horizon that is not substance. God is real, from eternity to eternity. His 'lovingkindness'—his willingness always to be my steady sure rock to lean upon—is from everlasting to everlasting!"

(May we meditate in quietness about times when we were not sure of ourselves, or of our plans; or when we were lonely; or when we needed a friend to lean upon. May we say to ourselves in thankfulness, "God is our refuge and strength." May we thank God for memories of times people have helped us, thus showing his love expressing itself through them; and may we pray that these remembrances may come to our minds and help us when we are tired, harassed, hurt, bewildered, even as "the shadow of a mighty rock" helps a weary traveler in its cool shade.)

HYMN: "A Mighty Fortress Is Our God." Amen.[5]

TRUE RELIGION
(Paraphrase of Micah 6:6–8)

With what shall I come before the Lord,
And how shall I worship the God of all mankind?
Shall I attend church and Sunday school?
Shall I be a faithful member of the youth fellowship?
Will God be pleased with many dollars pledged to missions?
Shall I give my pennies to salve my conscience
For idle and unkind words outside the church?

You have been told, O Man, what is good,

And what true religion is:

Merely to do just what is necessary and to have a pious charity

Toward my brothers far away,

And to stop with *talk* of the missionary spirit?

"He hath shewed thee, O man, what is good; and what doth the Lord require of thee, but to do justly, and to love mercy, and to walk humbly with thy God?"[6]

LIGHT THROUGH OUR DARK

Have you ever been lost in the dark? There are perhaps few country roads these days, infrequently traveled by cars, where a person might find himself groping on a starless night. We live in a country where light is much experienced, taken for granted.

Think what it must be like to be on a ship that has been blown off its course in a severe storm. To be sure, you have lights inside the vessel. But you're concerned that it find its way across the trackless, heaving ocean to a safe port. How thankful you are for a beacon from a lighthouse, showing direction and distance from shore. Or think of an airplane pilot searching for a landing field and seeing gratefully the airport beacon and then the boundary lights around the field. Think of a traveler in the night needing help, and seeing through the dark a lamp in a window.

Probably no one goes through life without some very bewildering, dark situations. One wonders what to do, which way to go. It is as if darkness closes in. When we become desperately worried and anxious, even our minds seem to dim out into darkness and our thoughts do not come clearly. Is there then no help, no hope? Maybe we are in the dark of a mood of despair, feeling that much we had hoped for is gone; maybe we are in the dark of a grief at the loss of one we have loved dearly who was the "light" of our lives; maybe we have failed in something we have tried to do, and we are in the dark of blaming ourselves.

God is light. He is there, if we but look upward in prayer. As rays of light across the water seem to come toward the very spot where we are, so God's ever-sure beam of "steadfast love" *finds* us; and in this light, we can move forward unafraid.[7]

8. PRAYER

PRAYER

Be not afraid to pray—to pray is right.
Pray, if thou canst, with hope; but ever pray,
Though hope be weak, or sick with long delay.
Pray in the darkness, if there be no light.

How many times we pray in the darkness of despair, when we can see no light . . .

How many times we pray in silence, when our lips can find no utterances for the deep murmurings which well within our hearts . . .

How many times we pray in confusion, when we cannot read the will of God as plainly or as immediately as we would like to.

But still, we have prayed. When we did not know that we prayed, or how, or why, still that voice within us could not be smothered. It cried out to its Creator.

And out of the chaos of our whirling minds, our struggle for existence, has emerged this fact: God is there. He has heard. He is answering.

We are not sure how it happens. We are not certain how

he answers our prayers. But we know that he does. And after years of aimless wandering, when at last we are grounded on a rock, we shout our joyous assertion: "We believe in prayer—really believe!"

PRAYER: Lord, teach us to pray. Amen.[1]

STANDING IN THE NEED OF PRAYER

Not my brother, not my sister, but it's me,
    O Lord . . . standing in the need of prayer.
Not the parson, not the deacon, but it's me,
    O Lord . . . standing in the need of prayer.

Why do you keep looking at the speck in your brother's eye, and pay no attention to the beam in your own? (*Read Matthew 7:1–5.*)

In every Negro spiritual, the emphasis is on the personal. The sweet chariot is "coming for to carry *me* home"; "the trumpet sounds within *my* soul." God cares for the singer *personally*, but God places responsibility on him personally too. So in spite of the evil around him, and in spite of spiritual need in others who did him wrong, the Negro sang, "It's me, it's me, O Lord, standing in the need of prayer."

Today when you pray for the world to be better, remember how great your own need is and begin your prayer there.

Not like the Pharisee, "Lord, I thank thee that I am not as other men," but like the publican, "O God, have mercy on a sinner like me!"

How much praying do you need to do about prejudice in your own life . . . about laziness . . . about selfishness

. . . about your relationships with friends . . . about your life vocation? How much will you do today toward winning others to Christ?

Yes, it's you and *me*—standing in the need of prayer, right now. Let us pray.[2]

WILLINGNESS TO RISK ADVENTURE IN PRAYER

There is no other way to explain Christianity. Because Jesus was what he was the Christian fellowship began and grew. Track Christianity down to its source, and you find Jesus the Christ.

It would seem, then, that the important thing to do would be to find the source of Jesus' life power. If we could do that, we would be at the heart of the most powerful movement in history. In a power age, we who search for power would have found the source of real power, power that shapes life and rules death . . .

And yet there is no secret or mystery to it all . . . He said it was the simplest and most natural way in the world for that power to be obtained . . .

Would anything please God more than for us to live as Jesus did?

Is there any trick to it?

Is God trying to make it difficult for us to live that kind of life?

If it is possible, then why can't we do it? . . .

You say, "This all sounds so simple it scares me." Men

have always tried to make a mystery of the plain fact Jesus illustrated and preached . . . Must we refuse him too?

Are you ready then? . . . Let's look at his life and see where the source of power for him was.

Here it is—in two words: He prayed!

"Oh, yes," you say, "but . . ."

. . . but what? Don't try to add anything, don't make it complicated. Keep your finger and your mind right there. This is the spot. This is the source: prayer.

The early Christian fellowship took the cue from Jesus . . . Why were so few able to do so much? Was theirs a secret power we cannot have? No. They simply centered their life in God, and were confident that His spirit in them could conquer the world. Through the centuries since that time, many forms and techniques of prayer have been developed. But the power, the tremendous world-saving power, has slipped away from many Christians. We ask: Has God changed?

Why cannot prayer today become as of old a source of power, of wonder-working, world-changing power?

It can![3]

WE DARE NOT PRAY—UNLESS WE'RE READY TO MEAN IT

There is nothing hid from the Eternal.

When we come to God with a neatly worded prayer—maybe one that we've fixed up to use in a service, aware that other people would be listening—*he knows* whether we're really reaching prayerfully toward him or just saying mostly words. *He knows,* when we "repeat" a prayer or benediction or offertory response, whether *we're praying it.* He knows when we sing a hymn whether we mean its message.

He knows when we say, "as we forgive . . ." whether we truly forgive the person who said something against us, or who cut us cold at a party, or who kept us from getting elected, or who disappointed us. And we know that unless we truly forgive, our own hardness keeps us from receiving God's forgiveness to us.

He knows when we ask for daily bread, whether we mean that "our" to include all his children the round earth over, and furthermore, whether we're willing to share, to help him answer others' prayers for bread.

He knows when we come to that part about "thy kingdom come," we're adding under our breath, "But wait—not yet! Don't rush me, God. Some later time, perhaps."

Read Psalm 139:1–2, 14–18, 23–24.[4]

NOT MY WILL...

Opening the door of the small chapel, I walked in and said good morning to God, for I felt his presence there. The gray stone of the walls, the arches, the stained-glass windows enhance that presence.

The gold-colored cross in the foreground reflected the rays of the sun, made blue as they filtered through the windows. Behind the cross, portrayed in multicolored glass mosaic, Jesus knelt in Gethsemane, lifting his arms outstretched—like the arms of the Cross—praying to God, "*Not my will, but thine be done.*"

I thought on those words . . .
Not my will, but thine be done, O Lord.
Not what I want, but what you want for me.
Not what I would do, but what you would have me do.
Not what I would say, but what you would have me say.
Not what I would think, but what you would have me
think.
Not what I would be, but what you would have me be.

O Father God, teach me thy will. Open my ears, my eyes, my mind, my heart to thy still calm voice, to thy will, and to thy abundant love. Give me the courage and strength to live, not as I will, but as thou wouldst have me live. I want my will to be one with thy will. Today, O God, I give myself again to thee.

I left the little chapel in its quiet splendor. I did not say "good-bye" to God, for he went with me.[5]

WITH ALL WE ARE

Read Romans 12:9–12.

We pray with all we are.
We pray with all our hate
As well as all our love.
Our angers, small and great,

And envyings, are heard
Louder than any word,
And often may defeat,
The good that we entreat.

We pray with all we are—
Lord, teach us how to pray
In spirit and in truth,
Living the words we say.[6]

AS WE FORGIVE—AND ONLY
AS WE FORGIVE

The Lord's Prayer is a hard prayer. Too many times we just repeat. . . . It is a humble prayer, giving honor to God and submitting our wills entirely to his care. In it we ask only for daily bread, for the elements essential to life, and for guidance away from temptation and evil.

The part that is so easy to mumble as so many excess words is "Forgive us our trespasses as we forgive those who trespass against us." Say it again. That's loaded.

In the manner that we forgive those who wrong us, forgive us, God. Pardon us of our sins as we pardon the world of its sins. Forgive our hatred as we forgive those who hate us. Forgive us of the judgment we pronounce as we forgive those who pronounce judgment on us. Forgive us our gossip as we forgive those who gossip about us. Forgive us our negligence as we forgive those who are negligent when we are concerned. As we forgive, God, forgive us.

. . . Forgiveness, friendship, and love are all akin. To be obtained they must first be given.

Muriel Lester of England has said, "I'm afraid of the Lord's Prayer," particularly the part where we must say, "Grant me that degree of forgiveness that I am willing to extend to my personal enemy." She tells of a highly respectable neighbor in Bow who, with hard heart, mouth, and voice, refused to allow a poor wretched woman come into her home—one who had been dragged out of a canal into which she had jumped as refuge from anxiety and shame. "Don't you really fear the prospect of losing God's forgiveness yourself?" Muriel Lester inquired of her. The woman, Muriel Lester said, looked at her wonderingly, as if the idea were a new one—yet how often had her lips said the words?[7]

> Thou canst not say the Lord's Prayer
> And make one selfish plea;
> Thou canst not pray the Lord's Prayer
> And even once say me—
> Thou canst not pray the Lord's Prayer
> And pray not for another—
> For when thou asketh daily bread
> Thou must include thy brother.[8]

GROUP PRAYER OF CONFESSION

(*Soloist may sing hymn of prayer for forgiveness, or "The Lord's Prayer," as group members engage in soul searching and preparation for prayer. Instead of a spoken group response in this "litany," let there be silence after the leader's spoken phrase, so that each individual might make his own response secretly and directly to God. As the sentences are unfinished, let individuals make their own completion. If desired, after every four thoughts, the soloist may sing very softly a stanza of a chosen hymn.*)

LEADER: When through most of the hours of my day, I keep my mind on small, selfish concerns,

When I make the little daily choices that come up hour by hour without stopping to seek God's guidance on my way,

When I am too busy to be kind, or too rushed to think of some needful person,

When I have a chance to speak up for the right conviction, but through timidity or fear of what others might think or just laziness, I let the golden minute slip by,

When I fail to take time for study of my Bible and for daily prayer, that I might grow in the faith,

When I envy others' success or popularity,

When I spend my money foolishly, and fail to give to certain crying needs which I try to push out of my mind,

When I fail to take part in church or other Christian activity, preferring my rest and leisure to God's work,

When I fail to show full forgiveness to others, yet expect God's full forgiveness of my own sinful self,

LEADER: Through the grace of Christ our Savior and the Father's boundless love, go forward forgiven, and forgiving.[9]

OUR DAILY BREAD

I am hungry, Father,
Feed me.

Feed my mind; it hungers.
Feed my mind
With kind words and thoughts,
With pure thoughts,
With a desire to grasp knowledge
Tempered with wisdom,
And understanding,
And sympathy.

Feed me.
Feed my heart; it hungers.
Feed my heart
With compassion, patience,
With gentleness,
With unselfish love.

Feed my soul, Father,
It hungers.
Feed my soul
With constant towering ideals
And motives,
With steadfast faith,
With unwavering hope,
With more than a sense of justice—
A sense of mercy and forgiveness,
Free from pettiness, jealousy, prejudice, pride.

Feed me, Father!
That my mind, my heart, my soul
May not die from spiritual malnutrition.[10]

TEACH ME

O Lord, teach me how to pray.

Teach me to know thee as a friend . . .
  to talk with thee,
    sharing my sorrow and my joy—
      gaining strength through thy companionship.

Give me a thankful heart
  for all good things from thee.
    I share my burdens with thee,
      but first, let me be thankful.

I pray for health of mind and body.
  Thou has given me a temple
    to live in and to do with.
      Let me keep it pure and holy.

I pray for good works in thy name—
  missions, schools, hospitals, and many more.
    Give me strength and a will to share.

When I fail to toe the mark of Christian service—
  when I drift into unclean ways—
    when my example is not thy example,
      Father, forgive me, for I know not what I do.

Am I selfish in my prayer, Lord?
  Do I pray for vain, personal gains?
    If I do, please answer, "No."
      Lord, teach me humility.[11]

"LISTENING"

SETTING: *A good picture of the young Samuel may call to mind the scriptural background for this service; a picture (or slide) of a person looking out from a hilltop, in a spirit of listening, prayerful thought may be better.*

CALL TO WORSHIP: Psalm 90:1, 2.

HYMN OF PRAYERFUL SEEKING: "Behold us, Lord, a little space"; or, "Master, speak, thy servant heareth."

CONVERSATION-MEDITATION:

One: When we prepare to pray, or when we gather for a service of worship as now, we imagine that God "listens" to our prayers, that somehow the great Creator-Father-God has so made us that our deepest concerns can be attuned to his wavelength, that, out of all the millions of his children, he can know and respond to us as individuals and in our groups.

Another: With the Psalmist, we can pray, "O Lord, thou hast searched me and known me," and in some mysterious way we realize that God *has*, and that we can hold nothing back from him.

Another: Yet in this knowledge of being known by God, without pretense or camouflage, is somehow a comfort. We can drop all defenses. We can be ourselves, in all our creatureliness and misery, knowing that he knows us at our worst yet loves us completely anyway. Such knowledge is too wonderful for us! We are all the more ashamed. We would run off and hide from such limitless love, for before it we are so unworthy. Yet this very love, that comes seeking us, like the "hound of heaven," draws us—as surely as the lights of our home draw us back from all our wanderings.

Another: When love draws us home, and leads us to confess our sins, we do so not in abject fear or in cowering before a merciless or vengeful Judge; we confess as children before a Father. God listens. He hears the deep voice of our *wanting* to be made whole, and he responds by creating within us cleaner hearts, renewing within us more rightful spirits. And as the wonder of this new creation dawns on our consciousness, we sense his listening to our thankfulness.

Another: Yet, should we, at such a holy moment of being forgiven, succumb to human pride and count ourselves now righteous in our own strength, he hears that, too! May we pray ever to be kept humble, responsive, ready for his remaking, giving him ever the praise.

First one: And thus renewed, we seek to respond, in listening love, that God may lead us—into whatever daily choices he would have us make, whatever paths of service he would have us follow, whatever convictions he would have us express, whatever life-commitment he would have us make. "As I was with Moses, so will I be with thee," God spoke to fearful Joshua as he embarked upon the tasks to which he had been brought. May we ever remember that the God who calls nerves us for following through, all the way. May we ever, daily, respond with Samuel, "Speak, Lord, thy servant heareth." And may we answer the call with our lives.

HYMN OF COMMITMENT: "Where he leads me," or "Lord, speak to me that I may speak."[12]

A LITANY OF QUIETNESS

(*When the worshiping group is ready to enter into a meditative unison-prayer, the leader may suggest that after each section he will give them the refrain to repeat prayerfully, or copies may be in the hands of all.*)

LEADER: O thou great Shepherd of our souls, we need thee to guide us into the paths of peace and unto the places of deep quietness.

GROUP: *Lead us beside the still waters.*

LEADER: O Lord, thou knowest how sorely we are beset on every side by the pressures of modern life. "The world is too much with us, getting and spending we lay waste our powers."

GROUP: *O thou great Shepherd of our souls, lead us beside the still waters.*

LEADER: O Lord, we confess unto thee our lack of peace within: the disturbing conflict between our ideals and our actions, the haunting sense of guilt for our sins and failures, the discords and dissonances that agitate and disturb the harmony of our lives.

GROUP: *O thou who art our Shepherd and our Guide, lead us beside the still waters.*

LEADER: O Lord, by thy grace forgive us our tenseness and nervousness, our quick irritability and our explosive angers.

GROUP: *O Shepherd, who knowest all our needs, lead us beside the still waters.*

LEADER: O Lord, fill us just now with a strange inner quietness, hush our spirits into the calm of tranquil waters, and let the miracle of the peace of God which passeth all understanding quietly enter every heart.

GROUP: *O loving Shepherd, lead us beside the still waters and now in thy presence help us to be still and know that thou art God.*[13]

LOOK UP TO GOD

I will lift up my eyes to the hills. From whence comes my help? My help comes from the Lord (Psalm 121:1–2, RSV).

Look up to God.

Lift yourselves to him that his strength and power and love may make you strong.

He is there always. Do not forget him.

If you feel the task too hard for you to do alone, remember that it is. For it is only with him that we can truly face Life and our tasks.

God is Eternal, Almighty, Everlasting, full of Grace and Glory.

He is our Refuge, and it is only as we look up to him and seek him and find him in our daily lives, that we may be sure of Life itself.

We may start the new day and forget God—
We may face our tasks of the day, and forget God—
We may come to the end of the day, and forget God—
But, he never forgets us.

And he is always there—not just in the morning, not just during the day, or just at night—but he is *always* there.

We can forever trust in him.

He is the Strength of our lives!

So, let us look up to God, and keep our hearts, our hands, our minds, our whole selves reaching upward for the Power that comes from above.[14]

* * *

ONE-LINE SERMON: "Young man, your arm's too short to box with God."[15]

* * *

IF
(*Read Matthew 9:16–22.*)

Today a friend came to me for help. His soul was uneasy, for a burden of habit lay heavily upon it. He came to me for help but I did not know how to help him. All I could do was offer a listening ear and a concerned heart. After he left I fell to my knees in prayer, for in his hour of need I had failed my friend. IF, IF, IF—

IF only long ago I had developed a strong personal faith that I might give of it to him now. But I had been too inclined to say, "It's late now, I'll just skip my devotions this evening. Don't see much good in them anyway."

IF only I had sooner noticed his difficulty. Perhaps I could have given him a word of encouragement in a troubled time. But I had been too self-centered to notice.

IF only I had made the fullest use of the resources at my disposal through four years of college. But I had been lax and heedless, just "getting by" and leaving the "weightier matters." So today when my friend cried to me for help I had little to give.

PRAYER: O Father, help me to study and pray that when next I meet a friend in need I may be a channel of thy love and guidance. Let me learn the understanding heart and the loving concern for all peoples.[16]

> Help me the slow of heart to move
>   By some clear winning word of love;
> Teach me the wayward feet to stay,
>   And guide them in the homeward way.[17]

DIRECTED PRAYER

Father, we have paused to think on thee, feel thy presence, and hear thy voice, that we might go forth renewed in body, heart, and mind, better to do our class work and other tasks.

Now we remember before thee those who have been closest to us:

Our mother in whatever she may be doing today
Our father in his work today
Our brothers and sisters in their activities
Our best friend
Our other friends

We pray for those who need thee especially at this time:
    Someone we know who is sick
    Someone who is in sorrow today
    Those we know who are still overseas
    Those we know who are readjusting into civilian life

Father, our nation is so in need of a consecrated citizenship:
    May our President ever rely more on thee for guidance
    The same petition we make for the Secretary of State
    The members of Congress
    Our Bureau heads

We also pray for the leaders of other nations:
    Of England
    Of France
    Of Argentina
    Of other nations (*name them, one by one*)

Father, we know that thou art the only salvation for this world. Help thy church on earth to stand forth at this crucial hour.
    We remember our church at home.
    We pray especially for the church here where we are, and other groups with whom we are working this year.
    O God, help us to put our best into our work.
    May we be so guided by thee that the best will result from thy working through us.
    We think of the pastors,
    Of the Sunday school teachers,
    Of the families . . . all over the world.

O God, there is much to do. Help us to find what task is ours that thou hast planned for us particularly. May we never let thee down, but give our very best.

We thank thee for thy uncountable blessings to us,
We humbly acknowledge our many sins.[18]

OUR PRAYER, MOVING OUT IN EVER-WIDENING CIRCLES

Let us pray for our church . . . (silence) . . .

We would thank thee, O God, for our church's influence, spread into unnumbered lives; we thank thee for what our church has meant and is meaning now in our own lives. Father, may the church put first things first always. May we of thy church worship thee wholeheartedly as we should. And may we each so band together in glad fellowship, and so give of ourselves to serve thee, that the church may truly bless our town and our world.

Let us pray for our homes . . . (silence) . . .

We would thank thee for all that our homes have meant to us. Probably times without number our parents and others have made sacrifices, giving up something they wanted or needed to make possible our happiness. O God, make us worthy of the highest dreams our parents and any adult friends have for us. Help us never to disappoint those who have loved us. May our parents and other adult friends find greater joy in thee, and keep our homes as centers for radiating thy love.

Let us pray for our school friends . . . (silence) . . .

We thank thee for memories of fun and friends, for what different personalities have to offer one another. Help us in school to be ever honest with our teachers, with each other, with ourselves and with thee, as we seek humbly to know truth and prepare to do well whatever tasks Life holds for us. May we not put frivolity and popularity ahead of serving thee.

Let us pray for leaders of government everywhere . . . (silence) . . .

We thank thee that mankind has learned, even as well as it has, how people can band together in large groups for mutual protection and benefit. We pray that leaders of governments over the world may realize their solemn responsibilities, and work unselfishly for the welfare of all the earth's peoples and the bringing of good will everywhere.

Let us pray for ourselves . . . (silence) . . .

O God who hast been speaking to us, seeking to get through to our thoughts even when we were not listening, still us inwardly that we may hear and sense more clearly what greater way thou wouldst have us live. Forgive our stubborn resistance to thy call. Lead us out of our littleness of mind and spirit. Awaken us to deeper love and whole-hearted willingness to care as thou dost care for those who have need—whether for physical necessities or for friendly assurance. If in thy dream for the world some task is needing our particular talents or personalities, help us to be attuned to discover this call and courageous to follow. That thou hast not created us with eager heroism and left us without hard challenge, we thank thee! Amen.[19]

* * *

Our Father, we want to lift to you, these moments in our prayer, persons who need you in special ways (*fill in as desired*)—persons who are sick or who will this week face some crisis or decision that is difficult; persons who are lonely or hurt or who imagine they are; persons working long hours to bring taken-for-granted comforts to us daily; missionaries in far places and near; our parents; our friends; any with whom we may have had a misunderstanding . . . (*Add other persons or situations as needed.*)[20]

* * *

O God, it must have wrung your heart, the way people were going around so complacently and willfully, thinking so little about you and your love; manufacturing a smoke screen of silly rituals and rules so that they wouldn't, perhaps, have to face up to your real challenge to love their neighbors more; being proud of themselves for their "righteousness," and looking down on poor publicans who had retained humility! And so, you sent your Son.

And how it must have delighted your heart the way he grew—so gladly, so happily, in wisdom-ways, stature-ways, and in gracious friendliness with others and with you. All through his growing, no doubt there were times when he cried or suffered or wondered or worked until he dropped from sheer tiredness or went hungry when there hadn't been payment for carpenter's wares. Your business was his high choice.

Then as he taught so wisely and wondrously, his keen mind untricked by Pharisee's wiles, his depth of insight probing into human frailty, yet always with the balm of love, how your heart must have been overjoyed.

But when the people kept their hearts cold, their eyes blind; when they doubled up their fists, when they hurt him . . . how your heart must have bled.

Do you still love as you did when you "so loved the world that you gave your only Son . . . ?" Then give us strength, we pray, to know that *this is the victory that overcomes the world, our faith. Who is it that overcomes the world but he who believes that Jesus is the Son of God?*[21]

9. UNDERSTANDING OURSELVES AND MAKING CHOICES

෴

WHO AM I?

(To the worship committee: The mood of reflection should dominate the service. A possible setting might be a shadow from cut-out of a person lighted from behind so that bulb is hidden.)

CALL TO WORSHIP: Isaiah 40:31.

HYMN: "God of Grace and God of Glory."

MEDITATION: "Who Am I?"

LEADER: This is a time for introspection, to look in upon ourselves in order that we may understand our motives, our desires, our goals for life. Shut out the other persons around you, and think about yourself. The questions are to help you examine yourself before God. The statements are for your prayerful thought.

VOICE 1 (*heavy voice*): Who . . . am . . . I?

VOICE 2: I am a person. I have a body, a mind, a soul. I have a name to distinguish me from other persons. I

238

belong to a family. I have friends. At least several persons are concerned about my welfare.

VOICE 1: How can I describe my personality?

VOICE 2: Let me think of what I am, and what I am not.

VOICE 1: What are my talents?

VOICE 2: I have likes and dislikes in material things, in activities, in other persons.

VOICE 1: What fears do I have?

VOICE 2: I fear powers greater than myself. I fear the unknown. I fear the possibility of failure in any task I pursue. I fear the loss of friends and loved ones. I fear the opinions others have of me, for I know their opinions of other persons.

VOICE 1: What are my standards for living?

VOICE 2: I believe in honesty, cleanliness, and fair play. I would like to live by the Golden Rule, to treat others as I would want them to treat me, but that is not easy to do.

VOICE 1: What are my ambitions?

VOICE 2: I want to find a place in the workaday world, to find a mate as a lifelong companion, and to build a home of which I can be proud. I have some ideals for living; I hope someday to see them become real.

VOICE 1: Do I desire to be with other people? Is it easy for me to get acquainted and, if not, what are the barriers between me and other people?

VOICE 2: I enjoy people who like the same things I do. I would rather be with people than to be alone, except at certain times.

VOICE 1: What are the elements of my personality that can be improved?

VOICE 2: Sometimes I find it difficult to give up my own way; other times I cannot stand on the convictions I have learned. I seldom take time to understand other people; instead, I form inaccurate opinions about them. I do not examine myself often enough to know what I really am. I surprise myself sometimes with my own thoughts and actions.

VOICE 1: What is my purpose in life?

VOICE 2: I have some ideas about an occupational and economic purpose in life, and I suppose I believe in "live and let live" for the other person. I have heard other persons state their purpose in life, especially people in church, and usually I agree with them. In fact, as a Christian, I would say my purpose in life is to be loyal to Christ and to serve him in all that I do. This is not easy and I often lose sight of this purpose, but I do believe I can find the most abundant life by living as God wants me to live.

I have come here today, partly because of friends, but also because I want a better understanding of God in my life. I need to know myself, and to know how God and the spirit of Christ can control my thoughts and actions. (*Moment of quiet*)

HYMN: "I Would Be True."

PRAYER: O God, help us to know ourselves for what we are, and for what we may become. Grant us the wisdom to live at peace with ourselves and with others. Encourage us to press onward and upward to the high calling of being children of thine. In the name of Christ, Amen.[1]

IN THAT MOMENT

Have you ever entered into a silence
  So deep
No other on earth could share it
  With you?
Have you ever felt so close to God that every
  Human being
Seemed far away by contrast?
  Then you have known peace.
Have you ever then said to yourself
  That if you had to choose between God and
Anyone else anywhere,
  Your choice would be
God?
  Then you have known religion.
Did you ever realize that God sees no such
Conflict nor decision you have to
Make,
  But rather is himself best pleased
When
  By loving others you show your love for him?

In that moment you have found the definition of
Christianity.[2]

* * *

O God, thou hast made me . . . Thou knowest of what
stuff I have been fashioned . . . Thou understandest my
passion, pride and hope, the desire for life abundant which is
the native air my spirit breathes. Help me, then, O God,

To turn my curiosity into a search for truth,

To turn my passion into endless service;

Awake the sleeping powers within me, O God,

And teach me how to lay them at thy feet.

O God, where have I been all the time that thou hast
been seeking me? Whom dost thou want me to help to
know thee? And how can I help others if I hardly know
thee myself?

From this hour forward, O God, help me to listen to
thee . . . and act on what thou sayest.

O God, I rush into everything. Always there are things
I wish I had not said or done. Help me now to let go . . .
let thee,

Put all my energies to work for truth, and right, and
happy holiness . . .

Help me not to think of myself more highly than I ought
to think . . .

And guard me against thinking of myself more lowly than
I ought to think.

Keep me from shallow pretense, jealousy, pride, bitterness,
or just plain contrariness or laziness . . .

This hour, O Lord, I open wide the doors and windows of my life,

I set my sails to the winds of God—
Thy winds, O Spirit of God! Amen.[3]

WITH THE STRENGTH GIVEN ME

I felt the glory of the wind this morning
As if I were one of the white-winged birds
Feeling keenly the coldness in flight,
Cheered and made beautiful by the sun.
I am the creature of my God.
I will live my life naturally as the birds do.
I will be strong and glad, and not fear the wind.
I will reach my heights, with the strength he has given me.[4]

MOUNTAIN-TOP MOMENTS
FOR GROWING

We individuals grow through high, holy moments. "Illumination" is one word. "Mountain-top experiences," we sometimes say. "Magnificent moments"—when God and our souls were strangely attuned. We saw life with more meaning; we could never afterward be the same. Some breathless, poignant moment of spring beauty . . . some still twilight prayer . . . some heart-rending concern and our eager effort to help, bringing new realization of partnership with God who cares for all. Jesus our Christ, when walking, laughing, sharing among people, helped folks to see their better, *upward* selves.

There was a night, there was a hill,
  There was a star-lit sky;
An upturned face that hardly sensed
  The night wind blowing by.

There was a Voice—no human voice—
  I heard it clear and still;
And since that night, and since that Voice,
  I've loved each star-lit hill.[5]

* * *

PRAYER

(*Leader says: "Will you please repeat after me each phrase of our prayer?"*)

Dear Creator of the Universe . . . And Father of us all, we pray to you because we need you . . .

Sometimes we think we don't need you . . . Sometimes we think we're pretty smart . . .

But we are only fooling ourselves, . . . because each of us has some problem, . . . each of us finds growing up difficult . . . especially in this world of ours . . .

And so we pray . . . that you will ease our growing pains . . . Help us to face life . . . and to be honest with ourselves; . . . help us to recognize temptations . . . and to overcome them . . . with our hand in yours . . .

And above all, . . . as we grow up, . . . let us not repeat the mistakes . . . of the grownups around us.

But let us follow Jesus Christ . . . and him alone . . .

In his name we pray . . . Amen.[6]

THE PERSON I WAS MEANT TO BE

Zacchaeus the collector of
Taxes for the Romans became
Rich through extortion.
Then he climbed a sycamore
Tree to get a good look at
Jesus, and thereafter could
Never be the same man. The
Reason for his conversion
Is thus phrased by the
Novelist Lloyd Douglas:
"Zacchaeus," said the
Carpenter gently, "What
Did you see that made you
Desire this peace?"
"Good Master—I saw
Mirrored in your eyes—
The face of the Zacchaeus
I was meant to be."

. . . .

The man God meant me to be—
With simple loving kindness,
Sensitive to the needs of
Others, considerate in all
Relationships, and ready to
Carry a full share of the
Burdens of the weak.
The man God meant me to be—
With faith in the right

Because it is right, with
Courage to walk with our
Lord wherever he leads,
With compassion and serenity
Blended into fervent truth
In the grace of God and
His mighty power.
The man I was meant to be,
Dear God, help me to be.[7]

*   *   *

O God, even though perhaps we can never feel completely satisfied with the way we are understanding thee and following thee . . . keep us ever close to thy purposes for our lives. Help us to study, work, pray, and play with glad spirits, confident that thy love leads us ever on.[8]

GRANT ME A VAST PURPOSE

God of Universal Matter, thou hast lifted the mountains out of the level of thy far-spread plains.

Thy hand hath held them aloft through the silent nights, wreathed them in mystery of clouds, touched them with the glory of the sunrise.

God of Universal Life, set thou a mountain in my mind.

Lift up within my heart, I pray thee, some mighty and selfless ambition.

Raise above the common level some cause to dominate me as this mountain does its world.

Grant me a vast purpose for which to live.

Hold it aloft within me through the dark and silent days
of life.

Wreathe it in the mystery of undiscovered truth.

Touch it into glory with the sunrise of thy will.

Let it redeem the littleness of life by the touch of its greatness.

Set thou a mountain in my mind. Amen.[9]

IN BENEDICTINE SILENCE

(*Note: in a retreat or camp, or indoors where space allows
for each individual to move a slight distance apart from
each other one, let all enter for a specified period into un-
broken silence. Explanations can be made that if there is an
emergency or need, one may ask the help of a neighbor, but
that otherwise all can depend upon it that all others will
be in silence also; no one need be ill at ease or afraid someone might speak.*)

Gifts Such As Might Come Through Silence

"Silence?" Does not the very word mean a cessation of
sound, a cutting off of the spoken word or of music, a
blank? Rather, let us approach the moments of quietness
ahead as a positive, not a negative time. True, at first, we
may seem to be giving up something: the usual small talk,
the sound of our own voices, the lines of communication
with others back and forth.

But silence, dedicated, can bring gifts that perhaps could
come in no other way—

First, perhaps, is the gift of an easing off of our inner

tensions. Perhaps we didn't realize how tightly wound up we were, how like a taut violin string ready almost to snap at any moment. Gradually, in the blessed uninterruptedness and calm, our bodies and then minds and spirits begin to relax and to expand.

Soon half-buried little tender thoughts will begin to whisper tentatively, to knock timidly on the doors of our minds —thoughts we may often before have put quickly away in the rush and fever of our days. Now they can blossom forth, thoughts God has all the while been ready to reveal yet we would not reach forth our minds to listen.

But silence, too, can roar and thunder with the clamorings of conscience, that we've tried to squelch so often, but that now must be heard! Whom have we hurt with our selfishness, jealousy, tendency to say a cutting word? Whom have we cut cold by our indifference? What not-quite-truthful statement did we make recently, so as to paint ourselves in a favorable light in the group with which we wanted to rate? What prompting toward giving a gift did we put aside, rationalizing that we needed our money, or time, or energy, for our own uses? What current situation in our city or community needs brave, courageous action, yet we have been sitting on the sidelines as if it were no concern of ours? Has some friend or relative been turned farther away from wanting to be Christian by our poor daily example? In a crowded bus or store or on the street, did we give a witness of harassment more than of Christian joy? Has our mind and creative effort been more on material things than on ways to express love and good will to family, friends, and on out into wider world reaches?

In silence, God's miracle-gift of forgiveness comes. No one can ever fully explain. Such is his nature, to reach into our sinfulness and need, our mixed-upness and hurt. His healing balm restores. From the very hand of God, through silence, the gift of another chance!

And from this holy awareness of the operation of the Holy Spirit within us, comes growing realization of how vast God's love, how limitless his caring to us so undeserving. Never again can we go back to small ideas of God. This stretching of our thoughts, this deepening of our awe and reverence, is also a gift.

And one more gift comes as we listen through the silence: a call! Something we may do, or some preparation we may make: a tap on shoulder. And we go out from the quietness, strengthened now for the new task ahead, or for the old task faced a new way![10]

WHAT DOES GOD REQUIRE?

"You have been told, O man, what is good, and what the Lord requires of you: only to do justice, and to love kindness, and to walk humbly with your God" (Micah 6:8).

TO DO JUSTICE?

Can I be merciful to my enemy and see that the cause for the enmity is to some extent my own fault?

Can I disagree with others and still acknowledge their right to disagree with me?

Do I have any idea of what tolerance means?

TO LOVE KINDNESS?

Do I bluntly say what I think regardless of the hurts I administer, and boast that I am not diplomatic?

Has kindness grown habitual with me or must I still stop to decide whether or not to do the kind thing?

AND TO WALK HUMBLY WITH MY GOD?

Do I, deep down, feel self-sufficient? Haughty?

Do I merely pray for God's approval of the things I am doing; or do I pray for guidance and then take the time to listen for the voice of God speaking to me?

Father of us all, help me to answer the questions of each day as Jesus would answer them, and help me to see that only in that way can I hope to extend my thinking to include the world community. Amen.[11]

LITANY OF SELF-MASTERY

Leader: For reverent and victorious conquest of duty through faithfulness and worthy effort,

Response: O God, we pray thy help, that we may gain self-mastery.

Leader: For the purpose to control our bodies, our thoughts, and our actions,

Response: O God, we pray thy help, that we may gain self-mastery.

Leader: For the power to rule our conduct in harmony with the standards of Jesus Christ,

Response: O God, we pray thy help, that we may gain self-mastery.

Leader: For the ability to keep back angry words and actions when provoked,

Response: O God, we pray thy help, that we may gain self-mastery.

Leader: For strength of character to stand for the hard right against the easy wrong,

Response: O God, we pray thy help, that we may gain self-mastery.

Leader: For the resolve to hold ideals of high conduct and character,

Response: O God, we pray thy help, that we may gain self-mastery.[12]

NOT FOR EASE

Oh, do not pray for easy lives. Pray to be stronger men! Do not pray for tasks equal to your powers. Pray for powers equal to your tasks! Then the doing of your work shall not be a miracle. But you shall be a miracle. Every day you shall wonder at yourself, at the richness of life which has come in you by the grace of God.[13]

SLOW ME DOWN, LORD!

Slow me down, Lord!

Ease the pounding of my heart by the quieting of my mind.

Steady my hurried pace with a vision of the eternal reach of time.

Give me, amid the confusion of the day, the calmness of the everlasting hills.

Break the tensions of my nerves and muscles with the soothing music of the singing streams that live in my memory. Help me to know the magical, restoring power of sleep.

Teach me the art of taking minute vacations—of slowing down to look at a flower, to chat with a friend, to pat a dog, to read a few lines from a good book.

Remind me each day of the fable of the hare and the tortoise, that I may know that the race is not always to the swift—that there is more to life than increasing its speed. Let me look upward into the branches of the towering oak and know that it grew great and strong because it grew slowly and well.

Slow me down, Lord, and inspire me to send my roots deep into the soil of life's enduring values that I may grow toward the stars of my greater destiny.

In Jesus' name, Amen.[14]

TWENTY-FOUR NEW HOURS

A brand-new day! A day that has never been lived in before! Twenty-four new full hours—presented to me by God for the purpose that I make the very best use of them that I possibly can. What a serious undertaking, twenty-four hours entrusted to me to be lived to their greatest possibilities.

I wonder what God has in mind as he hands me this day.

I wonder if I'll accomplish the purpose for which he is giving me this day. At the close of this day, will the world be any better because I have lived in it? If not, then why have I lived?

I wonder what Christ would do if he had this day? If he had twenty-four hours entrusted to him, it dazzles me to think of the things he could accomplish for God. Perhaps that is just what God has in mind as he hands me this day— to live it as though Christ himself had the opportunity of these twenty-four hours. Since it's too great an undertaking for me, why don't I let him have a chance at this day to see what he would do with it?

Shall I set out on such a quest this day—to live each moment as I think Christ would be living it? Let's take it one day at a time, though. It's a big enough order that way.

A brand new day—a bundle of responsibilities—mine! Tonight as I kneel before God to give back to him the hours he is entrusting to me this morn, I wonder if he will be able to smile and say, My child, you've earned a brand-new tomorrow for the Christlike way you've lived today. I wonder—[15]

LITANY OF THANKFULNESS FOR TIME

Affirmation (by leader, or by different voices around room): "In the beginning," reads our Holy Word, thus implying that before ever there was man to be conscious of Time, God the Creator-Giver lived and breathed a mighty Plan forth into pulsing reality. To each created person, since earliest beginnings, God has bequeathed some time for living, breathing, learning, doing. We live in time, and in turn awareness of time lives in us. How holy this gift! How sacramental each minute!

Group (or individual, responding slowly, thoughtfully as if expressing not only for the assembled group but for all mankind): God of Creation, instill within us a more reverent awareness that this gift of time does not wholly "belong" to us, but that both we and time are sustained in thy ongoing Plan.

Affirmation: God offers this gift of time, not all at once, but as we can receive: minute by minute, day by day. When we face difficulties, sorrows, trials, or heartaches, time may seem to move slowly; but because we must needs endure only one moment at a time, thus God helps us through. When we enjoy gladnesses and delights, God gives us "all things richly to enjoy," and endows us strangely with memory that we can relive the happy moments, while time mercifully softens the remembrance of sorrows.

Group: As we think of ways thou dost strengthen us in our joys and in our growing, yet dost soften that which is hurtful, we can but marvel and give thee the utmost thanks of our contrite hearts.

Affirmation: In time, we learn and grow. One who aspires to become a musician, by patient daily practice finds his mental and muscular responses becoming more quick and skillful. One does not change suddenly, but in God's good time, according to his laws of growing. Yet if we practice hateful, hurtful thinking and attitudes, we shall tend to grow in this direction. If we practice carelessness, thus we grow.

Time is good or evil as we choose to use it—as good as our thoughts and deeds, as evil as our thoughts and deeds.

Group: Almighty God, who art Lord of all life, triumphant over all evil, lead us into such fearful awareness of the challenge of time that we shall make choices from moment to moment, day to day, that may reflect thy goodness and love. "Grant us wisdom, grant us courage for the living of these days."[16]

HELP ME TO CONTROL MY TONGUE

Lord, I give thee thanks for speech. I praise thee for tongues—the tongues of eloquent men of all times, the tongues of friends.

I rejoice in my own.

For its power to carry my thought over the bridge between me and another's mind.

For its ability to call forth laughter, and action, and knowledge.

For these I give thanks.

So, O God, I ask thee for the power to control my tongue.

Leash it when my anger would cause it to wound my friend.

Hold it silent rather than have it repeat the story of another person's failure.

Save it from speaking a lie.

Make it a bearer of happiness and good will.

May it often commend my neighbor's good.

Make it a tool of clean fun.

Use it often for "words fitly spoken" which are like "apples of gold." Amen.[17]

SPEAKING OF SPEECH

(*Read Proverbs 15:23; James 3:5, 8–11.*)

Talking's fun. And talking's excruciating. Talking's friendly. And talking's hurtful. Talking's a help toward making meanings clear. And talking fogs over understandings between persons and groups.

Knowing the same language isn't always the key. Two people who speak different languages can, if their spirits are akin, achieve deeper understandings in a few minutes than others speaking the same tongue do in a lifetime.

Words have power—for good and God, or not. "Evil," *says Dr. Rall, is* "saying 'no' to God." Think what that little word "no" can shut out!

Words are little semaphore signals we mortals send out hopefully to each other; when a meaning is "caught" by another, his eyes light up. If that meaning is kindly, his heart lights up. The world is sick unto death for "a little bit of love"; for words that bring joy and assurance instead of threats; for humorous words; for warmhearted words. No word ever spoken or written can be erased, once another person has heard or seen. "Boys flying kites haul in the white-winged birds . . . you can't do that when you are flying words."

PRAYER: God, let the words of my mouth as well as the meditation of my heart be acceptable in thy sight . . . and if that is so, it will be acceptable in the sight of others. Amen.[18]

SAFE-DRIVER PRAYER

Dear God, Creator and Preserver of all mankind,
  Before I ever turn the key, or touch the wheel
Let me take inventory: . . .

Help me to realize that I hold beneath my hands
  An instrument that may bring destruction, mutilation, and death.

Let me appreciate the fact that I bear responsibility
  Not only for my own life,
But that of those who ride with me,
  And those whom I meet on the road.

Let me know that I hold the power to bring
  Not only misery and pain, and wretchedness,
But also tragedy and heartbreak to others in ever-widening circles—
Beyond my wildest imaginings and my ability to atone.

Give me a deepening consciousness that I must possess
  A clear head, the wisdom to choose wisely and often quickly
What is best for all concerned in moments of the unexpected.

Take from me any desire for bravado.
Give me always the abiding sense of thy presence and thy love.

And now . . . As I place my hands on the wheel
  May I feel yours above them,
  For into them do I commend myself. Amen.[19]

AIR TRAVELER'S PRAYER

God, who hast made all creatures for thy own Glory, and
hast destined all the things of this world for the service of
mankind, bless, we pray thee, this machine built for our
travel, that it may serve—without loss or danger—for spreading ever more widely the praise and glory of thy name, and
for quicker dispatch of the world's affairs; and may foster
in the hearts of those who travel in it a yearning for the
things above, through Christ our Lord.[20]

TO BE CHRISTIAN

Our God and King, we pray thee this day for courage:
Courage to be unpopular for the sake of truth and sincerity;
Courage to risk our lives in a cause that is greater than life;
Courage to declare our convictions at whatever cost to our-
  selves;
Courage to trust the truth, even when the battle seems to
  go against it;
Courage to be alone with thee in the right;
Courage to admit when we are wrong;
Courage to start anew when we have fallen;
Courage to do our best and leave the outcome in the hands
  of God;

Courage to walk with Christ along a lonely road;
Courage to be a Christian.[21]

*   *   *

O thou who art heroic love,
Keep alive in our hearts that adventurous spirit
Which makes men scorn the way of safety,
If only thy will be done.
For so only, O Lord, shall we be worthy of those
Courageous souls who in every age have ventured all
In obedience to thy call,
And for whom the trumpets have sounded on the other side;
    through Jesus Christ our Lord. Amen.[22]

*   *   *

God, give us the courage to live
By the inspiration of thy beauty:
That by that inspiration we may grow in energy and faith,
Faith in the knowledge that thy spirit lies in the depths of
    the least of us.
We, with false pride, have gone on unheeding that power,
Clouding ourselves in a pretense of distrust:
God, help us to gain that needed faith.[23]

10. OTHERS' NEEDS AND OUR RESPONSES

৶ঠ

HEARTBEAT

Quicken me through thy righteousness (Psalm 119:40).
Read Psalm 119:33–40.

In an adventure of silence I sought God. Thoughts of the world's great need compelled my spirit to cry out for a way in which I might be used of God . . .

I had heard a young prophet of this generation declare that somewhere in the world a person starved to death every time my heart beat.

Oh, could the stopping of my heartbeat put an end to this certain, creeping, slow death which overtakes my brothers and sisters in Germany, China, India, Hungary. Every place where a brother or sister or father or mother or child is snuffed out in the misery of hunger. Could the stopping of my heartbeat keep them alive, I would gladly ask God to let me be their substitute.

"But it is not that easy," whispered God in the silence. "Every beat of your heart that brings death to one of these must beat a summons to you to live sacrificially . . . to use your breath to help others see the immediate need of bringing food to the hungry . . . to discipline your own desires and wants under the shadow of starvation of your brothers."

"O God," my spirit cried, "Take my heartbeats, my breath, my food, my clothing, my opportunities, and live through them, that I may help you save these my brothers."[1]

MAKE STRAIGHT IN THE DESERT A HIGHWAY

When highways are built these days, engineers find ways to fell great trees, move homes that may be in the way, level hills, fill in valleys, tunnel through mountains or under rivers. Years ago, the roads "wound around." But today, "a straight line" is the effort, being the shortest distance from where people are to where they want to go.

Let us think now, of human relationships. We can travel. We can use mass media of communication. We can read. We can study others' languages. But none of these skills mean that we have achieved friendly understanding.

That is a matter of our inner attitude. Are there any barriers within us that not only shut others away from our friendship, but shut us up in narrow walls away from their friendship as well? Do we allow hills or rock-like mountains of prejudice to shut us away? Do we tend to notice too much people's outward appearance, as to whether they show signs of prosperity or "class"? Do certain names of nations or labels of groups cause feelings of hatred within us?

If highway engineers can "make straight in the desert a highway," can we, praying that God will make us forgiving and sympathetic, bridge through or tunnel through barriers of spirit? "Life is too short to waste hating somebody." Hatred *costs*—tragically. Portia in "The Merchant of Venice" said that mercy blesses him that gives and him that takes; so hatred hurts the giver as well as the receiver. Remembered and unforgiven wrongs cut into our bodily health as glass into tires. The tense spirit makes worship a mockery. It robs us of friends, of spiritual growth, of peace—and most of all, of full fellowship with God, for we can only pray, "Forgive, as we forgive."[2]

A PLEA FOR FREEDOM

God, call me louder!
Is that your voice I hear, so still, so small
That I can scarce detect it
Amid the clangor of this busy life I'm leading?
God, call to me—
Call above the noisy squabble of selfish desires
Which war within me so loudly
That I cannot hear you for them.
God, cry to me—
Through the lips of millions dying in the world,
Who, needing me, are mute because
They cannot speak above the loud voice of
My craving for comfort and well-being.
God, open their parched lips—
That they may bear
Loud testimony to the starvation within their bodies and
their souls,

That they may call me to leave my laden table,
My thick-carpeted church aisles,
My life of comfort's vices
In which I cannot be satisfied—
And yet which binds me close to it
So tightly I am almost suffocated by it.
Tear me loose, God!
Let your voice be as thunder within me,
Speaking for the starving millions whom I cannot hear!
Call me louder, my God!

   "Inasmuch as you have not done it unto the least of these, my brothers, you have not done it unto me."[3]

* * *

LET YOUR CONCERN BE DEEP, YOUR LOVE WIDE

Voice of Self-Accusation: Soul of mine, how careless have you become regarding the hungers and hurts of others, how careful of your own least whim! Did you pass quickly by the container on the drugstore counter marked "For CARE" and spend twice as much as you had meant to on a special brand of soap? And then did you sit right down, although it had not been long since you had had a good meal, to order something of refreshment?

Have you become so used to the privilege of enjoying comforts of civilization that you forgot the refugees over the world who are crowded into splintery, drafty barracks or even living through cold winters in tents? Do you take for granted the gift of sight, of school training so that you can read, or of intellectual stimulation such as many over the world might hunger for?

Once another must have been thinking in these directions, until the growing sympathies and concerns which God brought into her heart caused her to pray, "God give me eyes that I may see, lest I, as some folks will, should pass by someone's Calvary and think it just a hill." May I come to this kind of prayer, too:

"O God, let me not refuse to look, or refuse to let the hurt come deep into my own self; for I must realize that when others of thy children are in want or cold, in mental or spiritual darkness or in loneliness, in their cries is echo of thy great heart of love crying . . ."

(Moment of silence)

Voice of orphan: I cannot remember when I didn't live in the home. That's all the life I've known. The leaders have given me food and clothes and a place to stay. At some times during the year, people come in and give us parties, as at Christmas. But what makes us feel lonesome inside is not belonging to a special mother and father, and wondering who we are.

(Moment of silence)

Voice of Alcoholic: In the home in which I grew up, we were not encouraged to go to church, and I had very mixed-up ideas about right and wrong. As a teen-ager I began drinking, not because I liked the stuff but because I was trying to get in with that certain crowd. I kept telling myself I could quit any minute I wanted to, but the day came when I realized I couldn't quit. That was after I had lost my job, my wonderful wife and family, and my confidence in myself. Why didn't somebody warn me, help me before it was too late?

(Moment of silence)

Voice of Refugee: Can you who have homes imagine what it is like to be torn loose from the town and neighbors, the house and furniture, and all the things and people you've been accustomed to, and then with only a pack on your back, to search for some place to stay? Can you imagine what it would be like to have several hundred in one crowded building with only one bath? Can you imagine how slowly the hours creep through a day when there is no work to be had anywhere, and no hope of things ever being different? Can you understand why children and young people get into trouble because they have no school to feed their minds?

(Moment of silence)

Voice of Elderly Person: Life is precious to me, for I do love the beauty of the earth around me. I love to be with people, too. And when I was able I loved to work. I was unable to make much money, however, and couldn't put by anything for my old age. Now I'm on the shelf, and I have it hard, in a cheap old folk's home; I could make out with the same uninteresting food day after day, if only I could *do* something, not feel so useless, see more people!

(Moment of silence)

PRAYER: O God, I see now. Is it YOU who are crying to me through these you love? Help me to love them, too and somehow to help. Amen.[4]

PENNILESS

Penniless . . .
A while
Without food
I can live;
But it breaks my heart
  To know
  I cannot give.

Penniless . . .
I can share my rags,
  But I—
I cannot bear to hear
Starved children cry.

Penniless . . .
And rain falls,
But trust is true.
Helpless, I wait to see
What God will do.[5]

QUESTION AND RESPONSE

Can I feed myself
When the pinched hands of little children
Reach out with clawlike grasp to clutch at a falling crust of bread?

Can I clothe myself
When humanity is staggering down the aisles of time
In the tattered shreds of garments long since past repair?
Can I shelter myself
When orphaned Europe roams the streets,
Homeless, penniless, friendless, futureless?
Can I be at peace with myself,
Can I sing hymns joyously on Sunday
When I refuse to share my pew with my neighbor
Because he doesn't wear my kind of clothes, or speak my
    language, or have my color face?
No! I cannot feed or clothe or shelter myself;
I cannot sleep at night, or be at ease in my mind, or sing
    joyously.
I cannot do these things until my brother is fed,
Until my brother is warm and housed,
Until the Church of Jesus Christ can throw open its doors
    to seeking humanity
And say with our Lord, "Come unto me," regardless of your
    race, regardless
Of the clothes you wear, or the language you speak, or the
    wrongs you have done—
"Come unto me!" and through me ye shall have life and
    have it abundantly and eternally.[6]

POVERTY

I know the road to Jericho,
It's in a part of town
That's full of factories and filth.

I've seen the folks go down:
Small folks with roses in their cheeks,
And starlight in their eyes;
And seen them fall among the thieves,
And heard their helpless cries.

The priests and Levites speeding by
Read of the latest crimes,
In headlines spread in black and red
Across the evening Times.
How hard for those in limousines
To heal the heart of man.
It was a slow-paced ass that bore
The good Samaritan.[7]

THE MIGRANT SPEAKS

I am a migrant fruit picker from Mexico—
As I travel through Indiana and Michigan harvesting the
    crops
  I get the stony stares of American citizens,
But—
They don't realize what it's like to be a migrant.
It means traveling in an ancient jalopy—
Patching tires every few miles—
Washing your face in cold water—
Often going without a bath—
It means being looked on as a thief because you're poor,
It means being asked to get out of town each night by ten
    o'clock because you're a foreigner—

It means sleeping on the ground because there is no better place,

It means breakfast, lunch, and supper out of cans and sacks or—if you're lucky, at a roadside table.

It means, when you find work, being treated like something less than human—herded in a truck with others of your own kind as you're hauled to and from the fields—hearing the remarks of passing motorists in sleek cars—"there are some more of those dirty Mexicans"

But—

What they don't realize is that I, too, am a human being—

I, too, have a wife and children whom I love and who love me,

I, too, have the same hopes and longings as American fathers,

And—

Because of these I came to "the states" for better chances— even as your forefathers came generations ago,

And—

As I drive along the smooth highways I wonder about the Christian America I've heard of—

Is it really Christian?

How would a dark-skinned man called Jesus be treated today?

What would he think of America?[8]

WE SHARE WITH OTHERS

(Setting: Possibly a picture of Jesus—strong, dynamic, not familiar pictures depicting meditation merely. Each of the six speakers may bring, or have at table when they come,

*the following items as symbols: a loaf of bread, a baby
sweater or dress, a schoolbook, a package of seeds, a hymnal
and/or a brick, and a white pillow case. Other symbols may
be substituted.*)

PRELUDE: "Fairest Lord Jesus."

PREPARATION FOR WORSHIP: May we bow in prayer:
  Lord, may thy will be ours, no self to serve,
  No will that does not seek the welfare of the all. Amen.

HYMN: "Fairest Lord Jesus."

SCRIPTURE: Luke 10:25–30. (*Read and then continue into
  the following.*)
  We all know so well the story of the Good Samaritan
  as it came from the lips of the Master. Jesus said,
  "You shall love the Lord your God with all your heart,
  and with all your soul, and with all your strength, and
  with all your mind; and your neighbor as yourself."
  "And Who Is My Neighbor?"
  There was a youth of America who stood and said
  fervently, "Thee, Lord, I love with all my heart, and
  mind, and soul, and strength."
  But He answered, "That is not enough. You must
  also love your neighbor as yourself."
  "But who is my neighbor, Lord?" he asked.

FIRST SPEAKER: I heard a refugee child with hunger crying
  outside my door
  And I went out into the night,

And I said, "Why, this is my child,"
And I took him in and gave him food. (*Places bread on the worship table.*)

SECOND SPEAKER: I saw a young Arab girl crying her
Heart out in a camp in Jordan—expecting a baby
Without a stitch of clothing for it,
With no one in the whole wide world to turn to, in her hour of need,
And I said, "Why, this is my sister,"
And I gave her clothing and I gave her care and comfort in my home. (*Places baby sweater on the worship table.*)

THIRD SPEAKER: I stood beside a boy in a displaced persons' camp,
And I saw his shoulders shake with sobs
When they told him he had failed the semester's work
In a temporary university inside the camp,
And I said, "Why, this is my brother,"
And I took him to a youth hostel and gave him rest and food and friendship. (*Places schoolbook on the worship table.*)

FOURTH SPEAKER: I knelt beside an old Chinese woman where she lay swollen with disease beside the road near Hong Kong
Abandoned by the living who had failed to catch the plague,
And I said, "Why, this is my mother,"

And I took her to a mission and they placed her on a clean bed,

And washed her tired and filthy body and gave her tender and loving care. (*Places pillow case on the worship table.*)

FIFTH SPEAKER: I sat before a haggard, haunted man, who had come to ask for seed and farm tools

To make up the shortage of seed grain;

And the loss of breeding stock slaughtered in desperation,

To keep alive during the nightmare winter months.

And I said, "Why, this is my father,"

And I gave him implements and food and went to visit him

In his home with gifts of clothing for his wife and children. (*Places package of seeds on the worship table.*)

SIXTH SPEAKER: I heard the music of many voices singing hymns of worship

In a city in Korea where the war had been,

And I thought—I will go to church.

And I went and there were only the ruins of a church

And pale and shabby people were the singers and worshipers.

I sat with them in the cleared place before the altar,

And I said, "Why, this is my church,"

And I arose and said aloud, "We must rebuild,

Let many help to lift the stones." (*Places brick or hymnal on the worship table.*)

LEADER:

> While there is a soul in prison, I am not free.
> While there is a child hungry, I am not fed,
> While there is a naked one shivering, I am not clothed,
> While there is a soul without hope, there is no peace.
>
> Human beings! Neighbors all!
> And you are to love your neighbor as much as yourself.
> (*Pause*)
> Why does *He* make our hearts so strangely still?
> Why stands *He* forth so stately and so tall? Because *He*
>   has *no self to serve*, no will that does not seek the
>   welfare of the all.

HYMN:

> "Master, No Offering."[9]

GOD, GUIDE MY THOUGHTS ABOUT COLOR

Whatever my own skin color—red or yellow, black or white—

Am I ever in any way tempted to look askance at persons of another color?

What would God my creator have me think, about my own color, about others' color?

I lift up other concerns in prayer. Do I lift this one?

Am I willing to let God help me overcome any prejudging of others,

Which is what prejudice is after all: judging them on appearance before giving them a chance?

A blind junior high school boy was given an assignment to write his greatest wish.

He thought and thought. "*To see*—isn't that what I would wish most of all?"

"No . . . *most of all,*" and his wish grew into a prayer, prayed with his whole heart—

"I most wish," he wrote, "that all the people in all the lands

Might know how the other fellow feels inside! Then surely they'd be kind and not fight!"

A Negro poet wrote, "I am blind and cannot see, but in my night all colors are alike.

Why do persons with sight so torture themselves about differences, when inwardly all are molded by God's hand?"

O God, I must search my own soul. Forgive any smallness within me. Lend me thy eyes.[10]

A PRAYER FOR RACE RELATIONS

(*Read I Timothy 6:11–16.*)

Father of all of us, glory be to you that you have made us as we are. We acknowledge your all-knowing and loving power.

You have taught us, through Christ, that all are brothers. We ask your divine guidance to help us to do your will when facing the problems of race relations.

May your love shine into our hearts to give us the understanding to face the ever-increasing problems of race relations. We all—colored and white—want to further our education. In doing so we hope to help others find Christ. May we all seek your guidance and be willing to do your will rather than follow evil influences so often present.

Forgive us that so many times we allow petty prejudices to influence our actions more than your teachings. As we are willing to forgive and help others we ask that you do so for us.

Guide us and give us strength to overcome the temptation to act hastily and with no regard for your will. Bless all teenagers and may no group desire to do evil to any other group.

For yours is everything, God. We can do nothing without you, and everything with you. Amen.[11]

"SET THIS MAN FREE AT ONCE!"

How brave would you be if you were facing a line of rough-looking soldiers, ready to point guns at you and fire simultaneously at the barked command, "Fire!"

Even though he could not see, Reverend Young Sik Lee in Korea knew well that the guns were ready, that he was at the place of execution.

Who was he? He had been caring for more than a thousand leprosy patients; he had had a school and home for blind, deaf children at Taegu. That was his "crime." He had been teaching them the Christian way of life. He had been caught in the war, and sentenced to death by the Communists. Now, lined up before the firing squad, he fully expected to die.

But strangely, he found himself unafraid. What is more, he could sing. He had full faith in his God. He asked for a minute to speak and began. Ringingly, his words poured forth—he told about his call to the ministry when he was a young man, then his call to serve the leprous and the blind and deaf so that they would not have to beg on the streets. He gave a "will" for his family—that his children should study hard, be good to their mother, follow Christian teachings, and finish his work of caring for the blind and deaf and lepers. He said, "I fear nothing now. My only concern is, will this work to help people go on?"

Suddenly a voice was heard—the Communist official broke in. He had been so moved by the spirit of courage and calm faith of Sik Lee that he could not give the usual order. "Set this man free at once," he said.[12]

I STAND BEFORE THE MAP
OF THE WORLD

I stand before the map of the world; before its countries stretched wide and its waters deep. I stand before its rivers lying like long crooked fingers across the land, fed forever from the streams, the snows, and the rains of the mountains, pouring endlessly into the seas.

Up and down the rivers people have their mansions and their squatted huts. Children are born and families fish the waters for food, or till the soil of its valleys and countrysides. Some families work in factories and some in the dark interior of the earth.

How alike we are around the world: living in our families, working and playing, having fun and having sorrow, knowing fear and security, needing food and clothing.

On this day I send into families of the world my wishes

for good will. I will make more room in my heart for all my brothers and sisters everywhere.[13]

THEY'RE PRAYING ALL OVER THE WORLD!

(This is a brief radio-drama. Voices should be chosen carefully. They may be broadcast or speak from behind a screen. Rehearse; speak sincerely).

NARRATOR: Listen! The year is _____, the place, Antewok— South Pacific. A voice like the voice of destiny's clock is counting the remaining seconds, five, four, three, two, one. A blinding flash of light, a red ball of fire so intense one must look away, then slowly a billowy white cloud rises like a beautiful sun-kissed mushroom, miles wide, miles into the air, but with the kiss of death! A whole island disappears below the waters of the Pacific. Silence reigns, then, after what seems an eternity, a voice, "God, deliver us."

(Quiet, slow music, "Ton-y-Botel: Once to Every Man and Nation.")

NARRATOR: In a distant field where agricultural migrants gather food for you and me a voice is heard: it is a young mother, in prayer.

MOTHER: O Lord, in whose hands are life and death . . . look down upon me and my loved ones with pity and compassion . . . Forgive us all for neglecting thy work and grant that we who toil in these fields, and those for whom we gather this food, may yet become diligent in the performance of thy commands.

NARRATOR: You heard, she prays unselfishly—she hasn't much worldly goods—in fact not so much to look forward to, but she prays. Come now to Korea, a shell-torn village that was once home for many—over there that makeshift hut and thatched roof, and inside it a child, thin, emaciated, with the telltale sign of rickets. The mother raises her eyes and peers as if to see beyond the skies—

KOREAN: Help us, O Lord . . . My people starve and are sick. Remove from the minds of men that which is false to thy commandments.

NARRATOR: Come with me now behind the iron curtain—there, that desolate-looking building—it houses many. Here on the floor one prays for the deliverance of the people—

VOICE: Dear God, I raise my voice to thee. Help men to see the light. Save us from self-destruction. Bring back for our people thy great Church that we may be free to worship, that we may work to save civilization. Help me, Lord—help us, Lord.

NARRATOR: Never have so many people been faced with the possibility of destruction. But this need not happen. The strains and fears of a disordered world—life is a test of our love . . . Let us face it together and say, "In Him who strengthens me, I am able for anything" —even to forgive . . . to love . . . to melt barriers

. . . to build peace first in our hearts and then around the world![14]

WHEN LOVE WORKS THROUGH SKILLFUL HANDS

In the heart of Africa is the Ganta Mission, where Dr. Harley works tirelessly healing sick bodies and demonstrating how to make tools and needed implements for better agriculture, and a healthier, higher standard of living. Blama was a little boy when his father brought him to Dr. Harley. Blama knew something terrible was the matter with him, because of the sad look in his father's eyes. But when Blama saw the kind face of Dr. Harley he did not feel so afraid any more. His father's voice almost broke with urgency—

"Doctor, I've brought this boy to you. Those terrible blemishes on his skin look like leprosy to me. We Liberians have tried everything we knew. See if you can help him. He'll do what you say. He's a good boy."

Dr. Harley's face was grave. Often he heard this broken note of urgency as relatives pleaded for help for those they loved. Had they brought their sick to him in early enough stages of the disease? He examined Blama. He shook his head slowly—was it perhaps with a prayer?

Blama responded to the treatment. After a long while, he was able to help around the mission, then to go to its school and to learn useful work. Ten years after his father first brought him, Blama graduated from the Ganta school with the highest marks in his class, his valedictory address being on "Medical Progress in Liberia." Yes, he's training to be a doctor, too.[15]

WOULD YOU END WAR?

Would you end war?

Create great peace . . .

The Peace that demands all of a man,

His love, his life, his veriest self;

Plunge him into the smelting fires of a work that becomes
his child.

Give him a hard Peace; a Peace of discipline and justice . . .

Kindle him with vision, invite him to joy and adventure;

Set him to work, not to create *things*

But to create *man!*

Yea, himself.

Go search your heart, America . . .

Turn from the machine to man,

Build, while there is yet time, a creative Peace.[16]

PEACEMAKING?

Blessed are the peacemakers (Matthew 5:9) . . .

"Gonna lay down my sword and shield . . . down by the
riverside. Ain't gonna study war no more."

You are not going to study war any more in this kind of
world? That's wishful thinking, isn't it? That's not practical
or realistic.

No, I suppose that it is practical, realistic, to kill 40,000,000
of the world's finest men each generation. Yet some people
are asking why mothers must raise sons for slaughter, why
wives and sweethearts must lose their husbands and boy

friends, why little children must be blown to bits or starved to death.

Somehow they don't feel right when the leaders say, "Now we must start training your other boys because it looks as if our diplomacy is going to create another war."

We, the people, are ready to learn this Negro spiritual by heart. We are tired of studying war. Now we want to learn peace.

There is only one way for the lesson to begin. Prejudice, envy, selfishness, and all other things wars are made of must be put aside from my heart. I must make up my mind that peace is possible and that in God's strength the few of us who see his way can create peace. I ask God this day to help me play the part of peacemaker.[17]

PERSONAL COMMITMENT

We, the clean strong Youth of earth have the good right
To life and love and happiness and peace.
We would not be killers of men . . .
We want to walk the earth clean-handed,
Free from war with all its horrors, lust, and greed,
Its dark despair . . .
Lord, may there never be another war.
This is our prayer.[18]

LET ALL PEOPLES LIVE IN PEACE

About 200 years before Jesus (196 B.C.) Emperor Wen-ti of China was born. During his rule barbarians from the north broke their treaty with him and invaded his territory.

What he really did was to send to the barbarian chief a letter so beautiful that we have not reached its ideas today with all our boasted civilization:

"North of the Great Wall lies the land you rule over; south of that Wall are the families which are governed by me and are mine.

"Let all peoples live in peace. Let parents and children never be divided. Let us try dismissing our troops, melting down our swords. Let us direct our efforts toward giving rest to the aged; let children grow up to manhood and all be joyous.

"Your country lies far north, you will soon be suffering from the cold. I am having silk sent you, and cotton, rice, and wheat. We are now friends; our peoples are glad; you and I are now more than their protectors; we are the parents of our peoples.

"Let us reflect that the sky covers us all equally, the earth makes no distinction in bearing us; we are all one family.

"Our wish is that the world should be at peace forever. Thus would the fish swim more tranquilly, the birds fly more freely; while the insects would hum their gladness in the heart of the woods."[19]

THE TRIED AND THE UNTRIED

The tried—

   To build a world of brotherhood by the machinery of war;

   To establish fellowship by feeding racial rancor—by keeping the Negro and immigrant in place;

To use force and violence in guaranteeing national security;

To dispose of the criminal by a prison system;

To put money first in the purpose of life; and

To be a Christian without following Christ.

The untried—

To build a friendly world by faith and understanding—to put love where there is now hate;

To lead the race toward a juster, wiser, and more merciful social order, where each individual is evaluated in terms of his true worth;

To fortify the nation by the armaments of faith and the long-range canons of love;

To give guidance to those who err and in time redeem the environment of every little child;

To work for the good of all—not for the gain of wealth;

To make an earnest trial of Jesus' Way of Life.[20]

HOW BIG IS MY WORLD?

How BIG is my world?

What countries,

What peoples,

What languages does it include?

Only those countries, peoples, languages that are on your side? Dangerous politics, you say, to believe otherwise?

How BIG is my world?

Where are its boundaries,

Its roots,

Its demarcations?

Are they limited? Confined? Circumscribed?
How BIG is my world?
  Who is its Maker,
    Its Planner,
      Its Architect?
If I say, "It is God's world," then I must admit that we, *I*,
  have tried to take his Place!
For I have tried to make and to plan a world that is limited
  To certain peoples,
    Countries,
      Languages;
A world confined to
  Certain social and racial boundaries,
    Limited roots, and
      Lines of separation!

*"Don't let the world around you squeeze you into its own
mold, but let God remold your minds from within."*[21]

CAN FORGIVENESS CROSS NATIONAL LINES?

An outstanding young Filipino youth, whom we shall
call Y, thought long and deeply about what God's love
makes us want to do. He came to the conclusion that no
matter if people hurt us, we want to forgive them and to show
them kindness anyway. He knew, then, what he himself
had to do.

And so he went to Japan, as a member of an International
Work Camp Team of Christian youth. These youth from
many countries were showing by their joyous lives and by

their willingness to do hard, needed work that they held no grudges.

Y, himself, did some extra things. He visited the Japanese prisoners of war still jailed in Manila because of their acts of brutality, and chatted with them. He took down on his notepaper the names of their families. When he went to Japan to the work camp, he visited as many families as he could find and reported that he had talked with their loved ones. They in turn gave him messages to cheer the lonely criminals in the Philippines who had wronged his countrymen.

One group of Christian youth composed of Filipinos and others formed an experimental Christian community for the purpose of discovering the best methods of fighting malaria on a large scale. They dug drainage ditches, sprayed, and did all they could to teach people healthful practices. Their own "camp" was a model of kindly, brotherly living. Rather than bringing disputes or problems up in such a formal thing as a "council," they waited for worship, when together they could talk with God and then with one another freely and in friendly spirit. They shared one another's worries and problems; they lent a helping hand. They made brotherhood real.[22]

THE TWENTY-THIRD PSALM
FOR ALL RACES

The Lord shepherds all races,
Not one does he neglect;

He gives rest to everyone through the great pastures of this
   fact;
He leads his flocks away from prejudice,
He restores belief in the final fairness of life,
Even in the presence of injustices so grave that they deaden
   personality,
No one need fear! His justice lives!
His promises and their repeated fulfillments, comfort.
He gives the Bread of Life to all his hungry children,
Even in the presence of racial discriminations;
Impartially, he heals his bruised lambs,
The cup of living water overflows,
Surely understanding and kindness shall increase between
   races and between nations,
All the days of the world's life,
And we shall dwell in the presence of One Shepherd
Forever.[23]

HANDS OF YOUNG CHURCHMEN
BUILDING WORLD BROTHERHOOD

*(For setting, a picture not only of Dürer's "Praying
Hands" but also of hands at work—photographs or sketches.
Follow the meditation with a question, "What of our hands?"
and a moment for silent thinking of what further we can do
. . . must do . . . what God may be calling us to strive to
do . . . to become instruments for his spreading brotherly
ways around us.)*

Hands are building world brotherhood. What kind of
hands?

Hands that have let themselves become nerve-and-muscle for God's holy ongoing, creative, loving Purposes . . .

The hands of a woman who wrote her news commentator asking him to call them Japanese, not "Japs" . . .

The hands of a dime-store clerk in a northern town who stepped in and waited on two Negroes the other clerks had ignored . . .

The hands of thirty-six conscientious objectors who did hard labor on a six months' starvation diet in preparation for helping in the rehabilitation of Europe's starved peoples . . .

The hands of a tireless labor leader, giving her very life that Oriental, Negro, and Mexican workers should have working conditions equal to those of so-called "whites" . . .

The hands of youth work-campers in a slum area building a co-operative cannery . . .

The hands of people like ourselves who refuse to let custom or prejudice warp our living . . . who speak and act and give the work of our hands—that God's kingdom blueprints of more loving ways may be realized in our day.[24]

JESUS' PLATFORM FOR LIVING— AND OURS?

SCRIPTURE: Luke 4:16–19—Jesus' announcement of why he came to earth, and his vision for "giving his daily life."

VOICE: Jesus came that we might have life and have it more abundantly. He meant that life to be the lot of all people everywhere . . .

A German family last year flavored potatoes for a

week with a small sardine because it made them taste different . . .

A man in Poland became ill after eating a doughnut because he wasn't used to eating such rich food . . .

There are babies in Europe who have never known anything but the ache of hunger in their bones. In India and in many other places millions of people do not know what good food is like . . .

Yet He came that all may live and live abundantly.

ANOTHER VOICE: There are teachers of one race who receive less salary than teachers of another race, although their training may be equal . . .

Across America and around the world the personalities of young people are breaking. Many are feeling a sense of futility. Ideals and moral standards are being disregarded. Some think they must be excused because they are in the midst of a social upheaval. . .

We are part of that youth group in the world. In this one group there is enough latent ability and power to push the darkness back in many ways; to help Jesus bring healing to many who are hurt; to share his love with many embittered people; to give our resources so that some will look up in new hope; to give Christ a chance in this broken, chaotic world.[25]

BEING FRIENDS

All during the day, almost any day of your life, there will be many people around you. First, there are those of your own family or those nearest you. Then, others will be playing with you, talking with you, maybe working with you. Will they *enjoy* these contacts? Will their days be nicer because of you?

You want people to like you. Who doesn't? You want to be popular. Who wouldn't? But in these quiet holy moments of thinking with God, consider how to be a helpful *friend*. With his guidance, make your prayer about times or situations when you may be a better friend today—

—for example: in team games where there are some who are timid or do not play well . . .

—in the home, when someone is tired or cross . . .

—when you have work or worries and are tempted to complain or be grouchy . . .

—in study when, although you have finished preparing your lessons, a friend telephones for help . . .

—when in a group discussion you want your point to win so much that you are tempted not to *think* of others' . . .

—when you have spare time and are about to waste it, but remember suddenly a shut-in . . .

PRAYER: O God, as I continue this prayer-thinking with thee, help me to be the friend all day that I am seeing now in my prayers.[26]

PRAYER TO BE KEPT FROM HATRED

Our Father,

May we have the spirit of Jesus to say, "Forgive them, for they know not what they do."

We need the strength of something bigger than ourselves to keep our hearts and minds free from hatred.

May we be willing to drink of the cup, even as our Master did.

Guard us from the things or thoughts that would keep us from forgiving our brothers. May we realize their common kinship with thee, and face the fact that many wrongs are committed unwillingly.

Bless all thy children who are giving themselves daily for the advancement of thy loving spirit and thy principles of justice and brotherhood.[27]

FRIENDS AROUND THE WORLD

GUIDED MEDITATION

Let us now direct our thoughts to our many friends around the world. Some of them we may know personally; some of them we have heard about in one way or another; some of them are completely unknown to us; yet all are friends of ours because Christ works through them and in them.

Think prayerfully about those who serve faithfully in countries other than those which they call their own. Pray for the missionary who carries the Gospel of Christ to those who might not otherwise learn about God's "Good News." (*Allow about fifteen seconds of silence after each petition.*)
. . .

Pray for the Filipino teacher who teaches young people in Japan. Add your strength to hers to help her demonstrate the power of Christian love and forgiveness . . .

Ask God's blessing for the French social worker who labors in Hong Kong to ease the plight of and to give new hope to some of the thousands of refugees who crowd that teeming city . . .

Thank God for the nurses and doctors from Norway and Sweden who use their healing skills to help the unfortunate African. Pray that their strength may be equal to the task . . .

Request God's help for the American technicians who share their knowledge of agriculture and engineering and manufacturing with those in India who are eager to learn that they might improve the lot of their undernourished and underprivileged countrymen. Pray that the spirit of Christ might shine through them . . .

Turn to God in prayer for Christians everywhere throughout the world. Ask him to comfort and strengthen those in danger or difficulty. Request a renewal of faith for those who face discouraging times or tasks. Call for his presence in your own life to help make you conscious of your own task in the world today . . .

We have reached out through the fellowship of prayer to Christian friends around the world. Let us think of them often and resolve to add our own skills and knowledge and faith to theirs so that the kingdom of God may come closer to being.[28]

11. OUR LIFE VOCATION

₰

MY FATHER'S WORLD

My Father's world—and yet
For me he leaves stirring mighty tasks;
And bids me share with him
In building love and truth and joy
To make his dream come true.

My Father's world—and yet
On me waits part of all the beauty, love,
And tenderness the world
Might use in building other powers
To make his dream come true.

My Father's world—and yet
Not His until each willing child of his
For him and for his dream,
Gives love and toil and sacrifice,
To make his dreams come true.[1]

HANDS

Hands are funny things—
Four fingers and a thumb
   with palm attached.

Some think they're made
    to wear their diamonds on;
Others like them for their
    well-groomed look.

But God has given
    to this thing we call a hand
    the power and art
    to heal, to comfort, and to love.

Because of hands so busy all the day,
God's work on earth is being done.

Hands are funny things—
Four fingers and a thumb
    with palm attached—
What power God has given them![2]

MY HAND

This hand of mine is a wonderful piece of machinery—a queer-looking thing when you examine it closely—just a flat object with extensions, octopus fashion, radiating from it. Soft to touch, yet underneath a bony structure. There is blood—a deep red, healing fluid, flowing to the very tips of these fingers and back again.

This hand of mine can move without any outside force. I say "close up" and the fingers curl into a fist. I say "open" and they stretch taut—nor do I have to say this aloud—one finger, two fingers, three fingers can obey my thinking. That chair cannot move. I can scream and yell, yet each leg and arm and back remains motionless. It hasn't in it those intricate muscles and nerve fibers bound together in a way that makes it a machine all by itself.

The Inventor of this machine has a mind far beyond mine —for, though the machine belongs to me, I do not understand it; nor, given complete control of it, would I know how to keep its parts in running order. So I must rely constantly on that Inventor to keep the blood coursing, the skin growing, the nerves feeling.

I wonder why he made that hand!

And why he put that hand on me?

Who am I that I should have custody of such a wonderful machine?

It can do things—hold a clod of earth and touch the sky.

It can make things—which fly through the air, to destroy or bring together.

It can push a person—or lift.

It can twist and destroy—or it can heal.

It can get or give.

I wonder why the Inventor made that hand!

If I could discover that, and he and I could work together, there is no end to what that hand could do.[3]

OUR SKILL OF HAND AND STRENGTH OF LIMB

O God, who workest hitherto,
  Working in all we see,
Fain would we be and bear and do
  As best it pleaseth thee.

Our skill of hand and strength of limb
  Are not our own but thine;

We link them to the work of him
Who made all life divine.[4]

MISSING THE GOAL

Read Mark 12:32–33.

Once during a basketball game I watched a particular
player for a long time. He seemed to be an excellent player,
but he also seemed to be what one might term "a grand-
stander"—he played for the public. Many times I noticed
that he was so concerned with his dribbling, his fancy hand-
offs, and his tricks that he would miss the goal. But, making
the goal was the only thing that really mattered.

Are we as Christians not guilty of the same thing? We
become so concerned about ourselves, we lose sight of our real
goal.

Once I saw a church youth fellowship president refuse to
stop and talk with a boy who needed help very badly. The
boy was not a member of a church, but he was searching for
a purpose in life. The president could have witnessed to the
faith that he knew—but he didn't have time for *that*. He
had to get to church and get things ready for the program.
He must see that the candles are lit, flowers are in place,
hymnals are out. All these things were good, but are they our
real goal?

Is it not to love God and our fellowmen?

PRAYER SUGGESTION: Pray that you will not lose sight of life's
real goal and ask for strength to find and obey God's will.[5]

ATHLETES OF THE SPIRIT

THOUGHT: Paul's life was aflame and a-thrill with dynamic purpose: a "mark" he was "pressing toward," as a runner gives all in a great contest.

PRAYER: O God, to thy way I commit myself. Let me not make this step halfheartedly, but with all I have. Let this high purpose shine like a light before me. Help me to remember this always, especially when I get tired, blue, or careless.

THOUGHT: St. Ignatius of Loyola realized that, in order to organize and discipline one's daily life there needed to be system and "exercises."

PRAYER: O God, help me with will of steel to shut out all that would be unworthy, and to exercise my spirit daily in prayer and study, that when testing times come I may prove strong for thee.

THOUGHT: Learning to swim means learning first to relax on the water, that gravitational forces may bear one up.

PRAYER: O God, teach me to trust.

THOUGHT: In a hard game or race, the extra ounce of "keeping on keeping on" may make the difference.

PRAYER: O God, nerve me for whatever the need.

THOUGHT: God calls us to give our utmost, but not in stern duty but exhilarating joy! The systematic practice of prayer and dedicated action becomes, not an iron rule, but an adventurous Open Road!

PRAYER: O God, thy high call beckons, the way opens, the breeze of morning lends wings to my feet. Thy rod and thy staff comfort me. Amen.[6]

THERE WASN'T A MAN!

Time and again in crisis moments of the world's history, God has called—and *there wasn't a man*. This lonely God has needed a person—sometimes just one man, and that one has been lacking.

Where was the man or group or institution at the crisis of ancient Babylon? Who was there to save the Holy City of Jerusalem as the chosen people of God went out to captivity? Where the ten to keep Sodom from destruction? God called . . .

Where in our day the men of God who can avert a third and final World War? Where the workers, to strengthen the numbers of Christians—until the time comes when a prayer *can* be said at the peace-tables of the nations? Where the church, God-filled enough, to know in this our day the things which belong to our peace?[7]

ME TOO

(*Read Luke 18:9–14.*)

I read about the desperate need for missionaries over the world; missionaries to help new Christians get started and to keep older ones from being discouraged. (*Yes, I hope lots of people are inspired to do something about that.*)

I saw an account of the wonderful work some youth groups

are doing to relieve suffering in the world. (*It would be nice if someone in our youth group started something like that.*)

I listened to a speaker telling of the great service which a worker in a local church can give. (*I hope the people in the audience are being reached.*)

I glanced quickly through the page of the devotional booklet I was reading for the day. (*It's about a few traits that Christians should develop. I hope some of the folks I know take this to heart.*)

Then somehow, somewhere along the line, I stopped my "better than everyone else" pace. Into my thinking crept the disturbing thought that perhaps all of these things weren't just for others. Is it possible that some of this was meant for me?

My prayers and thoughts had been on a Christian vocation for myself. Always (I thought) I was striving to be a better Christian. Yet, here were the tools I needed and I had disregarded them. Unconsciously, I had become like the Pharisee, seeking salvation for others and neglecting it for myself.

Father, it seems so easy to exalt myself, just in my thinking. Teach me humility, that I may know you better. Amen.[8]

TOWARD PERFECTION

Michelangelo was working on a statue when some friends visited him one afternoon. A month later they returned and found him still working on the same statue.

"Why, what have you done since our last visit?" one asked.

"Oh, I've smoothed a line here, and polished an arm,

taken a few flakes of marble from the forehead, and so on," replied the great artist.

"But those are only trifles. Is that all you have done?"

"True, they are but trifles," Michelangelo gravely responded. "But trifles make perfection, and perfection is no trifle."[9]

—AS AN ANCIENT SOLDIER

The Roman soldier stood at the gate of his city—Pompeii.

The maddened crowd swept by—vainly trying to escape from the rain of burning lava from the deadly throat of Vesuvius.

"Flee!" they cried. "Save yourself," they said. "Our city is doomed!"

"A Roman soldier does not flee," answered the soldier.

"Who will know, and who cares?"

"Rome cares and I care."

When centuries afterward, Pompeii was dug out of the ashes they found the armor of the Roman, a dead soldier guarding a buried and lost city. Of such is the glory of ancient empires.

QUESTION FOR MEDITATION: What does it mean—to me—to-day—at the posts of duty that are mine—to "be about my Father's business"?[10]

A NEW ELEMENT

In the movie, Marie Curie says to Pierre, "Pierre, tell me again. It is true, isn't it, that there are a certain number of elements in the universe, and that they have all been discovered and classified, and this is fixed and forever?" Pierre nodded affirmatively with a sigh. Marie kept trying to tell herself it was so.

"But just suppose," her soaring imagination kept prodding her, "there were another element—unlike all the others—not inert matter but active energy." On that supposition, she and her companion Pierre worked until there was opened to the world the door to a universe not forever static and fixed but changing, dynamic.

Some day a new movie, maybe, is going to be written about some young person or young couple. They may, as the Curies did, try to tell themselves that what people say is true, that wars are to be expected, that it will take time to work out better race relations.

But just suppose there were a new element unlike these sad, hateful ways, maybe an element full of energy and life-giving force—peace, good will. Just suppose it were put to work. Like Gandhi, who did put it to work because he took Jesus' teachings at face value, they will find how powerful this is. There will be opened to the world, a new door to a universe not forever static in its old, outworn ways, but changing, dynamic, love-powered.

Father, let me help to bring about this new discovery.[11] Amen.

BUT WHAT CAN ONE PERSON DO?

We live in a time of numbers—big overwhelming numbers. Men and machines, money and powers. What can one person do against a sea of trouble?

From the beginning of the world, it has taken only one person to start a movement. "From the loving example of one family a whole state becomes loving; and from its courtesies, the whole state becomes courteous; while from the ambition and perverseness of one man, the whole state may be led to rebellious disorder—such is the nature of influence."

We must not underrate the power of a few. Eleven disciples turned the world upside down. One was apostle to the Gentiles. Two German students set the Protestant missionary enterprise going. One young English cobbler and Cambridge don awakened the church of England. Five American college boys started the missionary enterprise among students.

> I act, and faces I shall never see
> And lives that I cannot guess
> Will be faithful or false because of me,
> Will curse the world or bless.
> Think! I so weak and frail and small
> This deathless power am given,
> That by word or deed a host may fall
> Or a legion be raised to heaven.[12]

12. MAKING PERSONAL DEDICATION

GOD CALLS

Youth, oh youth, can I reach you?
    Can I speak and make you hear?
Can I flash my secrets on you?
    Can my spirit draw you near?

Is there a prophet among you?
    One with a heart to know?
I will flash my secrets on him,
    He will see my glory grow.

For I, the God, the Father,
    The Quest, the Final Goal,
Still search for a prophet among you
    To speak my words to his soul.[1]

IF WE REALLY FOUND THEE?

God—what would happen if we really found thee? We do not change very much with all our talking in prayer. We are just about where we were last year in making "thy kingdom come . . . on earth . . ."

"But we don't know what to say," we say.

As if saying words meant that we were in touch with thee!

"What have you done?"

Wait, God, do not ask us that—we are trying to say our prayers. You must listen to us: "Almighty and most merciful Father: We have erred and strayed from thy ways like lost sheep. We have followed too much the devices and desires of our own hearts. We have offended against thy holy laws. We have left undone those things which we ought to have done; and we have done those things which we ought not to have done . . . Have mercy upon us!" Through Jesus Christ our Lord!

There, God, we've said our prayers. It makes us feel better.

"What have you done?"

Done? Let me think.

Yes, God is asking what you have done this year to make the world more like the world that Christ revealed.

"But God, I am too young," we say.

Jesus was only thirty-three when he died.

"But God, I am too busy."

About what?

(Read no more . . . while you answer that question.)

God, help us to see that life is not a careless chance; that if we do not, by the strength of a purposeful spirit, move toward thee, we drift aimlessly away, and it is so much harder for the world to become thy Kingdom which we pray about. Amen.[2]

THE CALL

Hush, God . . .
It is my will to do thus and so.
I'll pick my own path, go
My way.

Hush, God . . .
I know which job I'll choose.
I must hurry now, or lose
A fortune.

Hush . . .

(That voice—so loud, insistent, clear!
It drowns out everything!) . . . I hear
You, God . . . yes . . . take me now.
I'll do your will—just show me how.[3]

SECONDS TICKING AWAY...

(Note: Let the meeting room be dimly darkened; a hidden metronome may be set to tick the seconds so that all may hear. A prelude in a minor key may set the mood; let a voice begin immediately without announcement, if any of the following "seed-thoughts" are used. This service may be planned to work up to worship expression in hymn and prayer, or in spontaneous sharing of personal thoughts at the close.)

Seconds!. . . ticking away . . . our life-time, moving out gradually into eternity . . . seconds . . . minutes . . .

This very minute someone is breathing his last . . . some new life is being born . . . someone is plotting some dastardly deed . . . someone is dreaming of doing a heroic act for God . . . someone is praying somewhere right now, for someone else . . . yet someone else is hating . . . seconds . . . *our* seconds. . . .

Here in this room as we have gathered, we represent many millions of seconds ahead. Will the seconds of our hours, and the days of our years bring the world one step closer to brotherhood and peace? Will ours be a pull forward or backward in better race relations? Will somebody be led by the influence of our example, to make a choice for the better? Will the home of which we dream be a haven of Christian love? Will we in our vocation uphold Christian ideals? Will we, in the days ahead this very week, use our seconds worthily? . . .

Let us, in quietness, as seconds go by, think of the *wonder of being alive,* of being given the mystery of heartbeat and breath whereby we are enabled to live, and move, to think, and do. These bodies of ours are composed of the ingredients of the dust of the earth, yet with the astonishing gift of self-consciousness, so that we may—as now—pause and consider ourselves, our ways and days. Let us thank God our creator, from whose breath we are endowed with this breath of life.

(*Silence*)

Let us, in quietness, as seconds go by, consider the way in which all of us as human creatures are bound up together "in the bundle of life," so that we can feel each other's joys, share each other's woes. Have we been trying too hard to live our own lives apart, unwilling to admit how dependent *we* are upon others, and hence unwilling to face up to their dependence upon us? When we are in grief or trouble, when we need help from out beyond ourselves, we are grateful for hands that reach understandingly and helpfully to us. Do we in turn reach toward those who may have some need? Is there someone now?

(*Silence*)

Let us face frankly the influences that would discourage us in seeking to dedicate our life-energies and our seconds to God. Someone will say, "But if you stand up for such a conviction you'll be thought self-righteous or holier-than-thou." Someone else will say, "But one person cannot make a difference; it's human nature to fight, isn't it?" Let us remember God's magnificent truths: "One with God is a majority!" "God doesn't need much of a man but he needs all there is of him." "I am only one, but I *am* one . . ." As the seconds merge with our heartbeats, let us pray, "Lord, I Want to Be a Christian in-a My Heart," singing this softly.[4]

WHO ANSWERS...

"Hail!" the ringing call came across the water where the weary young fishermen were struggling with tangled nets. Quickly they looked up. Could it be . . . he, their new-found friend, in whose company they felt so at ease, who opened to them such wondrous new thoughts? They could scarcely believe he had come, so early in the morning, down by their end of the lake. Straining their eyes through the fog and dimness they could see him striding strongly and purposefully along the shore. Again the clear friendly greeting. And now they answered back, already bringing their boats in as swiftly as they could.

For something in the tone of their friend sounded urgent, as if something more serious were in the air than just a casual chat. Soon they were to know. For as they neared the shore, he continued, "Come! Follow me!" No apology, no "Can you?" or "Would you consider?" "Come!" That was all they needed. Quickly, with the wholeheartedness of youth, they leapt over the side of the boat, waded ashore, and were at their friend's side. "What can we do for you?" they asked eagerly.

And for the rest of their lives they were to find what they could do for God. Had they foreseen what sufferings, what unpopularity, what physical hardships, and what persecution would await them at the end, would they have answered so readily, so zestfully? Yes! For their friend had called, had chosen *them*. That was enough . . .[5]

AN EPISTLE TO YOUNG PEOPLE —

(in the style Paul might have used if he were writing now)

To all young people, both those who are in Christ and in his church and those who should be won to him:

Grace be unto you, and peace, from God our Father and from the Lord Jesus Christ.

Your religious leaders and counselors thank God upon every remembrance of you and long to come to you with Christian counsel and command. We are grateful for your fellowship in the gospel and for your ministry of love and prayer to us.

You are a part of a troubled and uneasy generation. Called to serve your country in war as in peace, much has been required of you—wisdom beyond your years, skills beyond your capacities, and courage unlimited.

Many times have you been in rebellion at the stupidity of your elders, and discouraged and dismayed by their seeming inertia or indifference to critical issues. In your search for freedom, may you stand fast in the liberty wherewith Christ has made you free.

We would constrain you to be merciful, and in every way to serve the necessity of others.

Be patient under the silences of God. Face the future unafraid never losing faith in the power of ultimate truth.

Do not imagine vain things, but look on life with quiet eyes. Walk in humility and strength before God.

Never cease your quest to know the mind of Christ and to appropriate the power of a full commitment to his purposes.

In state as in church, approve only the things that are excellent.

We pray that you may be sincere and without offense, being filled with the fruits of righteousness, which are by Jesus Christ, unto the glory and praise of God.[6]

I WOULD SO LIVE –

(*Read II Timothy 2:22–25*)

I would so live that—
My faith in God would be beyond my own understanding,

My prayer would be continuous but regularly prayed,
My love of man would hold no prejudice, no discrimination,
My humbleness to the will of God would be as a child,
My love for God would know no bounds,
My wrath would be directed only toward evil,
My study of the life of Jesus would never end,
My goal in life would be to achieve a love of God such as he
    had,
And that truly my life would be lived in his name.
Father, accept my dedication of life in this same spirit.
    Amen.[7]

WHEN ABRAHAM WENT OUT OF UR

Men go out from the places where they dwelled,
Knowing not why or whither, but overborne
At midnight by some awful word, forsworn
Between one dark and day, called and compelled.

So have they gone for ages in the gleam
Of many a daybreak, turning troubled eyes
For one last look at home beneath old skies,
Their birthright bartered for a nameless dream.

Even as God's first adventurer stood forth
One star-wrought night, on a familiar hill,
And saw the Chaldean dawn, remote and chill,
Etching old Ur along the lonely north,
And bowed himself to his loved earth, and rent
His garments, crying he could not go . . . and went.[8]

GOD'S CREATIVE TOUCH
AND OUR ANSWER

In the Bible stories of creation, after each step we read, "And God saw that it was good"—but regarding man, *it does not say*. Blank. As if the evidence were not all in. Could it be that man is still "God's unfinished creation?" That "it doth not yet appear what he shall be"?

Man wandering alone . . .

trusting in his own powers . . .

forgetting or scorning God . . .

—still in blackness and void!

(*Voice, paraphrasing Genesis 1:2:* And man's life without God is without form and void . . . and darkness is upon the face of the deep.)

But there have been those who have lifted their faces to God, and his light and his love have done their holy work of new creation. These lives have blessed mankind. Their light still shines. For that light came from God's creative fingers into theirs.

There was Nicholas Herman of Lorraine, for example. He was a lowly and unlearned man. He had been a footman and a soldier. In 1666 he was admitted as a lay brother among the barefooted Carmelites at Paris. Afterward he became known as "Brother Lawrence."

Dark had been his days, wandering in futility and fear— until one morning when he was about eighteen years old, in midwinter he chanced to see a dry and leafless tree. But as he gazed, he seemed to see the tree springing to new life—blossoming, vibrating with the very touch of the hand of God.

He knew that spring would bring that new life. "If such can happen to a tree," he thought, "why not to me?"

(*Note: For setting, a soft dark green or blue "ground" may be arranged on a table, with a bare lifeless branch on one side and on the other, a blooming branch. At this point light may be shown on the setting.*)

Herman's life henceforth blossomed at the touch of the hand of God. In the monastery kitchen, among lowly duties, he learned through practice to know the Presence of God even there. There, among the pots and pans, with much confusion and labor, God's holy creation was continuing—as truly as in the trees or outer world.[9]

LUTHER STANDS

Time: a late afternoon in April, 1521.
Place: the first imperial diet of Charles V, at Worms.

Stillness reigns a moment in the great court chamber. The quiet figure of a monk, his eyes burning in his wan face, stands before the young emperor and his cohorts in their rich robes. On the table before them are stacked a number of books. To the left of the emperor stands Dr. Johann Eck. Pointing to the books, Dr. Eck speaks: "Martin Luther, will you or will you not retract what you have written?"

Luther takes a step forward. His loose, drab robe swishes powerfully, and his strong voice rings out: "*I cannot and will not retract,* for it is unsafe for a Christian to speak against his conscience." His eyes sweep over the bishops, the archbishops, the red-caped cardinals, the emperor, the princes in the black silk and brocade, the noblemen, the mighty ones of this world, who have his life in their hands.

"Here I stand. I can do no other! May God help me. Amen!"[10]

A TOMATO PLANT—AND A WORK WITH GOD

Chad Walsh in our own day was in darkness and void until he saw—*a tomato plant!* He held in his hand one tiny tomato seed and heard it "proclaim a God so big that he can tenderly see to little things . . . a God whose love is so abounding, so given to overflow, that it spills over in the form of human lives, cats, dogs, foxes, worms, trees, and tomatoes." . . . Then meditating on how changed this luscious tomato was from the tiny sour love-apple of earlier days, he remarked on "how mightily man has wrought since God first thrust the wild tomato into his hands."

"God has made a world," said Chad Walsh, "in which men can be his junior partners. He does the groundwork of creation, and then permits them to share his joy by taking a wild vine—and dedicating centuries to its improvement."

So we have the chance to work *with* God . . . His creation continues. In some ways our own lives—our thoughts, our attitudes, our concern for others, our actions—are unfinished . . . maybe like that little sour fruit that needed to grow toward the ideal of the lovely tomato . . . maybe like the lifeless tree in winter needing new life.

We feel God's brooding call, even now, this hour. In our garden, saying, "Mary!" By our fishing boat, saying, "Peter!"

Beside our seat of custom, saying, "Levi!" Under our sycamore tree, saying, "Zacchaeus!" At our supper table in the
breaking of bread, saying, "Cleopas!" By the tomb of our
dead selves, saying, "Lazarus!" May we pray now . . . each
silently in his own heart . . . that God's plan of creation
may continue through us; that we may be the selves our
Creator dreams us to be. Amen.[11]

CONSCRIPTS OF THE DREAM

Give thanks, O heart, for the high souls
That point us to the deathless goals—
For all the courage of their cry
That echoes down from sky to sky;
Thanksgiving for the armed seers
And heroes called to mortal years—
Souls that have built our faith in man,
And lit the ages as they ran . . .
These are the sons of sacred flame,
Their brows marked with the sacred name—
The company of souls supreme,
The conscripts of the mighty Dream.[12]

ENDLESS LINE OF SPLENDOR

There is a strange fact in the history of track. For as long
as there had been records of timing and mileage, it seemed
that there was a certain limit to the speed a human body
could reach. Any breaking of records was within a small
range of variation. Generation after generation of young
runners took for granted that they could not aspire beyond

this limit. But some years back, a certain young doctor broke well beyond this speed; then others, gaining courage and a new image of what they, too, might do . . . then many others.

One of the greatest glories of earth is the story of what dauntless persons have done for Christ and his way through the centuries. They show, like shafts of light, how the power of God cuts through what seem to be limitations. True, many of God's valiant souls—in the long ages past and now!—have been trampled, scorned, crushed, frozen into isolation by scornful ones who would pass by. But they rose to move forward, ever singing, hoping, believing, trusting; and their song blends in with Paul's: "This one thing we do, we press on. We count not ourselves to have finished our task, we press on. God has a greater work for us yet. We have here no continuing city. We press on."

Pioneers, climbers, courageous speakers for truth when it would have been far easier to keep still; ones who stopped to help weak ones along the way and to look unflinchingly into causes of war and hunger and hurt; yonder they go, God's brave pilgrims: Telemachus questioning gladiatorial fights, Francis questioning war, Wilberforce questioning slavery, Elizabeth Fry leading prison reform—the line goes on. Who is next?[13]

HERE I STAND—BECAUSE GOD CAN USE ME!

"Don't make Jesus a mere creed! Let him live—in history —in society—in you—in the whole world—today and forever."

PRAYER HYMN (*in unison*): "Breathe on Me, Breath of God."

VOICE: Hear the words of the Prophet Jeremiah (*here let Jeremiah 1:1–10 be read, if possible from Smith and Goodspeed translation*).

YOUTH: We are so young! If we should choose today to loiter on the Self-Road for a while, what would it matter? Could we hope to cure the old ills of the world? This is our playtime, these our days of mirth! (If thou, O Christ, wouldst turn away thine eyes!) We have a right to play!

VOICE: Do you remember the excuse Jeremiah gave? But God said, "Do not say, I am only a youth" . . . God needs you—he can use you!

YOUTH: I have been thinking about the theme, "Here I Stand"; it has led me to look into the life of Christ to see what he did when he met hard problems. I found that where people were suffering he was there to help. Where there was injustice because of difference in creed, or color, or class, or other reasons, Christ was there to stand for the right. Where there was sin or greed or strife of any kind, he was there to challenge people to a better life. I find *myself* in these places. Can God use me there? How?

VOICE: Yes, God can use you, but you must have certain qualities before he can use you effectively.

Do you have enough love in your heart? How much? Enough to give up a new dress in order that a girl somewhere else may be warm? (*Pause*) Enough that you are willing to share, to the point of sacrifice, that the hungry might be fed, the illiterate educated? (*Pause*) Are you willing to lay aside all prejudice which you hold toward those who do not live on the "right side of town" or are of a different color, class, or creed than you? (*Pause*)

Do you have purity in your life? What about the undesirable habits and grudges which have accumulated in your life? (*Pause*) What about the literature you are reading? Is it largely comic books, cheap love stories, trash? (*Pause*)

Are you keeping your devotional life well nurtured? (*Pause*) What about the temptation to say the unkind thing about another? Did you overcome it? (*Pause*) Did you cheat on that examination paper last week? (*Pause*)

Do you have courage? Enough to prepare yourself for Christian life service if God wants you to do that? (*Pause*) Enough to return good for evil? (*Pause*) How about last week when someone was unfair to you or told a tale about you? (*Pause*) Enough to put your church first when the high school club, the football or basketball team, the movies, the television program, the weekend outing gets first claim on so many of us? (*Pause*)

If you have such qualities, God can use you!

YOUTH: Do you suppose God thinks we can really do anything about war, intolerance, indifference of church members, corruption in government, profanity, immorality, as well as other evils of our day? Even with these qualities in our lives, can we do anything?

VOICE: I will not say it is going to be easy, but you can do something by beginning where you are.

YOUTH: I know it will not be easy . . . But if that is what God needs—youth who will stand for him—youth with courage and love in their hearts—pure in daily living and humble in spirit, action and thought, I want to be ONE whom God can use.

Here I stand, because God stands beside me,
Here I stand, because Christ calls me to a living fellowship.
Here I stand, because Christ calls me to be a neighbor.
Here I stand, because Christ calls me to witness.
Here I stand, because God can use me.[14]

YOUTH GIVES THE WORLD ITS PROPHETS

Youth gives the world its prophets,
Isaiah, John, Buddha, Francis, Jesus—they were all young men
When the Dream smote them, made of them living flames,
To purge and quicken humanity.
Now at this dim-out hour the world awaits your coming,
In shame it waits while one by one its lights go out;
Yet daring still to dream of a better day to come . . .
One thing—and one alone:

The Spirit of a certain Man who lived long ago,

Who was lonely and misunderstood, . . . because he loved his brother men.

This is the challenge that comes to Christian youth today:

To love men as He loved them;

All men, black and white, clean or dirty, white-colored or begrimed with soot and sweat,

American or English or German or Japanese;

Love men until our very beings are part of them;

Until our own flesh writhes beneath their burden and injustices,

Until we are molded and twisted like white metal upon an anvil,

Until we ourselves, consumed by a living fire,

Become the torches that shall bring light to this darkened world.[15]

TOUCH US WITH FLAME

Touch us, O God,

With the Flame of the Spirit!

Touch us

With burning consciousness of thee!

Create in us

An urgent need for giving!

Sear out the roots of our complacency!

Touch us, O God,

That we may truly live!

Bring to us all, should such need be,

Our own dark hour of Gethsemane,

Where in its crucible of pain
Alone we falter . . .
Reach out . . . and gloriously find
That we were never alone, but blind!
Where in its crucible of pain
Shall our petty hates and discords . . . fused
Into one great, burning ache . . .
One burning ache for all humanity . . .
An ache which thou dost bless
To ecstasy when it is laid
With all of life and love which we possess
Upon thy altar!
Touch us, O God,
With the flame of the Spirit . . .
The flame
Were it but kindled
In each heart, the whole world
In one quick tomorrow might
Forever be illumined by its light![16]

ONCE TO EVERY MAN AND NATION

(*This program*[17] *was intended for a campfire dedication service, but it may easily be given indoors if phrases such as "beneath the stars" or "before this campfire" are changed to "in the House of God" or "gathered in Christian fellowship" or some other appropriate phrase. The appropriate time is United Nations Day, October 24; but the dateline can be put in to suit any time when youth want to think together about "the moment to decide."*)

SCRIPTURE: Romans 12:1–2.

SOLOIST OR ENSEMBLE (*or special reader if no singers are available*):

> Once to every man and nation comes the moment to decide,
> In the strife of truth with falsehood for the good or evil side;
> Some great cause, God's new Messiah, offering each the bloom or blight,
> And the choice goes by forever 'twixt that darkness and that light.[18]

FIRST VOICE: "Once to every man and nation comes the moment to decide . . ." Here sit we (*number of those present*) strong, beneath the stars; here sit we who call ourselves Christian, gathered before a campfire. Supposedly, we have made our decision "twixt that darkness and that light." Supposedly, we are already committed in the strife of truth with falsehood. *Have* we faced our moment of decision? We of the fellowship . . . we of the inclusive Christian brotherhood?

Have we made our decision—and stuck by it? Have I? Have you?

SOLOIST OR ENSEMBLE (*or special reader*):

> Then to side with truth is noble
> When we share her wretched crust,
> Ere her cause bring fame and profit,
> And 'tis prosperous to be just;
> Then it is the brave man chooses while the coward stands aside
> Till the multitude make virtue of the Faith they had denied.[19]

SECOND VOICE: It is (*date*). What does that date mean—to you, to me, sitting with our friends before the campfire;

To Albert Schweitzer and his aides, in the thick jungles of Lambaréné;

To the head man of Russia, behind the stolid, grim walls of the Kremlin;

To the crooner of the hour, under the glaring spotlights of Hollywood?

THIRD VOICE: What does it mean to the financier putting across a deal in his plush Wall Street office;

To the Indian mother watching her child grow spindly and sick of malnutrition;

To the youth of Africa, meeting secretly by moonlight, not for the carefree comradeship of a social fraternity but for the solemn promise of winning independence for their people—by peaceful means, if possible; by violence, if necessary?

Today's date—and United Nations Day—what can such dates mean?

FIRST VOICE: Historians give names to periods of history: the Stone Age, the Age of Reason . . .

It will be interesting to see what name they give the age of which this day is a part. Perhaps they may call it "The Age of Paradox"; for look at today's world and the paradoxes contained therein.

SECOND VOICE: In Washington D.C., congressmen unashamedly debate over crop quotas, and rats gulp down our stored-up surpluses undisturbed; while over one-half of the world's population goes to bed hungry every night.

THIRD VOICE: In the American household, the two-car garage and the television antenna have become standard operating equipment, while the Asian plows his fields with a forked stick as did his ancestors thousands of years ago.

FIRST VOICE: One by one, medical science conquers physical disease: smallpox, typhoid, polio, pneumonia—all falter before the onslaught of vaccines and antibiotics. But the hospital beds are rapidly filled by mental patients, their emotions and minds shattered by the rush of a fevered world.

SECOND VOICE: Leisure has become not a privilege but an undisputed right; schools, church, city, and club hasten forth with recreational opportunities to fill those leisure hours (as do the movies, television, professional sports, and commercial recreation). Yet the psychiatrist's office, the divorce courts, and the reform schools are monuments to the boredom of modern American man and the emptiness of his life.

FIRST VOICE: Religion has become the national hobby as witness our mass evangelistic meetings. New churches spring up in the suburbs overnight to hold the overflow congregation; yet the crime rate mushrooms yearly; alcoholism and mental disorders continue to increase. There are those who say we have swapped the cross of Christ for peace of mind and that church membership has become merely a passport to business prosperity, a free ticket to social acceptance.

THIRD VOICE: The greatest single source of physical power yet known has been unleashed. Yet we threaten to end all life with it!

SECOND VOICE: This is the Age of Paradox; of amazing progress —and abysmal poverty; of scientific achievement—and spiritual confusion; of physical ease—and mental chaos: *this date . . .*

FIRST VOICE: "Once to every man and nation comes the moment to decide

In the strife of truth with falsehood for the good or evil side."

And what, friend, is your decision? It is not, as some would claim, a simple choice. It is not simply communism versus capitalism. It is not simply a struggle between those who call themselves Christian and those who do not.

The world is not just black and white. There is also an infinite number of shades of gray.

SECOND VOICE: To align oneself on the side of truth takes courage—not merely the sudden flash of bravery that enables a man to die for a cause, but the steady, persevering determination that enables one to *live* for a cause; to live for truth demands a rare type of courage!

SOLOIST, ENSEMBLE (*or special reader*):

By the light of burning martyrs, Christ, thy bleeding feet we track,

Toiling up new Calvaries ever with the cross that turns not back;

New occasions teach new duties, time makes ancient good
uncouth;
They must upward still and onward, who would keep abreast
of truth.[20]

THIRD VOICE: But I am only one—a single soul isolated in
this single personality. What can one soul do?

SECOND VOICE: I came to the Lord with that question: What
can one soul do?

The room was suddenly vast, with the stars set bright in
the ceiling.
"All else is cause and effect. All else is law."
The thunder withdrew from the Voice, and the words came
hushed and clear,
Like the first stars in the twilight, each star a new-born glory.
"There is only one miracle, and it is already accomplished.
That miracle is the human soul."
The Lord he lifted his head and the Milky Way was his
hair.
"The soul is like the atom," he said, "wonderfully like the
atom.
Consider the atom.
So minute no lens you can make can enlarge it to a point
where your eyes can see it, yet there's a whole solar
system inside it, whirling around a nucleus, like the
planets around the sun.
So feeble in its unreleased state, yet actually the greatest
force, save one, in creation.
The greatest force in creation, save one."
The Lord strode through his house so the timbers whispered
to each other,
"He's thinking of the soul tonight, of the soul of man, and
the power asleep in the soul.

He always shakes the house when he thinks of the power,
The Power asleep in the soul of man."

"But," said the Lord—and the stars in the sky seemed to
stand still and listen—

"The power must be released, as the atom-breakers released
the power of the atom.

They had to get past the electrons to get at the energy
packed in the nucleus.

And I have to get past a deal of ego to release the power
that is packed in the soul of man.

I keep shooting my rays toward the nucleus,

And the charged field keeps fending them off.

But now and then one gets by.

The nucleus is split, the power is released, and things begin
to happen on a scale that makes men gasp, and talk
about miracles.

But it isn't a miracle.

It's just the soul of man coming to its own.

It's just the soul of man freed at last to be itself."

The Lord he looked at me and his eyes pierced like hot wires.

"Perhaps," he said, "there's something in you and numerous
others that will be cracked open, if a hundred and thirty-
five million people are going to grow up overnight . . ."

"Something in you," said the Lord, "something . . . perhaps . . . in YOU."[21]

THIRD VOICE: So here we sit tonight before the campfire:
(*number present*) separate souls facing decision; (*number present*) potential miracles seeking courage. If God
could reach the soul of each of us, release the power in
(*number present*) souls, what might that power achieve?

FIRST VOICE: Have we the courage here to vow within our
hearts that our decision is on the side of truth—and

then to leave the safe secureness of this fellowship—to rise up and go back home where unbelievers may scoff at our belief, sneer at our standards, oppose with fierceness every goal we strive for?

SECOND VOICE: Have we the strength to go back home and work with all those who believe—but just a little—who think it's fine to call oneself a Christian as long as he's not too worked up about it; who think the church a pleasant place to meet one's friends and socialize awhile when there is nothing much on television?

FIRST VOICE: Can we without reservation freely present our spirits to the Master and then receive them back freshly kindled with sacred fire? To be alive in such an age as this—what *does* it mean? And more—what *should* it mean? To me, to you—to Christ's eternal kingdom?

SOLOIST, ENSEMBLE (*or special reader*):

Though the cause of evil prosper, yet 'tis truth alone is strong:
Though her portion be the scaffold, and upon the throne be wrong;
Yet that scaffold sways the future, and behind the dim unknown,
Standeth God within the shadow keeping watch above his own.[22]

GOD'S SIGNPOST

Who answers Christ's insistent call
Must give himself, his life, his all,

Without one backward look.
Who sets his hand unto the plow,
And glances back with anxious brow,
His calling hath mistook.
Christ claims him wholly for his own.
He must be Christ's and Christ's alone.[23]

13. THE HOLY COMMUNION

IN EVERY QUIET UPPER ROOM

Beneath the Forms of Outward Rite
Thy supper, Lord, is spread
In every quiet upper room
Where fainting souls are fed.

The bread is always consecrate
Which men divide with men;
And every act of brotherhood
Repeats thy feast again.

The blessed cup is only passed
True memory of thee,
When life anew pours out its wine
With rich sufficiency.

O Master, through these symbols shared,
Thine own dear self impart,
That in our daily life may flame
The Passion of thy heart.[1]

THE CONFORMED LIFE

(Preparation for Communion)

(For worship setting, place a crude vessel of earthenware on the table, as the "cup," and a loaf of coarse brown bread as the "bread." Use draped cloth of rough uncolored weave. Stream of light on the elements.)

CALL TO WORSHIP

We have begun anew the Search, Our Father.

We have emptied ourselves into simplicity and faith,
    knowing that with true humility we shall find thee.

Hide not thyself from us. Let us find thee anew in the
    symbols of the Holy Communion.

QUIET MUSIC: *(Suggestion, "He Shall Feed His Flock" from Handel's The Messiah).*

MEDITATION *(three voices in back of worshiping group. One is the Searching Voice; the Second is Conscience answering; the Third is the Confirmation)*:

VOICE 1 *(pensively, quietly, slowly)*: Such a simple act he performed, taking what he had at hand—coarse bread—breaking it and giving it to each questioning man. Why such a simple method and such simple fare?

VOICE 2: Everyone of every race and clime and creed has at hand, bread—it is a universal need—it is provided in some form throughout life. It is a recurring daily

need. What better thing could he have chosen to remind us of the Way?

VOICE 1: And wine—of course, this—once the bread was
chosen. Wine was used generally in place of water in
one's daily thirsting. Water was so often polluted. The
two together, a perfect combination to call us away
to the quiet ritual he performed. But how can these
peasant things have meaning for me?

VOICE 2: Except by faith can you understand. Is it so
much to ask of you to believe, and that in believing
you will come to know?

VOICE 1: It is that I am used to complications and his way
is so different, so simple that it is difficult.

VOICE 2: You were not left comfortless. The Father sent
the Spirit—he is in you to help you understand—
understanding comes only through quietness, love,
simplicity, faith, and prayer. Are these things so very
difficult, my child?

(*Long pause*)

VOICE 3:

As one unknown and nameless He comes to us, just as
on the shore of the lake he approached those men who
knew not who he was. His words are the same: "Follow
thou me!" and he puts us to the tasks which he has to
carry out in our age. He commands. And to those who
obey, be they wise or simple, he will reveal himself
through all that they are privileged to experience in his

fellowship of peace and activity, of struggle and suffering, till they come to know, as an inexpressible secret, who he is.

HYMN: "Break Thou the Bread of Life."[2]

A COMMUNION SERVICE IN THE OUT-OF-DOORS

FIRST STEP: A SACRAMENT OF PRAISE

CALL TO WORSHIP: O come, let us sing unto the Lord. Let us make a joyful noise unto the rock of our salvation.

HYMN: "For the Beauty of the Earth"

READING

O God, we thank thee for everything!

For the sea and its waves, blue and green and gray and always wonderful!

For the beach and the breakers, the spray and the white foam on the rocks.

For the blue arch of heaven, the clouds in the sky, white, gray, and purple.

For the green of the grass, the forests in their spring beauty, for the wheat and corn, the rye and barley.

For the brown earth turned up by the plow, the sun by day and the dews by night.

We thank thee for all that thou hast made, and that thou hast called it good . . .

We thank thee that thou hast placed us in a world to subdue all things to thy glory and to use all things for the good of thy children.

We thank thee. We enter into thy work and go about
thy business.

PRAYER

MEDITATION: "We are God's fellow workers. As we praise
the Creator we meditate on how we can co-operate with
Him more fully."

SILENT PRAYER

SECOND STEP: A SACRAMENT OF REPENTANCE AND DEDICATION

SCRIPTURE: (*Matthew 3:10; I Corinthians 3:10–15.*)

PRAYER: (*For cleansing that our bodies may be made
temples of God.*)

MEDITATION: (*Place leaves and brush upon the fire symbolizing selfishness, laziness, and other shortcomings, and
with the rising flame symbolizing our renewed dedication to God.*)

HYMN: "I Would Be True"

THIRD STEP: A SACRAMENT OF FEEDING

SCRIPTURE: (*John 6:4–13, 35; John 4:14; John 6:27–39.*)

MEDITATION: (*Need for food. Only the hungry seek it.
"Blessed are those who hunger." Symbols of divine feeding strengthen the soul.*)

PRAYER OF CONSECRATION: Father of all mercies and God of all comfort, we humbly beseech thee to grant us thy presence and sanctify this bread, which is broken before thee as thy Son broke the loaves by the Sea of Galilee. May thy Spirit be with us as we perform this act in his memory, that by faith we may receive Christ crucified in us, that we may feed on him in our hearts with thanksgiving, and that he may be one with us and we with him. Amen.

HYMN: "Be Known to Us in Breaking Bread." (*The congregation, or a soloist, sings until everyone has received the bread. Then the leader repeats as the bread is eaten:*) "This is the bread which cometh down out of heaven that a man may eat thereof and live. And the bread which I give is my flesh for the life of the world."

FOURTH STEP: A SACRAMENT OF GROWTH

SCRIPTURE: (*John 15:1–8.*)

MEDITATION (*necessity for pruning, abiding in the vine*): "As we grow in him we should be joined in brotherhood to every branch which abides in the same vine."

PRAYER: We give thee thanks, our Father, for Jesus, thy Son. As we partake of the fruit of the vine may we and all thy people abide as branches of the true vine which brings forth fruit unto eternal life."

HYMN: "O Love, That Wilt Not Let Me Go" (*as clusters of three grapes are distributed*).

PARTICIPATION (*one grape eaten after each of the following sentences*):

> As we partake of the fruit of the vine, may we grow in mind, coming into more of the knowledge of the truth that sets us free.
>
> May we grow in sensitiveness of spirit to all that concerns the needs of our fellow men.
>
> May we grow in the disciplined control of our emotional life and decisiveness of action for all that is good.[3]

BREAD

When we eat good bread, we are eating months of sunlight,
weeks of rain and snow from the sky,
richness out of the earth.
We should be great, each of us, radiant,
full of music and full of stories,
Able to run the way the clouds do,
able to dance like the snow and rain.
But nobody takes time to think that he eats all these things,
and that sun, rain, and snow are all a part of himself.[4]

* * *

> Be gentle
> When you touch bread.
> Let it not lie
> Uncared for—unwanted.
> So often bread
> Is taken for granted.

There is so much beauty
In bread—
Beauty of sun and soil,
Beauty of patient toil.
Winds and rains have caressed it,
Christ often blessed it.
Be gentle
When you touch bread.[5]

THE SACRAMENT OF BREAD

Before me is the Sacrament of *Bread*. In this bread, I see the fellowship of man—for, throughout the ages, the sharing of bread together has been the public act of friendship between men. It is a means of communion between men.

I look at this bread—and sense a wonder and a mystery. For to nourish men is not the same as to fatten cattle; and this bread, eaten by man, is mysteriously changed into the laughter and love of a person.

With what awe does one stand in the presence of this miracle—that bread becomes personal life; becomes the mighty deeds of a nation.

And so, as I look at this bread, I see in it the boys and girls, men and women of all countries; their hopes—their homes—their friendship with my family and my country.

What then shall I do with this bread?

Just as many grains of wheat, scattered abroad over the plains, being gathered together, become one in this bread,

So may we, through its gift, become one with the people of the earth.

And may our partaking of a meal together

Be as the gathering together of the peoples from the ends of the earth

Into the feast of the kingdom of God. Amen.[6]

THE SACRAMENT OF WINE

Before me is the Sacrament of *Wine*. In this wine, I see the fellowship of man who through the ages has found sustenance in the fruit of the vine; and made the partaking together a ceremonial of friendship.

The very essence of God's mysterious creation is contained in one drop of this wine—the tiny vine beginning to reach upward through the soil, later curling its tendrils toward the sun, putting forth branches, drawing strength from soil and sun and air, until finally the fruit appears—cool, luscious grapes of the vine.

With what awe does one stand in the presence of this miracle—that from soil and sun and air, through this vine, should come food to enrich the life of man.

And so, as I look at this vine, I see in it God at work in his world, providing all around his children good things for their life and health—if they will but share his bounties freely with one another until all may have enough. Wherever one child of God shares with one other, I see man and God working together—partners.

The grape gives up its lifeblood, when compressed, to become wine. May we in the partaking, become willing to give up self—that God may use all our forces to bring saving health to others—until the time may come when all the peoples of the earth partake freely of the wine of true brotherhood in the feast of the kingdom of God. Amen.[7]

ARISE, GO IN PEACE

Remember the times you have risen from the altar with
   these words:
Arise, and go in peace.
Above the thoughtless deeds,
Above selfish and jealous desires,
Above indifference toward world peace plans,
And above racial and national misunderstandings.
Arise, without sorrow's detaining grasp,
Arise without false idols of fame or money,
Without misgivings or hypocrisy.
Arise, and may the peace of God go with you.

Arise, and go in peace;
Arise, to lift those who would fall,
To give to the hungry, to lead the lost,
To support things that make for peace,
And to live in Christlike humility.
Arise, with true faith, thanksgiving, prayer,
With willingness, courage, and joy;
And arise with pure bodies and hearts.
Arise in favor with God.

Arise, think, dream, work, and love;
Arise today and follow Christ.
Arise . . .

*"And the peace of God which passes all understanding, will
   keep your hearts and your minds in Christ Jesus."*[8]

14. THANKSGIVING

&

FROM "SONGS OF THANKSGIVING" IN *THE DEAD SEA SCROLLS*

(*In addition to the many Psalms expressing thankfulness, found in our Bibles, we have further similar devotional meditations from the Jews of the Dead Sea community, on scrolls buried before the time of Christ and recently found.*)

I thank thee, O Lord,
Because thou hast put my soul in the bundle of life;

.   .   .   .   .

thou hast brought me up to an eternal height, and I walk
in an unsearchable plain.
I know that there is hope
for him whom thou hast formed from the dust for an
eternal company.

.   .   .   .   .

For God thunders with the noise of his might.

.   .   .   .   .

I thank thee, O Lord, because thou hast sustained me with
thy strength,
and hast shed abroad thy Holy Spirit in me.

338

I thank thee, O Lord, because thou hast made me wise in
    thy truth
and in thy wondrous mysteries hast given me knowledge.
I thank thee, O Lord, because thou hast done wondrously
    with dust,
with a thing formed of clay thou hast done powerfully.
I will praise thy name among those who fear thee,
with songs of thanksgiving and prayer.[1]

A SACRIFICE OF THANKSGIVING

We beseech thee, O God, that our whole life may be a
sacrifice of thanksgiving unto thee.

May all that is within us be stirred up to praise thee forevermore.

We thank thee for blessings around us and within:

    For all that thou hast granted,

    For what thou hast withheld,

    And for everything yet in store for us.

Most of all we bless thee for everything through which
thou drawest us to thyself, and by which thou makest us
thine own: Through Jesus Christ our Lord. Amen.[2]

NOW, WAIT A MINUTE

(*Preparation: Four members of the group should be
chosen well in advance of the meeting to make brief statements about our need to give thanks for four different areas
of life. These areas are suggested in the service under the*

headings of Voices 1, 2, 3, and 4. These suggestions are intended only to start the thinking of those who are to take part. The worship setting might consist of one object representing each of these four subject areas—a picture of friends or of a family, a flag, a model church.)

MEDITATION

> *Leader:* Now, wait a minute, will you? We're all so busy rushing here and there and back again. But slow down just a minute. Slow down and ask yourself a question. You ready? Here it is. Should you give thanks? If so, for what, and how? I told you it was simple. For what should you give thanks and how should you express your gratitude?

> *Voice 1:* Thanksgiving for friendship, for the joy of being with friends, for the fact that a true friend is really interested in what you're doing, for the privilege and responsibility of working together with those you like on important projects, for the influence for good which friends should have on each other.

> *Leader:* Yes, each of us has friends. So let us pause to give thanks unto God for them, and in our prayer to dedicate ourselves again to show our thanks by acts of thoughtfulness. (*Moment of quiet meditation*)

> *Voice 2:* Thanksgiving for our country, the opportunities it provides, the responsibilities we have as citizens; our freedom to think, to meet, to report, to worship; the religious concern of our founding fathers and of present leaders.

Leader: So let us now give thanks for the America we love and pledge that we, its future citizens, shall make it even better. (*Moment of quiet*)

Voice 3: Thanksgiving for our families, the patience of our parents, the concern which they had for us when we were too young to know or care and that concern which still surrounds us, the countless tasks which mother does, the countless bills which father pays, the fun we have had together and the disappointments and sorrow which have made us feel closer together, the love which we have for each other despite our scraps and our different ideas and interests.

Leader: For families, then, let us give thanks and make a promise to ourselves and God that we will work at being thoughtful in our homes. (*Moment of quiet*)

Voice 4: Thanksgiving for the church, the building which it provides for our use, the leaders who help in our program, the help it gives in thinking through the things that bother us, the chances we have for study and fun and worship.

Leader: The church deserves our thanks. So let us in this quietness rethink what we have done for it. (*Moment of quiet*)

So, wait a minute, will you? As you rush around from here to there and back again, slow down and ask yourself a question. You ready? Here it is. Should you give thanks? If so for what, and how? (*Moment of quiet*)

HYMN: "Now Thank We All Our God."[3]

THANKS FOR WONDERING HEARTS

O God, Maker of Beauty,
For wondering hearts,
We thank thee.

For questions that reach out,
How old is the beginning?
Do the stars that shine so far
Give light to worlds we cannot see?
What is beyond the universe?

For deep wonder,
That makes our thoughts strong,
To find out, and to understand,
Maker of Beauty,
For wondering hearts,
We thank thee.

We do not know thee, God,
Our thoughts reach toward thee.
Our hearts look for thee.

O God, Maker of Air and Light,
Maker of Rhythm and Beauty,
For wondering hearts we thank thee.[4]

PRAYER OF PERSONAL
THANKSGIVING

Father God, right now—this still, holy now when we feel
close to you—we want to thank you for all quietness, every-

where. It's fun to have noise, to hear music, to talk back and forth, to sing. But sometimes we like it all hushed and quiet. Thank you for snow, and the softness of it that stills even the tiny rabbit's footfall. Thank you for late starlight and the still shine coming from some distant star so far, right into our very hearts. Thank you for friends to be buddies with, who understand what we mean when we *don't* speak. Thank you for the rests in music, the pauses in between the notes that rest our ears and help us hear the melody. Thank you for rest from work and for deep peaceful sleep. We want to pray now that somehow you and we working together, may help the ugly noises now over the world to hush—people quarreling, discords, wrecks, explosions, wars. May we all turn back to you, where all lovely quiet comes from. Amen.[5]

15. CHRISTMAS

❧

EMMANUEL—GOD'S LOVE WITH US

With us? Yes, wherever there is a need—even for such little things as a drink of water or a breath of air—his love has foreseen and provided. And needs we may have in years to come, he has remembered.

With us? Yes, in the beauty of the universe all about us, the laughter of the waters, and the crisp coolness of wintry days; the patterns of the snowflakes, and the promise of warm springs. And that we may see, he gives us eyes; that we may hear, he gives us ears. But most remarkably, he gives us hearts to be aware . . . even in memories.

With us? Yes, in the kindness we have received, from our dim early days of life when we were scarcely aware . . . in all the thousands of little daily acts whereby our parents and others have kept life aglow in us . . . in the healing arts and those who dedicate their skills of hand and training to helping sick people be well and happy . . . in friends who love us just as we are, who remember our birthdays and who share our sorrows . . . in teachers who, even though sometimes they seem difficult, hold before us higher ideals and make us want to be greater selves.

With us? Yes, in the work of our churches, our youth fellowships, our work camps, our far-flung ways of spreading the word about God's love to the ends of the earth . . . in the lives of all who are representing Jesus' way everywhere . . .

PRAYER: O God, you have been with us all along, more than we have been aware. But now, as we open the windows of our hearts with these thoughts, we see more clearly. Keep us aware, in the coming days every hour, that you *are with us*, and that every evidence of our lives points toward this astounding truth: that your nature is loving.[1]

A CHRISTMAS STORY

And there were in the same country children
Keeping watch over their stockings by the
Fireplace. And lo, Santa Claus came upon them; and
They were sore afraid. And Santa Claus said unto
Them, "Fear not, for behold, I bring you good
Tidings of great joy which shall be to all people
Who can afford them. For unto you will be given
Tomorrow, great feasts of turkey, dressing, and
Cake; and many presents; and this shall be a sign
Unto you, ye shall find the presents wrapped in
Bright paper, lying beneath a tree adorned with
Tinsel, colored balls and lights." And suddenly
There will be with you, a multitude of relatives

And friends, praising you and saying, "Thank you
So much, it was just what I wanted." And it shall
Come to pass as the friends and relatives have
Gone away into their own homes, the parents shall
Say one to another, "What a mess to clean up." . . .
"I'm dead tired, let's go to bed and pick it up
Tomorrow." . . . "Thank God, Christmas only
Comes once a year!" And they go with
Haste to their cold bed and find their desired rest.
Is someone missing? No, I think you can see Him
Back in the shadows, not that He matters. Or
Does He? This is Christmas, but why shouldn't
We change it to Familymas or Giftday instead of
Christ's day? We were too busy to attend church
This morning. Are we too busy? Too busy to seek
Rest from this war-tired world? Can we be living
Too fast to live that which is life? Can we continue
To exist when God is not the center of our existence?
Are we just superintelligent animals or men with
Eternal souls? Wherever we turn, "Hell Bombs,"
"Germ Warfare," "Third World War." Let us put
Christ in front this Christmas. Let us hear again
An angel's voice, "For unto you is born this day,
A Savior, which is Christ the Lord."[2]

THE CHRISTMAS CHURCH

*"Glory to God in the highest, and on earth peace among
men with whom he is pleased!"* (Luke 2:14)

On a small tropic island in the South Pacific an American

airstrip was built. The chaplain and his crew tried to tell the natives about religion, but somehow they responded slowly. Christmas of 1943 came with orders to move on. The Americans gave a big farewell Christmas party with makeshift presents, and several tried to explain the origin of the Christmas spirit.

A few years later the same chaplain stopped at the island on his way to India as a missionary. He was greeted with excitement and taken to see something beautiful, a church. Over the doorway was written this crude inscription: "This is our church built on the faith and brotherly love which we know is."

The chaplain stayed for a service. There were no seats in the church; everyone stood in the presence of God. The songs were all Christmas carols, for these were the only ones they knew. One explained, "After you leave we build the church to worship Jesus. We worship him with the only service we know, Christmas, the day he was born. Every day is Christmas here. Every day Christ child born anew. Our gift to give is love. Our church we call her Christmas church."

What better way to worship than to sing Christmas carols all through the years? What better way to serve than to give gifts of love? What better way than to rule out all cruel wars forevermore, to show the faith of brotherly love which we know is?[3]

FORGIVE US OUR CHRISTMASES

—as we forgive those who Christmas against us (prayed a little child).

And we might all well pray it; and all through this holy month, we might strive to live so that others will not need to "forgive us our Christmas" ways. Pressures mount. Our shopping list grows. Radio voices remind us that we have only so many more days. School and clubs and other activities have extra programs.

We say each year, "*Next* year I won't get caught in the rush." But here we go, clutching our purses and tearing through the crowds, thinking, "Now what on earth would so-and-so like?" The late Peter Marshall puts into words that deeper inner feeling we've had all along:

You can't think of anything they need
  (which is rather strange when you take time to think of it).
Maybe there is nothing in a store that they need.
But what about some token of love—what about love itself . . .
  and friendship . . .
    and understanding . . .
      and consideration . . .
        and a helping hand . . .
      and a smile . . .
    and a prayer?
. . . Christmas is not in the stores—but in the hearts of people.

Suppose we started this very year. First, we'll think much about the *person* . . . we'll lift our thoughts to God in prayer . . . we'll seek to be guided by deeper impulses of love from within ourselves . . . maybe our final choices of gifts won't be as costly in money, but they'll come from our hearts. We'll think especially of persons who are in need—

the hungry in our own towns and over the seas; the lonely-hearted; the aged.

We'll discover that each day, no matter how rushed, we can look at the people around us and respond to them with sympathy, forgiveness, understanding. These we may take as our three gifts, even as the Wise Men brought three to the Christ child! When a sales girl is too tired to smile, we'll smile and make the chore of waiting on us as pleasant and easy as possible. When a waitress makes a mistake, we'll try to remember that perhaps her feet hurt, or her husband is sick. When a teacher gives a grade lower than we know we deserve, we'll try to extend to him the forgiveness we'd want if we had made a mistake ourselves.

And on from Christmas, through the coming days of the year, these three gifts passed on, will multiply as in turn the receivers pass them on to others. We'll find our own thoughts growing deeper, our compassion and human understanding stretching and strengthening—even as our muscles strengthen when we exercise. We'll grow to be delightful persons to give the world: persons with that rare quality of understanding that everybody needs so much all year long.

But surprise! As on Christmas morning when we hadn't anticipated a special gift, there will keep coming back to us in full splendid measure—joyous response and understanding from others: the true Christmassy feeling, *lived* all year long.[4]

16. WATCH NIGHT AND
NEW YEAR'S

ﾠﾟﾟﾟﾟﾟﾟﾟ

RELIGION IN LIFE

(*Read Luke 6:38.*)

As we seek to tie religion and life together by focusing our attention on the Christian way of life, let us pause to examine prayerfully what our needs and our objectives in religious living should be. We need to meditate at some length in silence on the full, challenging implications of each need we have . . . Perhaps you can add others.

. . . to deepen my own spiritual awareness by rethinking my own faith and its implications in each day of living, with all its complex situations.

. . . to consecrate myself wholeheartedly to the service of God, dedicating my talents, abilities, and education as my brick in the ongoing construction of his kingdom.

. . . to seek strength and guidance for my job in the youth fellowship program, realizing that individual persons do matter and that I have a great opportunity to help make religion-in-life become a reality.

. . . to extend myself humbly, yet with genuine Christian

350

concern to others, that I might share with them a measure of the fullness which I have found in Christian experience.

. . . to keep before me as my daily reminder, *"I am come that they might have life and that they might have it more abundantly."*[1]

A STEP INTO THE UNKNOWN

Each life is a center, from which concentric circles radiate out to the farthest light-year at the edge of the universe.

Each morning is the dawning of a new year, a new country, a new thousand years.

Such is the mighty chain of influence that from the thoughts of one person, on one day, millions may be affected both now and in time to come. Suppose you should begin to work for a certain institution with the understanding that on the first day you would receive a penny, doubled on the second day to two pennies, on the third to four, and so on. By the thirtieth day, you would make something like five million dollars! Or suppose you influenced two persons, these in turn two more, by the thirty-second day, such influence would have spread over the earth's population! This is what is meant when we say God has placed us here in the bundle of life, intricately related with one another. We are all both senders and receivers.

Now in the holy, mysterious, awesome time of the turning of the year, we look back over our days of the past year. Viewing your ways only yesterday, as if through a window of clear honesty, were these actions or failures, these words, these thoughts worthy? Did they express the real YOU, the dedicated YOU of your highest and holiest moments? If the influence of your yesterday had been multiplied, would others have been in any way hurt or turned away from God, or led a little nearer to him and the ways of kindly love?

As any new year, or day, or minute begins, we step over a threshold into the unknown. We tremble in the dark. Our strength is but weakness. Of our own power we might repeat yesteryear's errors or worse. O God, how we need thee! We reach out timidly . . . and yes, wondrous mystery—Someone has taken hold! How much better than a light! How much safer than a known way![2]

MY NEW YEAR'S RESOLUTIONS

How shall we face the New Year?

With Faith—the inner spirit with which we win moral victories over chaos, unrest, and evil.

With Belief—a belief in God, his creation, and the life everlasting.

With Prayer—as regularly as night follows day.

With Conscience—the counterpoise between right and wrong.

With Courage—the indomitable quality that keeps us going forward.

With Honesty—because it is an obligation within ourselves.

With Content of the simple things—so that we may defeat selfishness and keep personal concerns from undermining the high plane of his will.

With Love for one another—the new philosophy of life.

With Christian living—that which we can attain only through thinking and doing what is in accord with Christ's teachings.

With Trust in this credo—for it is God's will.[3]

17. LENT, GOOD FRIDAY
AND EASTER

ঙ

BETRAY HIM?

*And as they were eating, he said, "Truly I say to you, one
of you will betray me." And they were very sorrowful, and
began to say to him one after another, "Is it I, Lord?"*
(Matthew 26:21–22)

Today, too, Jesus' voice is saying, "There are those among
you who will betray me in many ways," and we answer,
"Lord, is it I?"

"Some of you will betray me by clouding your thinking
with prejudices of all kinds; by molding your characters for
the public rather than for me; by neglecting to make effective
places for yourselves in your church."

. . . I, Master?

"Verily I say unto you that some of you will betray me by
refusing to respect and help the dirty, uneducated, underprivileged of other races and nations along with those who
have had opportunities equal to your own . . ."

Master, is it I?

"Indeed, many of you will betray me by failing to seek

my Father's guidance for your daily lives through prayer;
by making your goals the things you want without considering God's wishes."

. . . I, Lord?

"There are those of you who will betray me in failure to
think and act with an open and Christ-motivated mind
concerning economic systems. In countless ways you are un-
true to me. Search deep into yourselves."

Master, grant me the consecration, the strength, and the
love to follow after thee alone. Amen.[1]

WERE YOU . . . THERE?

"Were you there when they crucified my Lord?"

I was there when they crucified my Lord, for I heard a
twelve-year-old boy crucify him anew by using his holy name
as a vent for his furious anger while playing with some other
little boys.

"Sometimes it causes me to tremble" . . .

"Were you there when they nailed him to the cross?"

I was there when they nailed him to the cross, for I saw
four young men and women, made in the image of God, fill
their strong young bodies with harmful drink and their
minds with degrading thoughts.

"Sometimes it causes me to tremble" . . .

"Were you there when they pierced him in the side?"

I was there when they pierced him in the side, for I knew
the group of young high school students who deliberately

struck a feeble-minded boy to hear him cry out and then laughed at his weakness.

"Sometimes it causes me to tremble" . . .

"Were you there when he rose up from the tomb?"

Yes, I was there when he rose up from the tomb, for I beheld a young man, who had lived a life of sin, who had reached the lowest hell, become whole again. This young person knew his Redeemer and praised him by saving others.

"Sometimes it causes me to tremble."[2]

PRAYER ON GOOD FRIDAY

(*Symbol: the Passion Cross, with each of the bars shaped into a point, symbolizing Jesus' final suffering.*)

Eternal, loving God, hear my prayer for all those in Good Friday experiences of life—

the mother who has just learned that her child has leukemia . . .

the young man frustrated by temptation . . .

the alcoholic who has hit bottom . . .

the woman with incurable cancer . . .

the young man who has lost his eyesight . . .

the husband and wife with a broken love-relationship . . .

the youth with a gnawing, unforgettable memory of a despicable deed he has committed . . .

O Thou, who canst break the crippling power of sin, help all who are depressed and beaten. In the midst of their suffering, give them courage to say, "Into thy hands I commit my life."

Speak to me, O God, as I meditate upon the drama of contrasts around the cross—

> mockery and meekness . . .
> pain and prayer . . .
> forgetfulness and forgiveness . . .
> reviling and revealing . . .
> force and faith . . .
> treachery and trust . . .
> rebuking and redeeming . . .
> matter and mystery . . .
> gloom and glory . . .
> agony and atonement . . .

Grant me great resources of faith and trust as I stand confronted with the eternal mystery of thy power and glory and seek to understand the meaning of the cross for me now.

Through the redeeming Christ who died for me. Amen.[3]

PRAYER AT EASTER

Almighty and everliving God, give us today the great gladness of Christians—

that thou hast raised our Lord, Jesus Christ, from the dead,

that through him all our failures, and all bodily death are conquered for us.

Keep us evermore from all fear that thou hast left us to the death we draw upon ourselves.

In daring faith in the Easter promise, help us to commit ourselves again in obedience to thee.

Make our hearts sure by this Easter sign, that thou dost perform thy will, and that in thy will is our life.

Through Jesus Christ our risen Lord. Amen.[4]

"LIGHT OUT OF DARKNESS"

An Easter Service which may be used at sunrise

(*This service may be held out of doors or in a dimly lighted meeting room. The form is semidramatic—narrator's voice heard, choir singing from side or back. When Narrator says, "Darkness covers the earth," etc., several figures may appear in black robes, groping as if blind . . . searching for light. As Voice 2 and Voice 3 are heard near the end, the pantomiming figures corresponding to 2 and 3 drop their black robes showing full white garments; they reach toward the central Cross where they see Light. The other figures remain in darkness—imparting a challenge of unfinished work yet to be done, that sometime they, too, may be led to the Light.*)

NARRATOR: Out of the East comes new light after the darkness of night. We call it morning. On the first Easter morning came a wondrous new light—the light of life—after the darkness of sin's night. And it has been the gleam of a morning, the morning of a new day, for all men.

Contrasts make things stand out. Black touching white seems blacker, white touching black seems whiter. Sorrow makes joy seem gladder. Joy makes sorrow seem sadder. The deeper the sorrow, the greater the uplift of joy following. The greatest of all contrasts is between life and death. All sorrow and darkness, all heaviness and despair, brood in the black word, Death. All gladness and brightness, all lightness and joy gather into that bright word, Life.

CHOIR: "Light of the World We Hail Thee" (*or other hymn of light*).

NARRATOR: The people that walked in darkness have seen a great light; they that dwell in the land of the shadow of death, upon them hath the light shined." Light had come into the troubled world during the tyrannical days of Roman rule, in the form of the babe, Jesus, lying in a manger.

CHOIR: "Joy to the World."

NARRATOR: And the child Jesus increased in wisdom and stature and in favor with God and man. As a young man he began to teach. Many followed. At one time there were five thousand who listened spellbound by his words.

CHOIR: "O Young and Fearless Prophet."

NARRATOR: But there came that night when he took bread, and blessed and broke it, and gave it to them and said, "Take, eat, this is my body." And he took the cup also, and when he had given thanks he gave it to them, and they all drank of it. And he said to them, "This is my blood of the covenant which is shed for many."

CHOIR: "Bread of the World in Mercy Broken."

NARRATOR: And then they went to the Mount of Olives to a place called Gethsemane . . . and he prayed . . .

And immediately, while he was yet praying, Judas came . . . and they laid hands on him and seized him . . . And Pilate, wishing to satisfy the crowd, delivered Jesus to be crucified.

Light had come into the world, but they comprehended it not. Again darkness crept into the world . . . at the noon hour. Darkness covers the earth! Everywhere . . . darkness! Is it . . . Death? In our day, voices of men cry out as they cower in fear and darkness! (*Figures appear, groping.*)

VOICE 1: Darkness penetrates my life—I have no purpose— my attempts all meet with failure—is there no one to whom I can turn? Is there no hope? No light anywhere? Must there always be poverty, misery, war, suffering, darkness?

NARRATOR: Yes, there is darkness, even in the souls of men. But wait! The story of Jesus was not ended with the darkness at noon. For on the first day of the week, he arose . . . as he said.

CHOIR: "The Strife Is O'er, the Battle Done."

NARRATOR: Christ is ever rising again. Day by day men seek to bury him under sin, selfishness, ignorance, and stupidity. But always he rises—from the ashes of fires of selfishness and carelessness in which we allow him power over our lives. Ever and again he is lifted up out of the common things of life, a triumph over the powers that did him to death. All men are drawn to him as irresistibly as the earth is held in its orbit around the sun. The empty tomb opens before the world, telling us it is God who still has the last word, not ourselves. Morning light comes and life looks forward, onward, upward, Godward!

VOICE 2: I have seen something happen in the lives of those of my people who have seen his way. Can he lead me, too, into light and life? I stretch out my hand to be led by him. I shed my garments of blackness and despair. I open my eyes to the light of his glory.

VOICE 3: I, too, want to catch the glory of the morning light. His hand has touched mine. His eyes have looked into mine. His voice has answered my cries of despair and has given me hope. My path has a light upon it now. I, too, will leave behind my robes of dark despair . . . and onward . . . to the new day.

CHOIR: "Joyful, Joyful, We Adore Thee."[5]

NOTES FOR PART ONE
(By Chapters)

ஒ

INTRODUCTION

1. William Temple, *The Hope of a New World* (New York: The Macmillan Company, 1942). By permission, Mrs. William Temple and publisher.

I. RESOURCES FOR INWARD PREPARATION

1. *The Table Talk of Martin Luther*, T. S. Kepler, ed. (Cleveland, Ohio: World Publishing Co., 1952).
2. From "Brother Lawrence," *The Practice of the Presence of God: Conversations and Letters of Nicholas Hermann of Lorraine*, tr. from French (Westwood, N.J.: Fleming H. Revell Company, 1895).
3. I Thessalonians 5:17.
4. *The Spiritual Letters of St. François de Sales*, Sidney Lear, tr. (London: Longmans, 1920). See also "Treatise on the Love of God," in *Oeuvres* VI, Dom B. Mackay, tr. and ed. (O.S.B., 1928), p. 217.
5. Walter Rauschenbusch, *Prayers of the Social Awakening* (Boston: Pilgrim Press, 1910).
6. Fred D. Gealy, "What Do We Do When We Worship?" in MOTIVE, January, 1961, p. 13. By permission, MOTIVE magazine, copyright owner.

7. Unknown young man from Nebraska, in youth worship meditations.

8. Augustine, *The Confessions*, E. B. Pusey, tr. and Ernest Rhys, ed. (New York: E. P. Dutton & Co., Everyman's Library, 1946). See pp. 397, 30, 168 on strugglings of spirit.

9. Ignatius Loyola, 1491–1556, in *Spiritual Exercises, with the Central Idea of the Imitation of Christ* (London: Society for the Propagation of Christian Knowledge). See modern modification of exercises for spiritual athleticism in Albert E. Day, *Discipline and Discovery*, copyright, 1946, by The Upper Room; copyright transferred to Disciplined Order of Christ. By permission, Albert E. Day.

10. Jeremiah 29:13.

11. By Jacquelyn Kovacevic, in POWER, April–June, 1958, p. 46. By permission, National Conference of Methodist Youth.

12. Third stanza of hymn, "There Were Ninety and Nine," by Elizabeth C. Clephane, 1830–1869.

13. Douglas Horton, *The Meaning of Worship* (New York: Harper & Brothers, 1959), p. 16. By permission.

14. From "Saul," in *Robert Browning* (London: Walter Black, Inc., n.d.), p. 89.

15. *Epistle to Diognetus*, first half of second century. See Kenneth S. Latourette, *A History of Christianity* (New York: Harper & Brothers, 1953), p. 254. By permission.

16. Evelyn Underhill, *Worship* (London: James Nisbet & Company, Limited; also New York: Harper & Brothers, 1937), p. 3. By permission.

17. William Law, *Selected Mystical Writings of William Law*, Stephen Hobhouse, ed. Copyright, Stephen Hobhouse. First issued, 1728. By permission, Barrie and Rockliff, Edinburgh, publishers.

18. By unknown young person, in POWER. By permission, National Conference of Methodist Youth.

19. Alfred, Lord Tennyson, "The Higher Pantheism," stanza 6.
20. Anonymous. In frontispiece, A. W. Palmer, *Aids to Worship* (New York: The Macmillan Company, 1944). By permission.
21. St. John of the Cross, *The Dark Night of the Soul* (New York: Frederick Ungar Publishing Co., 1957). See also Georgia Harkness, *The Dark Night of the Soul* (Nashville, Tenn.: Abingdon Press, 1945).
22. John Campbell Shairp, 1819–1885, " 'Twixt Gleams of Joy and Clouds of Doubt." In public domain.
23. Psalm 139:10.
24. Evelyn Underhill (see Note 16 above). See also pp. 15 ff., 44, 46.
25. William J. Schmidt, "Damascus Road," in THE CHRISTIAN CENTURY, Dec. 19, 1956. Copyright, 1956, Christian Century Foundation. By permission of THE CHRISTIAN CENTURY.
26. Author and source unknown. CMB found this used in youth camp in Oregon, overlooking the Pacific.
27. Frank C. Laubach has dealt with the idea that "laws" or "principles" underlie the devotional life, in *Prayer, the Mightiest Force in the World* (Westwood, N.J.: Fleming H. Revell Company, 1946).
28. CMB (Clarice M. Bowman) on idea suggested by R. C. Smith, *Rural Church Administration* (Nashville: Abingdon Press, 1943), pp. 94–95. By permission.
29. Dorothy Jane Conway (Indiana) in POWER, April–June, 1958, p. 72.
30. Hymn by William F. Lloyd, 1791–1853, "My Times Are in Thy Hand."
31. See particularly Sören Kierkegaard, *Training in Christianity* Walter Lowrie, tr. (Princeton, N.J.: Princeton University Press, 1944); and *Purity of Heart Is to Will One Thing*, Douglas V. Steere, tr. (New York: Harper & Brothers, Torchbook, 1956).

32. This does not mean human arrogance, but humble trust. See J. Rufus Moseley, *Perfect Everything* (St. Paul, Minn.: Macalester Park Publishing Co., 1949).

33. Edwin Hatch, 1835–1889 (New York: Oxford University Press, copyright no longer in force).

34. Paul Tillich, *Systematic Theology*, Vol. I (Chicago: University of Chicago Press, 1951).

35. Grace Noll Crowell, *Flame in the Wind* (New York: Harper & Brothers, 1938).

36. Frederick W. Faber, 1814–1863.

37. Author and source unknown. Quoted in Laubach, *Prayer, the Mightiest Force in the World* (*op. cit.*), p. 40.

II. RELATING WORSHIP WITH ALL LIFE

1. John 3:8.

2. Halford E. Luccock, *Marching Off the Map* (New York: Harper & Brothers, 1952), p. 147. See also *The Acts of the Apostles in Present-Day Thinking* (New York: Willett, Clark and Co., 1938), p. 13.

3. Philippians 1:9–10, in *The Bible: Smith-Goodspeed Translation* (University of Chicago Press, 1935). See also II Timothy 2:16 and II Corinthians 2:13; 13:58.

4. Joshua 24:15. John Oxenham, "The Cross at the Crossways," in *The Collected Poems of John Oxenham* (Boston: Pilgrim Press).

5. Title of hymn by Earl Marlatt, based upon Matthew 20:22.

6. A. J. Gossip, *In the Secret Place of the Most High* (New York: Charles Scribner's Sons, 1947), p. 117. By permission.

7. Irwin G. Paulsen, *The Church School and Worship* (New York: The Macmillan Company, 1940), p. 75. By permission, Theodore F. Paulsen, administrator.

8. Mark 12:11.

9. Billy K. Fowler, Houston, Texas, in report in course on youth worship.

10. Douglas V. Steere, *Prayer and Worship*, Hazen Books on Religion (New York: Association Press, 1938), p. 41. By permission.

11. Willard Sperry, *Reality in Worship* (New York: The Macmillan Company, 1925). By permission.

12. Frank C. Laubach, *Prayer, the Mightiest Force in the World* (Westwood, N.J.: Fleming H. Revell Company, 1946), p. 35.

III. FINDING AN INNER ORDER OF SPIRIT IN WORSHIP WITH OTHERS

1. Luke 15:8, Luke 15:4–7, Luke 15:11–32, respectively.

2. Thomas Kelly, *A Testament of Devotion* (New York: Harper & Brothers, 1941), p. 83. By permission.

3. Erwin Shaver and Harry T. Stock, *Training Young People in Worship* (Boston: Pilgrim Press, 1930), p. 18.

4. Georgia Harkness, *Prayer and the Common Life* (Nashville, Tenn.: Abingdon-Cokesbury Press, 1948), p. 151. By permission.

5. For explication of this idea, see Sören Kierkegaard, *Purity of Heart* (see Note 31 in Chapter I), particularly "The Listener's Role," pp. 177–184.

6. Henry Sloane Coffin, *Communion Through Preaching* (New York: Charles Scribner's Sons, 1922). By permission.

7. A. W. Palmer, *Aids to Worship* (New York: The Macmillan Company, 1944). By permission.

8. Herbert H. Wintermeyer, *Rural Worship* (Philadelphia: Christian Education Press, 1947), p. 5. By permission.

9. Horatius Bonar, 1808–1889.

10. G. A. Studdert-Kennedy, *I Believe: Sermons on the Apostle's Creed* (Doran Co., n.d.). English version, *Food for the Fed-Up*, p. 22.

11. By a senior high school group as reported to Gertrude Sheldon, in "Putting Its Message into Words," in the INTER-

NATIONAL JOURNAL OF RELIGIOUS EDUCATION, Nov., 1955, p. 12. By permission, National Council of the Churches of Christ in America.

IV. AIDS FOR PLANNING AND PARTICIPATING IN WORSHIP

1. Romans 8:16.
2. Orene McIlwain, *Worship God* (Richmond, Va.: John Knox Press, 1947), p. 29. By permission.
3. C. H. Heimsath, *The Genius of Public Worship* (New York: Charles Scribner's Sons, 1944). By permission. See also references on silence in Douglas V. Steere, *Prayer and Worship* (*op. cit.*), pp. 20–21, 26–27, 31.
4. Evelyn Underhill (see Note 16 in Chapter I).
5. C. H. Heimsath (see Note 3 above), p. 39.
6. Sidney Lanier, *The Marshes of Glynn* (New York: Charles Scribner's Sons, 1949).
7. Ezekiel 2:1.
8. Paul Tillich, *The Courage to Be* (New Haven, Conn.: Yale University Press, 1952).
9. Attributed to E. Stanley Jones.
10. Gamaliel Bradford, 1863–1932, "God," from *Shadow Verses* (New Haven: Yale University Press, 1920). By permission.
11. von Hügel's phrase "perennial freshness" was a theme from Gerard Manley Hopkins. "Marks of apostleship," a theme from Thomas Kelly in A *Testament of Devotion* (see Note 2 in Chapter III).

NOTES FOR PART TWO
(By Chapters)

૭ફ્રે

Editor's Note: To conserve space, initials are used for four of the most frequent sources as follows:

    CMB   Clarice M. Bowman
    IJRE   International Journal of Religious Education
    MPH   Methodist Publishing House
    NCMY   National Council of Methodist Youth

1. Calls to Worship, Offertory Sentences, Benedictions

1. CMB.
2. Henry Hallam Tweedy in hymn, "Eternal God, whose pow'r upholds both flower and flaming star" (The Hymn Society of America, copyright, 1929). Now in public domain.
3. Hermann Hagedorn, "Lift Up the Curtain," from Prologue to *The Heart of Youth* (New York: The Macmillan Company, 1955). By permission of author and of The Macmillan Company.
4. CMB.
5. CMB.
6. Author and source unknown.
7. Jeanne Hatch Michie, "The Open Door," in newsletter of the Disciplined Order of Christ, Vol. II, No. 6, Oct., 1953, p. 2. By permission of Albert E. Day.
8. Samuel Johnson, 1822–1882.

9. Nelle Morton, in PROPHETIC RELIGION, Fellowship of Southern Churchmen. By permission.

10. Psalm 84:5.

11. Milton S. Littlefield, 1864–1934. From *At Worship: Hymnal for Young Churchmen* (New York: Harper & Brothers, 1951). By permission.

12. CMB.

13. CMB.

14. CMB.

15. Jeanette Perkins, *As Children Worship* (Boston: Pilgrim Press, 1935), p. 47. By permission.

16. Betty J. and J. Martin Bailey, in THE INTERNATIONAL JOURNAL OF RELIGIOUS EDUCATION (hereafter designated as IJRE), Oct., 1958. By permission of the National Council of the Churches of Christ in the U.S.A., copyright owners.

17. CMB.

18. Jean McKenzie (further information as to source unknown).

19. CMB.

20. Author and source unknown.

21. CMB.

22. Marathi hymn by Narayan V. Tilak, Christian leader of India, 1862–1919.

23. From "Light from the Heights," by unknown author as used by Dr. Martin E. Carlson, Augustana Lutheran Church.

24. CMB.

25. CMB.

26. John Ellerton, 1826–1893.

27. From "Prayer of the Quest" by Eleanor B. Stock. By permission of the author.

28. Warren Wheeler Pickett, "Liturgy of Malabar," in *Worship Services for Young People* (Boston: Pilgrim Press, 1931), p. 58. By permission.

29. From *The Book of Common Prayer*, The Protestant Episcopal Church (Greenwich, Conn.: The Seabury Press), p. 114.

30. CMB.
31. In public domain.
32. CMB.
33. In public domain.
34. CMB.
35. In public domain.

2. GOD IN HIS GREATNESS AND MAJESTY

1. John C. Trever, IJRE, Feb., 1953, p. 3. By permission. Meditation based on Psalms 19 and 8, respectively.
2. Jeanne Nall in POWER, March 23, 1947, p. 82. Copyright owners, National Conference of Methodist Youth (hereafter designated as NCMY). By permission.
3. Job 37:5-14, *The Bible: A New Translation by James Moffatt.* Copyright 1922, 1935 and 1950 by Harper & Brothers. Used by permission.
4. Job 11:7-9, 13-15, 17, Moffatt translation (*op. cit.*).
5. Adapted from prayer by Allan Hunter, Mount Hollywood Congregational Church, Los Angeles, California.
6. W. E. Orchard, *The Temple* (New York: E. P. Dutton & Co., 1918). By permission.
7. From WORKSHOP, Nov., 1947. Copyright, The Methodist Publishing House (hereafter designated as MPH). By permission.
8. CMB in IJRE, June, 1956. By permission.
9. CMB in POWER. NCMY. By permission.
10. Ian J. McRae, in IJRE, Sept., 1956. By permission.
11. Arranged for choral speaking by CMB.
12. From *The Didache*, one of the earliest Christian writings. *Didache: Ancient Christian Writers*, Vol. 6 (Westminster, Md.: Newman Press, 1948). By permission.
13. From the *Divine Liturgy of James the Holy Apostle and Brother of the Lord*, in *The Ante-Nicene Fathers*, Vol. 7 (New York: Charles Scribner's Sons, 1908). By permission.

14. Augustine, *Confessions*, Vol. I, 1. First published about 397. (London: J. M. Dent & Sons, Ltd., copyright owners; Everyman's Library No. 200, E. P. Dutton & Co., Inc.). By permission.

15. From the *Divine Liturgy of the Holy Apostle and Evangelist Mark*, in *The Ante-Nicene Fathers* (see Note 13 above). By permission.

16. A. Ninde, *Nineteen Centuries of Christian Song* (Westwood, N.J.: Fleming H. Revell Company, 1938), p. 18. By permission.

17. From unknown writer sometime between third and fifth centuries.

18. CMB in *Ways We Worship*, pamphlet elective (MPH, 1942), p. 26. By permission.

19. Russell Dicks, *My Faith Looks Up* (Philadelphia: The Westminster Press, Copyright, 1949, by W. L. Jenkins). By permission.

3. GOD AS CREATOR

1. Harris Franklin Rall. By permission. Introduction and choral arrangement by CMB and acceptable to author.

2. CMB in IJRE, Sept., 1955, pp. 33–34. By permission.

3. Ellen B. Stillwell in HIGHROAD, Copyright, MPH. By permission. Quoted matter within: (a) from *This Green World* by Rutherford Platt, reprinted by permission of Dodd, Mead & Company, copyright 1942); (b) *Ibid*; (c) "What I Believe," in THE FORUM, Oct., 1930.

4. Roy A. Burkhart, in *At Worship: Hymnal for Young Churchmen* (New York: Harper & Brothers, 1951), p. 58. By permission.

5. Introductory two paragraphs and closing line by CMB. Factual material by A. Cressy Morrison, New York Academy of Sciences, *Man Does Not Stand Alone* (Westwood, N.J.: Fleming H. Revell Company, 1944), pp. 9, 15, 27, *passim*. By permission.

6. Webb Garrison in ROUNDTABLE, Feb., 1956, p. 61. Copyright, MPH. By permission.

7. Guy Murchie, *The Song of the Sky* (Boston: Houghton Mifflin Co., 1954), pp. 411–412. By permission.

8. Prose, CMB. Poem, by Eleanor B. Stock, used by permission.

9. Walter Rauschenbusch, *Prayers of the Social Awakening* (Boston: Pilgrim Press, 1909, 1910), p. 47. By permission.

10. Jeanette E. Perkins, *While the Earth Remaineth* (Boston: Pilgrim Press, n.d.). By permission.

11. Jean Scott, in POWER, March 25, 1960, p. 87. Copyright, NCMY. By permission.

4. JESUS THE CHRIST

1. Prose by CMB. Poem by Henry C. Barnett, in THE ADULT STUDENT, April, 1954, p. 15. Copyright, MPH. By permission.

2. CMB in IJRE, Oct., 1955. By permission.

3. Introduction by CMB. Responsive reading by George Harper for convocation of Methodist youth. By permission.

4. Ivan Sergyayevitch Turgenev, "Christ" in *Dream Tales and Prose Poems*, Constance Garnett, tr. (New York: The Macmillan Company, 1920). By permission of The Macmillan Company.

5. CMB in IJRE, Oct., 1955, p. 36. By permission.

6. CMB in IJRE, Feb., 1956, pp. 36–37. By permission.

7. Rosalie Carter, D. D. S. By permission of the author.

8. *Pioneer Conclave.* Copyright, 1941, Presbyterian Church in the U.S., Board of Christian Education. By permission.

9. Barbara A. Cochennet, in POWER, Jan. 6, 1947, p. 12. NCMY. By permission.

10. Nenien C. MacPherson, in THE CHURCH SCHOOL Magazine. Copyright, MPH. By permission.

11. Fred Eugene Stom (New Jersey), in POWER, Feb. 6, 1956, p. 39. NCMY. By permission.

12. Chandran Devanesen, *The Cross Is Lifted* (New York: Friendship Press, 1954). By permission.

5. OUR BIBLE

1. Percy R. Hayward. By permission.
2. Lynn Harold Hough, from Introduction to A *Living Book for a Living Age* (New York: Association Press, 1918). By permission.
3. Paul Minear, in *Eyes of Faith* (Philadelphia: The Westminster Press, copyright, 1946, by W. L. Jenkins), p. 19. By permission.
4. Warren Wheeler Pickett, *Worship Services for Young People* (Boston: Pilgrim Press, 1931), p. 15. By permission.

6. THE CHURCH

1. Stanza adapted from hymn, "Rise up, O men of God!" by William Pierson Merrill. Copyright, The Presbyterian Outlook. By permission. Prose by CMB.
2. From IJRE as quoted by Orene McIlwain, in *Worship God* (Richmond, Va.: John Knox Press, 1947). By permission.
3. Charles B. Purdham, in POWER, Jan. 7, 1951, p. 11. NCMY. By permission.
4. William R. Terbeek, in IJRE, Dec., 1952. By permission.
5. Fred D. Wentzel, *Once There Were Two Churches* (New York: Friendship Press). By permission.
6. Mary Helen Culbreth, in POWER, Jan. 27, 1947, p. 33. NCMY. By permission.
7. Betty Berenthein, in POWER, Nov. 16, 1947, p. 50. NCMY. By permission.
8. CMB in IJRE, Feb., 1956, p. 37. By permission.
9. Sam Walter Foss, *Songs of the Average Man* (New York: Lothrop, Lee & Shepard Co., Inc., 1907). By permission of Lothrop, Lee & Shepard Co., Inc.

7. OUR BELIEFS AND CREEDS

1. Statement of Faith of the United Church of Christ. By permission of Co-Presidents Rev. James E. Wagner and Dr. Fred Hoskins.

2. CMB in IJRE, March, 1956, p. 62. By permission.
3. Helen F. Couch, in WORKERS WITH YOUTH, Feb. 1, 1959, p. 32. Copyright, MPH. By permission.
4. Peggi Johnson, in POWER, July 19, 1957, p. 21. NCMY. By permission.
5. CMB.
6. Roberta Dillon Williams. By permission.
7. CMB.

8. PRAYER

1. Rosemary Boston, in POWER, April–June, 1958, p. 59. NCMY. By permission. Opening four lines by Hartley Coleridge.
2. George Harper, in POWER, Feb. 22, 1947, p. 59. NCMY. By permission.
3. Clarice Bowman and George Harper, *Power Through Prayer* (Nashville, Tenn.: Source Press, 1947). By permission.
4. CMB in IJRE, Jan., 1956, p. 30. By permission.
5. Barbara Anne White (Stewart), in POWER, Jan. 17, 1947, p. 23. NCMY. By permission.
6. Jane Merchant, *The Greatest of These*. Copyright 1954 by Pierce & Washabaugh. By permission of Abingdon Press.
7. Gayle Graham (Mississippi), in POWER, Sept. 10, 1957, p. 74, with exception of last paragraph by CMB. NCMY. By permission.
8. Author and source of poem unknown.
9. CMB.
10. Frances Ragsdale (Texas), in POWER, Feb. 11, 1960, p. 44. NCMY. By permission.
11. Donald Marsh (Nebraska), in POWER, Nov. 1, 1947. By permission.
12. CMB.
13. Lynn J. Radcliffe, church bulletin of Hyde Park Community Methodist Church, Cincinnati, Ohio, Oct. 15, 1950. By permission.

14. Helen Butner, in POWER, April 1, 1947, p. 3. NCMY. By permission.

15. James Weldon Johnson, *God's Trombones* (New York: Viking Press, 1927), p. 21.

16. Betty Jo Jacobs (West Virginia), in POWER, Nov. 17, 1950, p. 51. NCMY. By permission.

17. Stanza of hymn by Washington Gladden, 1836–1918.

18. Orene McIlwain, *Worship God* (*op. cit.*), pp. 145–146.

19. CMB.

20. CMB.

21. CMB in POWER, Sept. 7, 1953. NCMY. By permission. Bible passage at end from I John 5:3–5, RSV.

9. UNDERSTANDING OURSELVES AND MAKING CHOICES

1. William Terbeek, in IJRE, March, 1953. By permission.

2. Mims T. Workman, in THE CHURCH SCHOOL, Oct., 1954, p. 32. Copyright, MPH. By permission.

3. CMB.

4. Patricia Bever, *Stepping Stones of the Spirit* (New York: Association Press, 1951), p. 22. By permission.

5. Prose by CMB. Poem by Ralph S. Cushman, in *Spiritual Hilltops*, p. 109, copyright renewal 1960 by Ralph S. Cushman. By permission of Abingdon Press.

6. Felice Lewis, in WORKSHOP. Copyright, MPH. By permission.

7. Kirby Page, "Living with Peace of Mind," in CONCERN, p. 31. NCMY. By permission.

8. CMB in IJRE, April, 1956, p. 33. By permission.

9. Percy R. Hayward. By permission.

10. CMB.

11. Anonymous meditation in POWER, Dec. 16, 1946, p. 79. NCMY. By permission.

12. CMB.

13. Phillips Brooks, *Visions and Tasks* (New York: E. P. Dutton & Co., Inc., 1910), p. 300. By permission.

14. Author and source unknown.

15. Dorothy Hubbard (Seoul, Korea), in POWER, July 18, 1953, p. 20. NCMY. By permission.
16. Attributed to Betty Lou Rose Stroud, Atlanta, Ga. For Alpha Delta Theta retreat, High Point College.
17. Percy R. Hayward. By permission.
18. CMB, in POWER, April 19, 1950, p. 22. NCMY. By permission.
19. Ruby Jones, in TOGETHER, May, 1958. Copyright 1958 by Lovick Pierce. By permission from TOGETHER.
20. Displayed in Aer Lingus passenger planes. By permission, Irish International Air Lines.
21. Owen Geer, in WORKSHOP, Nov., 1946. Copyright, MPH. By permission.
22. From *The Kingdom, the Power and the Glory* (New York: Oxford University Press, 1925). By permission.
23. Bob Sink, in EPWORTH HERALD, Oct. 19, 1940, p. 633. Copyright, MPH. By permission.

10. Others' Needs and Our Responses

1. By the late Royer Woodburn, in POWER, June 17, 1947, p. 81. NCMY. By permission.
2. CMB.
3. Carolyn Cleare, in POWER, Jan. 21, 1947, p. 27. NCMY. By permission. Bible quotation at end, Matthew 25:45.
4. CMB. In third paragraph, author and source of prayer, "God give me eyes . . ." are unknown.
5. Toyohiko Kagawa, *Songs from the Slums* (Copyright, 1935, by Whitmore & Smith), p. 70. By permission of Abingdon Press.
6. Mary Elizabeth Griggs, in POWER, May 7, 1947, p. 39. NCMY. Used by permission.
7. E. McNeill Poteat, "The Jericho Road," from *Over the Sea, the Sky* (New York: Harper & Brothers, 1945). By permission.

8. Eugene R. Balsley, "The Migrant Speaks," in THE CHRISTIAN ADVOCATE, Aug. 18, 1949.

9. From *Workers with Youth*. Copyright, MPH. By permission. Four-line insert by Eugene V. Debs, as quoted in *The Bending Cross*, biography by Ray Ginger (New Brunswick, N.J.: Rutgers University Press, 1949). Also by permission.

10. CMB.

11. By anonymous young person from Arkansas, in POWER, April–June, 1958, p. 81. NCMY. By permission.

12. From *Christian World Facts, 1953*, p. 5. Published for the Division of Foreign Missions, National Council of the Churches of Christ in the U.S.A. by Friendship Press. By permission.

13. Abbie Graham, in *Ceremonials of Common Days* (New York: Woman's Press and Whiteside, Inc.) By permission.

14. CMB, adapted from aids for observance of World Day of Prayer, 1955.

15. Adapted by CMB from *Christian World Facts, 1953* (see Note 12 above), page 55. By permission.

16. From James Oppenheim, *War and Laughter*. Reprinted by permission of the publisher, Appleton-Century-Crofts, Inc.

17. George Harper, in POWER, Feb. 21, 1947, p. 58. NCMY. By permission.

18. Mayme Garner Miller, in WORLD CALL, International Magazine of Disciples of Christ. By permission, Christian Board of Publication.

19. From EPWORTH HERALD, Oct. 1, 1938, p. 599. Copyright, MPH. By permission.

20. Roy A. Burkhart, in IJRE. By permission of the magazine and of the author.

21. Barbara Eskew (Fisher), Missouri, in POWER, Aug. 28, 1957, p. 61. NCMY. By permission. The closing Bible quotation is from the J. B. Phillips translation of Romans 12:2.

22. Adapted from story in NEWSLETTER of Youth Department,

World Council of Churches. By permission of Ralph Weltge, Geneva, Switzerland.

23. Mary Dickerson Bangham. By permission of the author.
24. Written by youth for national gathering, adapted by CMB.
25. M. Leo Rippy, Jr., in HIGHROAD, Oct., 1949. Copyright, MPH. By permission.
26. CMB in unit, *When I Worship*, Vol. 9, Part 2, pp. 1–4. Copyright, Christian Board of Publication. By permission.
27. Roberta Dillon Williams. By permission of the author.
28. Ian J. McRae, in IJRE, Jan., 1957, p. 37. By permission.

11. OUR LIFE VOCATION

1. Author and source unknown
2. Mildred Evadne Stevens, in EPWORTH HERALD, Oct., 1940. Copyright, MPH. By permission.
3. From PRESBYTERIAN YOUTH, Feb., 1944, p. 6. By permission, Board of Christian Education, Presbyterian Church in U.S.
4. Thomas W. Freckleton, in E. McR. Shields, *As the Day Begins*, meditation for July 23. (Richmond, Va.: John Knox Press, 1944). By permission.
5. Irene Thornton (Arkansas) in POWER, July 14, 1957, p. 16. NCMY. By permission.
6. CMB.
7. CMB.
8. Lorner Delay, in POWER, Aug. 14, 1953, p. 47. NCMY. By permission.
9. CMB.
10. CMB.
11. CMB in POWER, Nov. 20, 1948, p. 54. NCMY. By permission.
12. CMB. Author and source of eight-line poem unknown.

12. MAKING PERSONAL DEDICATION

1. Eleanor B. Stock. By permission of the author.
2. Allan Knight Chalmers, *Adventuring in Prayer* (Phila-

delphia: The Westminster Press, 1942), pp. 24–25. By permission of The Westminster Press.

3. Helen F. Couch. By permission of the author.

4. CMB in IJRE, Dec., 1955, p. 31. By permission.

5. CMB.

6. Bishop John Wesley Lord, in CONCERN, 1953. NCMY. By permission of magazine and of Bishop Lord.

7. Anonymous, in POWER, Nov. 22, 1948, p. 56. NCMY. By permission.

8. Nancy Byrd Turner, *Star in a Well* (New York: Dodd, Mead & Company, 1935). Reprinted by permission of Dodd, Mead & Company, Inc. and of the author.

9. CMB, in IJRE, June, 1956, p. 31. By permission.

10. From the jacket of *Monk in Armour,* by Gladys H. Barr (Nashville, Tenn.: Abingdon Press, 1949). By permission of Abingdon Press.

11. CMB, in IJRE, June, 1956, p. 31. By permission.

12. Edwin Markham, *Conscripts of the Dream* (Doubleday, Doran, and World, Inc.). Reprinted by permission of Mr. Virgil Markham.

13. CMB.

14. Methodist Youth of Central Kansas Conference. By permission of Miss Louise Dutcher and of Rev. Milton B. Holcomb.

15. Dorothy Clarke Wilson, "From This Small Candle," in CLASSMATE, May 2, 1943. Copyright, MPH. By permission of magazine and of Mrs. Wilson.

16. Pearl Carling Campbell, in POWER, Jan. 19, 1948, p. 21. NCMY. By permission.

17. Mrs. R. A. Buckner, in ROUNDTABLE, Sept., 1949, pp. 18–21. Copyright, MPH. By permission of the periodical and of Sally Buckner.

18. Insert by James Russell Lowell, 1819–1891.

19. *Ibid.*

20. Insert by Hermann Hagedorn from *The Bomb That Fell on*

America (Copyright, 1946, Hermann Hagedorn. Published in 1948, by Association Press). By permission of publisher and author.

21. *Ibid.*
22. James Russell Lowell.
23. John Oxenham, from "Follow Me," in *Selected Poems of John Oxenham*, Charles Wallis, ed. (New York: Harper & Brothers, 1948). By permission of publisher and Mr. Oxenham's daughter, Miss Theo Dunkerley, Sussex, England.

13. THE HOLY COMMUNION

1. James A. Blaisdell, b. 1867.
2. Marjorie Lasley. By permission of the author. The inset "As one unknown . . . who he is" is quoted from Albert Schweitzer, *The Quest of the Historical Jesus* (New York: The Macmillan Company, 1948), p. 401. By permission.
3. From mimeographed service, possibly from a worship workshop and presumably in public domain. The reading "O God . . . thy business" is "The 1000th Psalm," by Edward Everett Hale.
4. Author and source unknown.
5. Author and source unknown.
6. Everett C. Parker, Elinor Inman, and Ross Snyder, *Religious Radio: What to Do and How* (New York: Harper & Brothers, 1948), pp. 169–170. By permission.
7. CMB.
8. Marvel Conkling (Nebraska), in POWER, July 11, 1948. NCMY. By permission. Closing Bible quotation, Philippians 4:7.

14. THANKSGIVING

1. Adapted by CMB.
2. Arranged by Charles M. Laymon from *The Dead Sea Scrolls,* by Millar Burrows. (New York: Viking Press, 1955). By permission of publisher and of Charles M. Laymon.

3. Ian J. McRae, from IJRE. By permission of the magazine and of the author.

4. From *Thoughts of God for Boys and Girls*, by Edith F. Welker and Aimee A. Barber (New York: Harper & Brothers, 1936). Copyright, 1936–1948, Connecticut Council of Religious Education. Originally by fifth grade children, Riverside Church, New York City. By permission of Riverside Church.

5. CMB.

15. CHRISTMAS

1. CMB, in IJRE, Nov., 1955, pp. 45–46. By permission.

2. Adaptation appearing in THE CHURCH SCHOOL, Dec., 1954, p. 30, of "A Christmas Story," in MOTIVE, Dec., 1951, by Wiley Kim Rogers. Copyright, The Methodist Student Movement and MOTIVE. By permission.

3. CMB, in POWER, Dec. 26, 1950, p. 90. NCMY. By permission.

4. CMB, in IJRE, Nov., 1955, p. 46. Insert from "Let's Keep Christmas," by the late Peter Marshall. Copyright, 1952, 1953, by Catherine Marshall. Reprinted by permission, McGraw-Hill Book Co., Inc.

16. WATCH NIGHT AND NEW YEAR'S

1. Bob Payne, in POWER, Aug. 17, 1947, p. 50. NCMY. By permission.

2. CMB. Data adapted from W. Earl Biddle, *Integration of Religion and Psychiatry* (New York: The Macmillan Company, 1955). By permission.

3. From PROGRAM QUARTERLY, Jan.–March, 1950, p. 6. Copyright, MPH. By permission.

17. LENT, GOOD FRIDAY, AND EASTER

1. Nickey (Helener Kane) Currier (Texas), in POWER, Jan. 30, 1947, p. 36. NCMY. By permission.

2. Carol Jett (North Dakota), in POWER, March 26, 1948, p. 89. NCMY. By permission.
3. Wilbur Howard, in WORKERS WITH YOUTH, May, 1948, p. 13. Copyright, MPH. By permission.
4. Abigail Acker Johnson, *Prayers for Young People* (Philadelphia: The Westminster Press, copyright 1947, by W. L. Jenkins). By permission.
5. By students of High Point College, High Point, N.C., 1956. By permission of adviser, Mrs. Franklin Daniels.